I0814475

The Women Writers' Revolution: More than Bloomsbury

The Women Writers' Revolution: More than Bloomsbury

The Success of Female Authors during the Interwar Years

Stephen Wade

AN IMPRINT OF PEN & SWORD BOOKS LTD.
YORKSHIRE – PHILADELPHIA

First published in Great Britain in 2025 by
Pen & Sword History
An imprint of
Pen & Sword Books Ltd
Yorkshire - Philadelphia

ISBN 978 1 39903 645 0

A CIP catalogue record for this book is available from the British Library.

Typeset in INDIA by IMPEC eSolutions
Printed and bound in England by CPI (UK) Ltd.

Pen & Sword Books Limited incorporates the imprints of Archaeology, Atlas, Aviation, Battleground, Digital, Discovery, Family History, Fiction, History, Local, Local History, Maritime, Military, Military Classics, Politics, Select, Transport, True Crime, After the Battle, Air World, Claymore Press, Frontline Publishing, Leo Cooper, Remember When, Seaforth Publishing, The Praetorian Press, Wharncliffe Books, Wharncliffe Local History, Wharncliffe Transport, Wharncliffe True Crime and White Owl.

For a complete list of Pen & Sword titles please contact:

PEN & SWORD BOOKS LIMITED
47 Church Street, Barnsley, South Yorkshire, S70 2AS, England
E-mail: enquiries@pen-and-sword.co.uk
Website: www.pen-and-sword.co.uk

or

PEN AND SWORD BOOKS
1950 Lawrence Rd, Havertown, PA 19083, USA
E-mail: uspen-and-sword@casematepublishers.com
Website: www.penandswordbooks.com

Dedicated to Kate Walker,
romantic novelist and inspiration

Contents

Nesbit, Potter and Gilman

Beatrix Potter (1866–1943), author of some of the bestselling children's books of all time, and Edith Nesbit (1858–1924), who has the same claim to fame, emerged into publishing in the boom years for writers in the nineteenth and early twentieth centuries. Yet for all their similarities, they represent the two basic types of women writers on the eve of the First World War: Potter cultivated an internal world and shaped that imagination into creatures through art and words; Nesbit was a natural storyteller with a strong sense of the contemporary. The two imagined worlds here could be the template for understanding women writers as they came into the new professionalism of the interwar years. The contrast depends on the two concepts of imagined worlds: one always seeks a vision and the other finds a vision within the social world.

The situation for aspiring women writers before 1919 and the major changes in literary life during the interwar years, was in some ways ground for optimism. Yet, as always, there are many different routes to success, and in this case, if success means having one's work in print, then there were definite extremes. So much depended on status and money, and today we try to insist that this no longer applies. The truth is that circumstances are very influential. In the late Victorian and early Edwardian years, there was plenty of room in publishers' lists for both male and female novelists, and indeed also for non-fiction writers of both genders. But contrasts are instructive.

One interesting contrast is when we look at Edith Nesbit, author of *The Railway Children* (1906), and Beatrix Potter. Nesbit moved in Fabian socialist circles; she met famous and fashionable authors, including George Bernard Shaw (1856–1950). Her husband, Hubert Bland (1855–1914), was one of the leading writers of the day who had left-wing leanings: a powerful speaker and an adaptable writer. Together, Mr and Mrs Bland were a force to be reckoned with. Throughout the 1890s, E. Nesbit became a familiar name in the literary journals such as *The Idler* and *The Harmsworth's Magazine*. She was steeped in literary culture.

There were many like Nesbit; after the arrival of the sensation novel and the 'yellow back' novels from the mid-nineteenth century, the three-volume novel to stock the shelves of Mudie's Circulating Library and the railway bookstalls, there had been a decline in the 1890s, but a rise in the printing of newspapers and journals to satisfy the new readers of the commuter class who wanted a twenty-minute read on the way into the city. A search of the female writers in many of these journals yields very little beyond a handful of stories. Equally, the women novelists in the publishers' lists of the time indicate a pattern of brief successes and then obscurity. One might argue that it was always this way and is so today, but there is one massive difference: from 1890 to 1900 there was no television or radio, and no internet or cinema. Books and periodicals were proliferating, and the opportunities for women writers expanded as the market grew and publishers came on the scene regularly. Nesbit was very much of that established scene; she was in a coterie of writers and artists and she had encouragement.

If we turn our attention to Beatrix Potter, born into a well-heeled London family who had plenty of leisure and resources to help her into a comfortable life, we find a true individual. But like Nesbit, she had a creative urge, and this began with illustration; she was a talented entomologist and artist. But unlike Nesbit, Potter was a case study in the internalised artist, the person with inner resources, a steady inspiration and limitless imagination. Whcrc Nesbit saw opportunities opening up for her early fiction, Potter began with illustration, and her first story, *The Tale of Peter Rabbit* (1901). Her biographer, Margaret Lane, explains her deepest resource: 'She was solitary because she was an only child until she was five years old ... and she had limitless leisure for she was very rarely sent for out of the nursery.'

Potter was born in 1866; Nesbit in 1858. By the end of the nineteenth century, both had their fictional terrain. *The Tale of Peter Rabbit* was privately published in 1901 (before Frederick Warne (1825–1901) came on the scene). The Warne edition, familiar to all Potter fans, came along in 1902. At the same time, Nesbit's stories were coming into print. But in Potter's case, she entered the scene with a self-publishing venture; she had hit on a wonderful commercial idea, and her instinct to transmute any potential subject in front of her into a story of very wide appeal was faultless. For Nesbit it was a case of more relationships with editors and plenty of talk in a context of networking.

The late Victorian and early Edwardian years provide the modern reader with a fascinating case study in fiction and the reading public, and both Nesbit and Potter illustrate the nature of the savvy writer, whose instinct for an engrossing and charming tale matches the contemporary readership. A contrast of the two provides us with several informative insights. First, Nesbit represents the writer who is deeply involved in commercial genre fiction. The readers of the new periodicals were not difficult to define. A study of *The Idler* for instance, shows who it was aimed at: the intelligent, enquiring minds of the well-off middle class – the ones who enjoyed a night at the theatre and a weekend read of a broadsheet newspaper and an improving book. The journal covered that fairly new concept: the 'celebrity'. It also educated its readers with accounts of lawyers, artists, singers, men of industry, political personages and stage characters.

In contrast, Potter was a natural to supply that new being in the readership: the child. But this was not simply any child defined by arithmetic. No, this was the childish mindset, essential to the new modern family; both Potter and Warne knew very well what was missing in nursery reading, and they also knew that adults wanted to be involved in the image, appeal and creative nature of the new animal tales.

Both Nesbit and Potter had much in common and some differences, but what their writing shows the modern reader is that before the First World War, in that Edwardian summer when Britons relished journeys abroad as well as adventures down the River Thames and in the Norfolk Broads, there was a new version of those standard foundations of 'a good read': escapism, whimsicality and intrigue. After all, the 1890s and the first decade of the twentieth century was the period in fiction when detective tales flourished, as did the male adventure yarns of H. Rider Haggard (1856–1925) and G.A. Henty (1832–1902); it was also the time when poetry attained a new romanticism alongside a very much more inward looking personal landscape of angst and suffering. Readers queued up for *A Shropshire Lad* (1896) by A.E. Housman (1859–1936) and its nobility of youth, as well for Henry Newbolt's (1862–1938) masculine ethos.

To understand the fundamental challenge that came along from the modernists James Joyce (1882–1941), Virginia Woolf (1882–1941) and others, this commercial, reader-directed world of print has to be conceived. Before 1919, there were novels available for every niche in the reading public when it came to women writers and readers. Some publishers concentrated on fiction with a strongly moral and religious nature; others promoted exotic locations. Until the modernists, the fiction most often noticed in the reviews and talked about – Arnold Bennett (1867–1931), Joseph Conrad (1857–1924) and H. Rider Haggard etc. – had strong elements of realism: that is, there was usually a firm basis of naturalistic and recognisable reality. But this 'reality' of fiction was soon to be challenged.

Though the fictional worlds of Nesbit and Potter were well established and would stay that way for a long time, there was a revolution shaking the foundations of British literary culture and of the 'common reader'. The revolution came along with the First World War and into the 1920s, but there was far more to this than the thinking behind Bloomsbury, with its highbrow ideals and its worthy but elitist forms and often hermetically sealed fictional or poetic worlds. Before charting the progress of the hundreds of women writers who came into print in the interwar years, we need to explain why, for instance, there was T.S. Eliot's (1888–1965) poem, *The Waste Land* (1922), which required, in order to be read and understood, a reader who knew something of classics, myths, modern languages, and European high and low cultures, along with a substantial awareness of Christian scripture.

Through modern eyes, a glance at the reading on the shelves in the years just after the First World War appears to suggest a profound division in the writer-reader relationship. Some books wanted the reader to experience a close sharing of the story and material, while others clearly excluded that commuter on the omnibus who wanted and entertaining read on the way to the office. But what stands out in the interwar years is that the numbers of aspirants to creating writing was increasing noticeably. In an advert in *The Listener* in 1934 under the heading, 'How Many Stories There Are' there was this announcement from the London School of Journalism: 'One woman student recently reported that she had sold over 250 contributions ... Another informed the school that in his first year after completing the course, he had made, by spare time writing, nearly £400. And these are examples typical of many ...'

In 1933, novelist Hugh Walpole (1884–1941) was reported in a piece for *The Times*, asking, 'Why write a novel?' and in his talk he made a central point in the ongoing distinction between 'writing' and 'literature' saying, 'He believed that the novel was different from all other writing arts, in that it was something that could be quite good without altogether being literature.' He also reviewed the previous ten years regarding the novel and opined that the novelist 'must now be an artist and his novel must be something beautiful in form and must deal with things he knew to be true, and because his experience was necessarily limited, there had come about the elaboration of small incidents such as taking an aspirin and so on.' This report of the talk might seem a little clumsy at times but the argument is more important than it seems on the face of it. Fiction, after Virginia Woolf and others who used it as a product of a search for writing the truth of what might be called 'deep reality' had become, by the 1930s, a house with many mansions, and one of these was the story or novel's potential for creating a deep reality in contradistinction to a surface naturalism, a world in which recognisably social human beings move around in a matrix of duty, affection and hierarchy.

One might clearly see one of the key origins of this potential in the work of Charlotte Perkins Gilman (1860–1935), who wrote *The Yellow Wallpaper* (1892) and showed what could be done (even in miniature) with a fiction that reached out to multiple interpretations and offered a parable for the woman writer's situation. Maggie O'Farrell (*b*.1972), in her introduction to a recent edition of Gilman's writings, makes high claims when she writes of the narrator: 'The answer is that there is nothing for her to do. Kept from "society and stimulus", denied the freedom to write ... forbidden any kind of mental activity at all, she is quite literally bored out of her mind.'

The Yellow Wallpaper is partly the product of what happened when her doctor prescribed for Gilman a tough treatment for her depression – a treatment resembling solitary confinement in a prison. Perhaps she never realised this at the time, as the story seems to be written totally on the edge and with a sense of disintegration within a mind abundant with life and creativity, but *The Yellow Wallpaper* provides a powerful allegory of the woman writer in a world run by men, as the publishing world was in *c.*1900.

The narrator exists in what is effectively a prison: barred windows, locked door and a warder: her husband. He is a warder with apparent kindness on the surface; he is also a medical doctor. Whenever the narrator suggests an element of freedom the response is a block; even the smallest move brings something repressive: 'I got up softly and went to feel and see if the paper move, and when I came back, John was awake.' His response is to crush even that scrap of individuality. 'What is it little girl?' he said, 'Don't go walking about like that – you'll get cold.'

The crux of the story is that the woman begins inventing a life and a story behind the yellow wallpaper, and from this comes the exceptional imaginative power of the story. It is a fiction with claims for a highly creative allegory about women and creativity, of course. The narrator is trapped by 'kindness' but also by a medical science manufactured by men. The theme runs parallel to the actual medical practise of the nineteenth century regarding such concepts as 'hysteria'. This had been conceived a long time before Sigmund Freud (1856–1939), but took it up and made it a popular concept for all kinds of theory.

Now, reading the story, one may see the nature of the woman's thinking as something that would be taken as insanity, but there is a fascinating double layer of meaning, which makes this story a foundation work for the coming century of women's writing. This is because the 'madness' is in fact, an inverted version of the specifically female creativity we observe in storytelling. As Maggie O'Farrell puts it, '*The Yellow Wallpaper* is a cry, not so much of defiance, but of demand. A demand to be heard, a demand to be understood, a demand to be acknowledged.' This is a template for what is to come. To understand this, we have to recall that women reading and writing fiction had been denigrated and suppressed for many centuries. It was not productive, and worst of all, it was not contributing to the feminine virtues, which we see in particular in Victorian writing and culture.

At its most direct and explicit, the thinking behind this treatment of women may be seen in Coventry Patmore's (1823–1896) poem, *The Angel in the House* (1858), in which we have these lines:

Man must be pleased; but him to please
Is woman's pleasure; down the gulf
Of his condoled necessities
She casts her best, she flings herself.
How often flings for nought, and yokes
Her heart to an icicle or whim,
…

So much from social history backs up this view of woman as a creature to be cocooned and swaddled in stifling care and concern. Gilman makes this ideology twist into a kind of jail keeping, with a smiling warder jangling the keys of the home.

Here we have three versions of the women writers who will feature in this social history: Nesbit who was embedded in the literary and political world of the Fabians, married to a writer and speaker; Potter who had a unique imaginative fire in her, which created a 'market' and Gilman, who surely represents the writer who sees, in a vision, the link between a stifling mindset and a society that must, eventually, 'throw away the keys' of the door where she has need, in the words ofVirginia Woolf, of a 'room of one's own.'

Introduction

Themes and Reputations

'By the middle of 1920 she was sending poems to university journals and sketching out short stories.'

Vera Brittain (1893–1970)
on Winifred Holtby (1898–1935)

In the aftermath of the First World War, as author Marius Hentea has shown in his research on the writers of that generation, thousands of young people wanted to write and to be published. Fortunately for them, publishers and agents were very keen to encourage this and consciously cultivated and invited the youth of the land to take up their pens. Hentea points out that for the period between 1920 and 1933 a list of British novelists who had a debut work published in these years shows that there were at least twenty-four names, and of these, only six were women writers. These included several names still well known, but also on the list were Mary 'Mollie' Panter-Downes (1906–1997), who published *The Shoreless Sea* (1923) and Pamela Frankau (1908–1967), who debuted with *Marriage of Harlequin* (1927).

Some of these women, like Panter-Downes for instance, achieved remarkable success; she even wrote for *The New Yorker*, and she was only 16 when *The Shoreless Sea* was published. In this she ranked alongside Georgette Heyer (1902–1974), who, in her teens, published *The Black Moth* (1921). Panter-Downes has been reprinted: her work was re-issued by Persephone Books.

Hentea makes it clear that publishers 'targeted and advertised youth' and that 'The British public was enthralled by young authors who represented, in the 1920s, the future of the nation's cultural identity.' There were even publications of series devoted to young writers. There were dozens of works in print with 'youth' in their titles such as *The Wings of Youth* (1918) and *Wild Heart of Youth* (1925).

There had, of course, been the loss of a generation of young men, and works such as Wilfred Owen's (1893–1918) *Anthem for Doomed Youth* (1920) expressed a universal emotional sense of tragedy, with these lines:

> No mockeries now for them; no prayers nor bells,
> Nor any voice of mourning save the choirs,
> The shrill, demented choirs of wailing shells;
> And bugles calling for them from sad shires.

But there were also novelists and other writers, all crowding the mass influx of aspiring scribes to the channels of submission to the publishers. Many of these were women. There was no universal encouragement though: the papers liked to run features on the crowds of possibly new arrivals on the literary scene and many of the established 'old guard' were protective and defensive, not at all keen to have the flood of competition to deal with.

Who, then, is this new version of the woman writer? Was there a typical profile of her at work? Who was this woman who was neither a figure at salons and literary parties, nor a worker producing nothing but the least original works of popular narrative? She was a person who worked hard at the type-face, contributed to the household, family or her own survival. She had a talent with words and knew how to make a story successful. In many cases, she had done other work before discovering her writing talent, and often she had social causes, charities and 'good works' to attend to.

She was, in effect, someone like May Sinclair – born Mary Amelia St Clair (1863–1946) – who became the jobbing writer but also kept in touch with the freshest products of modernism; she walked with the Suffragettes but also managed to work across a number of genres. She was born in 1863 at Rock Ferry in Cheshire, the daughter of a ship owner in Liverpool, but he died when she was very young. By the mid-1890s Sinclair was writing to earn an income, as her mother needed her, and in fact, Mrs St Clair died in 1901. The independent Sinclair set to work, and as well as her fiction, she wrote on feminist and political subjects, and some were published by the Women Writers' Suffrage League. Central to much of her writing and thinking was the new science of psychoanalysis. Sigmund Freud was translated into English in 1900, and from some of his work on consciousness and dreams, and from early life emotional experience came the growing interest in the subconscious among writers and artists.

During the First World War, Sinclair did what thousands of women did: she joined an ambulance corps, but she could not cope with this for long. By the Georgian years, she was in her stride, writing highly valued fiction, such as *The Combined Maze* (1913), which was received and appraised as a story of relationships beyond a plain genre romance. Sinclair managed to stride over both worlds – the higher cultural discourses and more popular narratives – and her psychological interests filtered into both her fiction and her criticism.

There was more. She also wrote in the supernatural genre, and one of these titles in particular, called *Uncanny Stories* (1923), has been highly rated. Her interest extended to activities with the Society for Psychical Research, and this was at a time when the subject was attracting a much wider interest than in its first years. Arthur Conan Doyle (1859–1930) and W.B. Yeats (1865–1939) had interests in the area.

Sinclair died in 1946, highly respected in the world of literature, and she published over forty titles, covering fiction, philosophy, the supernatural, criticism and politics. There were many like her between 1918 and 1945, and this profile has to end with the sad fact that her works are all but forgotten in terms of general readership; this statement applies to very many similar writers of the period, and Sinclair is surely the absolutely typical woman writer in Britain in the years covered in the following pages.

There are plenty of books dealing with the critical assessment involved in understanding the women writers of the interwar years. I have no wish to add to that. My aim is to provide a social history of the subject. What was it like to be a woman aspiring to get into print at that time? What experience and skills were required for that success? The media myths and hype centred on the lone, suffering artist or the great original, writing in an attic, cut off from life, might be the stuff of an entire literary genre, but in actual life, embedded in all he trials of existence, there are writers and artists who have to cope with everything thrown at them day by day, and yet still write.

The survey following then, will often be concerned with the material life of the woman writer, and so will cover everything from editing, selecting, re-writing, liaising, networking and finding a pathway into print. But the epic trek to success is still not complete. After publication, the aim is for the book and the writer to be noticed. Therefore, along the route to what will be partly a social history of the subject, the reader will encounter all kinds of practical by-ways, off-shoots from the main course of writing itself.

This book has massive aspirations. For many years I have considered writing an account of the years between the two world wars with regard to the women writers who emerged then. The more I reflected on this topic, the more the scope of the project expanded. As soon as the literary historian scans and surveys the potential of this period for its artistic and aesthetic interests, more names and reputations begin to appear. But there is one strand in that literary history I wish to explore: the works of writers, in both fiction and non-fiction, who had nothing to do with Bloomsbury and the cliques, sisterhoods, brotherhoods, social sets and *avant-garde* credos coming from what we think of now as modernism.

Writing – Almost a Religion

This does not mean that I am not concerned with modernism; on the contrary, that gathering of new initiatives in writing narrative is very much present in the following pages. But my focus is on the writers who came out from the middle class, and those who came from the working class also, at a time when documentary and the facts of a working life became of central interest. After all, the years between *c.*1920 and 1940 saw such classics as George Orwell's (1903–1950) *Down and Out in Paris and London* (1933) – concerned with the life of the lowest café worker – and such landmark reads as James Hanley's (1897–1985) *Grey Children: A Study in Humbug and Misery in South Wales* (1937), which opened up knowledge about the workers on the South Wales coalfields; it was also the time of Christopher Isherwood's (1904–1986) writings from Berlin during the rise of the Nazi ideology, and the arrival of John Lehmann's (1907–1987) paperback anthologies, *New Writing* (1936–1950), which also explored working lives and little-known contemporary themes.

Those twenty-five years, between say Katherine Mansfield's (1888–1923) first short stories and Dorothy Parker's (1893–1967) first writings for *Vanity Fair* (1918–1920) and the later novels of Storm Jameson (1891–1936), contain one central literary revolution: it produced writings by British and

American women that brought into the light whole slices of previously hidden lives. Women were becoming visible as writers and artists. Alice Duer Miller (1874–1942) wrote *Come out of the Kitchen! A Romance* (1916), and the cover image shows a pinafored young woman servant, standing by a black cat, and she is peeping out at the wider world.

Matters delve deeper than this, however, because there is a philosophical dimension to the revolution in writing and art, and this relates to 'reality'. Virginia Woolf, in her seminal essay, *A Room of One's Own* (1929), wrote something that is at the roots of a division:

> Thus when I ask you to write more books I am urging you to do what will be for your good and for the good of the world at large. How to justify this instinct or belief I do not know, for philosophic words, if one has not been educated at a university, are apt to play one false. What is meant by 'reality'?

This is totally at the core of this book: most of the women writers discussed here would see themselves primarily as storytellers, and the reality they shared with their readers is the acceptable one of homes, rents, nine-to-five work and family groups. Their reality was largely one built around childbirth, courtship, marriage, family, the home and deeper beliefs. What had philosophical speculations to do with that shared readership of a novel or a memoir?

Yet for Virginia Woolf the question is central. Much of the work resting on this basis of two great contrasts acts deeply on the actual writing. In her memoir *Giving up the Ghost* (2003) Hilary Mantel (1952–2022) has fun playing with two voices and discourses standing before the aspiring writer:

> I will just go for it, I think to myself, I'll hold out my hands and say, *c'est moi*, get used to it. I'll trust the reader ... Remember what Orwell says, that good prose is like a window-pane. Concentrate on sharpening your memory and peeling your sensibility ...

But then she admits that embellishing is natural: 'but do I take my own advice? Not a bit.'

In other words, those women who set out their stalls, sometime around the end of the First World War, to make their living by writing or perhaps simply to see their name in print in a magazine, had that same decision regarding voice and style. In any narrative, at the heart of the verbal structures created there is a sharing of the events and introspections; the choice made then relates either to a genre with its tropes and conventions, or to something new. My book looks at both routes to success, but when I consider the well-off writer in the midst of a literary coterie, a support group, as opposed to say Storm Jameson with her seafaring father up in Whitby, I am acutely aware of what was needed in order to work at being a writer at that time.

One outstanding feature of the interwar years for writers is that as morality experienced the sea change brought about by the First World War, the trials of the Great Depression and the growth of fascism, new versions of identity came through into scrutiny and so had more chance of being understood. This means that in such works as *The Well of Loneliness* (1928) by Radclyffe Hall (1880–1943) and *Lady Chatterley's Lover* (1928) by D.H. Lawrence (1885–1930), may be seen accounts and revelations of identity and sexuality, which had previously been erased from public awareness. Of course, there were legal reasons for this, but nevertheless, the legal and moral suppressions were bound to have sideways effects. The same may be seen in the publishing history of E.M. Forster's (1879–1970) novel, *Maurice* (written in Edwardian times but not in print until 1971).

Putting all these thoughts together entails facing up to several contradictions and paradoxes in the writing by women in these two decades: on the one hand there is a profound concern for the family values so widespread before the immense sacrifice of the First World War, and on the other hand there is the realisation by so many writers and artists that there are widespread social changes in progress, and that political instability across the world will transform every aspect of life. With those thoughts in mind, of course, the subjects and treatments of writing themes will change radically, and indeed they do.

The Edwardian years display a wide and profound preoccupation with literary journalism and what used to be called *belles lettres*; the latter is a term applied to the work produced by a generation who could write well about a broad range of topics embraced by art, culture and literature. The genre for its readership (and success) depended on a base knowledge of such subjects as the classics, cultural vogues and intellectual history. That is to say, at the beginning of the period covered in this book, the world offered to the aspiring writer had more than a taste of this background. Writers had to be immersed in this cultural history, and that history was defined as high culture, and its products referred to as highbrow.

Writers generally fussed and fiddled about how the new woman writer would manage in this male world – one of brotherhoods, dining societies and higher journalism in which writing and writers were discussed over the port and cigars after a hearty ten-course dinner. This scene was dominated by such men as G.K. Chesterton (1874–1936), Hilaire Belloc (1870–1953), E.V. Lucas (1868–1938) and scores of similar characters who could produce a short essay for a journal editor, produce a book review on almost any subject, and speak with authority on the literature of the Western world. Such a man was Edward Thomas (1878–1917), and there were many like him, who, when young, strove to exist on literary journalism and series books.

The new versions of female writers were matched by women in other artistic spheres also: in music, as Leah Broad has shown in her book, *Quartet: How Four Women Challenged the Musical World* (2023), where she brings to notice Ethel Smyth (1858–1944), Rebecca Clarke (1886–1979), Dorothy Howell (1898–1982) and Doreen Carwithen (1922 2003). As critic Dr Flora Wilson wrote in a review of that book, the composers' contexts could well be the same as are included in the following pages: '*Quartet*'s four lives span 145 years, two world wars and a dizzying mess of social, cultural and political upheaval.' Arguably, most of the women writers dealt with here deserve to be re-read today, for all kinds of reasons.

Later, after the Second World War, there were still doubts about the social revolution of the Edwardian years. Philip Larkin (1922–1985), asked by the interviewer in a piece for *The Observer* what he meant by an 'invasion' of women into the men's colleges, replied, 'I would like to know what the result is in ten years' time ... whether it will boil up into shootings and tears and failed exams and nervous breakdowns.'

Women and their Aspirations

When women tried to cope in this world, what would they do? G.K. Chesterton faced this question in an essay of 1905, called simply, 'Woman'. He took issue with those who explored the subject of how a woman, who had to be busy with children, the home and looking after her husband, could possibly be any kind of figure in the arena of 'high culture'. Chesterton was snooty and condescending on this at first in the essay, writing, '[a] Woman does work which is in some small degree creative ... she can put the flowers or the furniture in fancy arrangements of her own …' but then he turns the focus onto the positive, and uses his familiar tool of the paradox to highlight the issue, arguing that high culture is not desirable anyway:

> And then the higher culture. I know that culture. I would not set any man free for it if I could help it. The effect of it on the rich men who are free for it is so horrible that it is worse than any of the other amusements of the millionaire – worse than gambling, worse even than philanthropy. It means thinking the smallest poet in Belgium greater than the greatest poet in England. ... It means taking literature seriously, a very amateurish thing to do.

Although this is humorous, and written to entertain, turning around a major assumption of the time – that high culture is to be desired – has the effect of provoking thought, and he leads his thought towards his closure, applied to the new women writers: 'Woman [*sic*] have been set free to be Bacchantes; they have been set free to be Virgin Martyrs; they have been set free to be Witches. Do not ask them now to sink so low as the higher culture.' This theme must have been impressed on the many women of the early twentieth century who were tempted by authorship as a profession. E.M. Forster, in *A Room with a View* (1908), integrates this duality also. His character Lucy Honeychurch has this new awakening in her: 'It was not that ladies were inferior to men; it was that they were different. Their mission was to inspire others to achievement rather than to achieve themselves. Indirectly ... a lady could accomplish much.' She then is also aware that 'In her heart also there are springing up strange desires.' Forster gives us a very telling contrast. First there is Lucy Honeychurch, immense with potential and with yearning to do something remarkable. Then we have the aspiring woman novelist, Miss Lavish. Both are there for the 'higher culture' of Florence and 'authentic' Italy, but Miss Lavish is used in the novel as a figure of fun and amusement. She is cultivating her aesthetic sense in Florence, and she has suffered a heavy blow in her first attempt to be a novelist. She had written something, and Mr Beebe explains:

> It was a novel ... and I am afraid, not a very nice novel. It is so sad when people who have abilities misuse them ... Anyway she left it almost finished in the Grotto of the Calvary ... while she went for a little ink ... and the grotto fell roaring onto the beach, and the saddest thing of all is that she cannot remember what she has written.

In fact, if we look at the situation for women writers *c.*1919, when women had proved to the world that they could take active roles in the masculine domain of warfare, it is clear that the media of the time suggest that the option of taking up creative writing could very well lead to that 'life of service' that Beatrice Webb (1858–1943) wrote about becoming manifest in other ways. The perfect case study for this is Marie Corelli (1855–1924), who settled in Stratford-upon Avon; she went there in 1899, and after fourteen years there, her strong desire to help with a movement for conservation had brought about the making of extensive gardens at her home, The Firs, to be used by the general public. Corelli had seen what earnings from her pen could achieve in the very needy wider world, very much as Beatrix Potter did in the Lakes. As the website for Stratford's culture notes,

> When she [Corelli] first moved to the town, she rented Hall's Croft ... During the next couple of years she paid for the whole Grammar School to go to the circus; for nearly 2,000 children to attend parties in the Memorial Theatre and for over 600 National Schools children to visit Rugby Park.

The urge to help with the betterment of social conditions for the labouring class was strong during the time of the settlements at the end of the nineteenth century, and many successful writers and artists twenty years later took up the same philanthropic initiatives.

What was happening was partly a desperate and determined effort on the part of women who attained success in the arts and culture to contribute in some way to that exhausted land around them that had suffered years of horrendous war, followed by the staggering level of suffering and death effected by the flu epidemic of 1918 to 1919. The post-First World War world was also one in which thousands of male combatants came home to depression – in more than one sense. In one survey of families in Bradford, West Yorkshire, a wife and mother made it clear that the First World War erased all religious belief in her and her family; she vowed never to go to church again, as their God had taken away every adult male in her street.

Nevertheless, writing as a way of earning money clearly had an appeal in that milieu in which commuters, and leisure enthusiasts in boats, on bicycles and in charabancs all saw that reading the periodicals was a wonderful element in their recreation time. The facts on the surface of the biographies of women writers do not necessarily convey the economic reality they existed in. Angela Thirkell (1890–1961), for example, presents a salutary lesson here. Her life suggests a world of privilege and good connections: her mother was Margaret Burne-Jones (1866–1953), daughter of the artist Edward Burne-Jones (1833–1898); she was related to Rudyard Kipling (1865–1936) and Stanley Baldwin (1867–1947). Her godfather was J.M. Barrie (1860–1937). But, as Alexander McCall Smith (*b*.1948) points out, regarding a reprint of her novel, *High Rising* (1933): 'Financial exigency meant that she had to make her own way, first as a journalist, and then as the author of a series of novels produced to pay the bills.'

The new social freedoms and the exciting opportunities may have offered something to question, as G.K. Chesterton did; however, the years between *c*.1900 and 1919 had shown that an independent woman, relying on her own resources, had options to consider from all kinds of new occupations and openings. James Milne (1908–1997), reflecting from the 1930s on the changes for women from mid-Victorian to modern, summed up:

> Perhaps the long spinsterish reign of the English 'three-volumer' had something to do with the insurgent fiction which followed its

> disappearance. Writing and reading must not be too good 'for human nature's daily food' and convention and conservatism swathed in immaculate morality and silvery wedding bells, would naturally result in a swing to the left. That bred the 'problem novel' of sex, the 'hill-top novel' of woman's freedom and generally the fuller text of human life, as novel writers paint it today, without the needs of any labels.

That *fuller text of human life* is the key to reading and understanding the new fiction by women through the decades delineated here.

The 'three-volumer' referred to is the railway novel, the sensational fiction of the 1860s primarily, and in this phase of fiction women writers such as Mary Braddon (1835–1915) came to the fore. What Alan Walbank called 'the queens of the circulating library' – mainly Braddon, along with Charlotte Yonge (1823–1901), Mrs Humphry Ward (1851–1920) and Mrs Oliphant (1828–1897) – had been a phenomenon, which escalated the reading of fiction from something seen as undesirable for a young lady of good breeding, to an educative, productive part of a wider education for women.

A readership had been created back in the days when Mudie and Smith's libraries became established and, in fact, up to the early 1960s such lending libraries were still around. My own early reading was helped by Boots' library off an arcade in central Leeds, West Yorkshire.

But the readership of 1919 was something different. The women who had nursed the wounded, controlled elements of administration, driven buses and handled trams, now demanded art and culture to match the new lives being revealed. That demand was inevitably met. When Agatha Christie (1890–1976) had her first taste of professional publishing, she sat opposite John Lane (1854–1925), the great entrepreneur, as he explained what was needed to make her novel, *The Mysterious Affair at Styles* (1920), into a work fit for print, and Lane had a contract ready, claiming rights on her next five novels. Christie handled this alone, with no agent and no advice. She walked home elated and excited, having created Hercule Poirot, but also having trusted her new publisher with her intellectual property for years to come.

Christie was one of the new women professionals, and she reflected in her autobiography: 'I had been dared to write a detective story; I had written a detective story; it had been accepted and I was going to appear in print. There, as far as I was concerned, the matter ended.'

One constant theme in the interwar years regarding writers and artists is the effort to be noticed and to make contacts. This was noticed before 1919 also. The literary context around the Bloomsbury coterie is one of many. Some were prominent and influential – such as Edward Marsh's (1872–1953) circle of poets, known as the 'Georgian Poets', which was a shifting concept, as it included D.H. Lawrence for instance. But the small magazines, ready with their manifesto and their eagerness to explain their aesthetics along with their politics, are a marked feature of literary life before the changes brought about after the First World War.

Allying oneself with the editors of such magazines meant that one would be invited to parties, afternoon teas, even excursions and performances. Choosing a typical example is not difficult. A.R. Orage's (1873–1934) leftist *The New Age* provides a narrative of its own, and its promotion of Katherine Mansfield (1888–1923) shows exactly how networking and friendships helped immensely in the writer's path to being published. Mansfield, fresh from European travel and several affairs of the heart, had been seriously ill but had managed to exist on the support of friends and lovers for some time. She had come to live in London from New Zealand, along with her family, as her father was a prominent banker; he gave her an allowance, and she tried various stratagems to be noticed and published.

Together with Orage, Mansfield was published but with no remuneration. However, she had contacts in the publishing world; there was also another friend in John Middleton Murry (1889–1957), who became a partner in life, and he also had a small magazine to run, *Rhythm*, which started in Oxford. He was a scholar and aspiring writer, as Mansfield was. They began to mix with D.H. Lawrence and his wife, Frieda (1879–1956), and with other roving writers and editors. Gradually, small steps after small steps, Mansfield's stories began to find print, and through another contact who started a small press, her first book, *In a German Pension* (1911), was published.

Just before the start of the First World War, Mansfield had lived a life that shows all the hallmarks of the woman writer who has limited funds and support, but who works hard to find her niche – commercially or aesthetically, of course. Between 1920 and 1924 several of her story collections found print, largely owing to the publisher Constable, who even reissued *In a German Pension* at the same time.

What strikes the modern reader about Mansfield's long road to recognition is that she had immense personal charm and also had a rare talent for making friends as well as cultivating literary contacts. Yet there is a true integrity in her writing, something that came from within her and gave her fiction the classic stamp. Arguably, one defining feature of the kind of writer Mansfield aimed to be, can be explained by Eckhart Tolle (*b.*1948), who wrote, 'You find peace not by rearranging the circumstances of your life, but by realising who you are at the deepest level.' This lies behind the great shift of sensibility that was taking place in the first twenty or so years of the twentieth century: the writings and cultural transmutations we now call modernism.

What happened in this literary microcosm in which Virginia Woolf, James Joyce and T.S. Eliot (1888–1965) emerged as most prominent was a challenge to the assumptions behind the Victorian naturalistic novel. In the fiction of most writers of the Victorian age there is an assumption that people in real life may be explained, and 'explained away' by various methods of description, and therefore fictional characters may also be similarly explained. But this was challenged by modernism. After all, do we know other people? Do they know themselves? Are we not creatures who present social selves, while deep inside there are bundles of doubts, morals, emotions and aspirations that never become visible to others?

What came into modern writing in the late Edwardian and Georgian years was a series of writing that took away the literary certainties about human beings and their worlds of supposed reality. In Virginia Woolf's *Mrs Dalloway* (1925) the reader joins in the writer's presentation of her character as her mind flits around from thought to thought. The term 'stream of consciousness' was conceived to explain this interiority: there are no real words of explanation behind actions, and, as in reality, the character's mind floats around according to stimuli from around or within.

However, this style and voice must not seem artificial; there has to be a natural sense of actuality for the reader. The effect when read is that there is some semblance of logical progression running through the person's mind, but along the way, a myriad sensations move in, similar to what most people would be familiar with in a situation in which they have to wait for a length of time, but they have nothing to maintain their interest. What happens there is that our minds have free range to wander, and then time switches, memory comes in, new events around us distract, and so on. The earlier notion of fictional characters as creatures who exist in a given, understood social context and are subjected to analysis or commentary is alien to the modernist approach.

One facet of this was highlighted in the 1960s when the playwright Harold Pinter (1930–2008) was asked if he could explain one of his characters in his play *The Caretaker* (1960). His answer was that he had no explanation: like real people, they were inscrutable, and even their words gave no real clue to their deep sense of who they were.

The words quoted above from Eckhart Tolle explain a great deal of this revolution, and it will be applied as I progress to look at dozens of writers' lives and work: the drive beneath the writing is to 'discover who you are at the deepest level.'

Before 1919 however, there were severe limitations on women's careers as writers. One of the most comprehensive studies of this situation has been produced by Cambridge University Press, and Alexis Easley (*b.*1963) gives some useful insight here:

> The *Cornhill Magazine* was particularly welcoming to women writers, yet, as Janice Harris has shown ... from 1860 to 1900 women contributed only about 20 per cent of its content. The rates of pay for journalists also tended to be lower for women than for men. Indeed, in 1891 W.T. Stead [1849–1912] created a stir when he announced that the female staff of his weekly periodical the *Review of Reviews* would be paid at the same rate as male journalists.

Easley also points out, by quoting Marie Corelli, how hard it was for the women writers: 'Corelli warned the young woman writer to expect to "fight like the rest, unless she prefers to lie down and be walked over."'

Who is the Creative Writer?

There is another way of looking at the dichotomy separating the middlebrow storyteller and the writer of 'literary' works. This is to question what is meant by the term 'creative writer' and to decide on other distinctions. In

Richard Hoggart's (1918–2014) seminal work on popular culture, *The Uses of Literacy* (1957), he does exactly this hiving off from the body of popular genre practitioners. Here, he describes the 'candy-floss world' of the popular writer of pulp magazines and cheap romances:

> Presumably most writers of fantasy for people of any class share the fantasy worlds of their readers. They become the writers rather than the readers because they can body those fantasies into stories and characters, and because they have a fluency in language. Not the attitude to language of the creative writer, trying to mould words into a shape which will bear the peculiar quality of his experience; but a fluency. A 'gift of the gab' and a facility with thousands of stock phrases which will set the figures moving on the highly conventionalized stage of their readers' imaginations.

Here, Hoggart is saying that writers of popular genres are not creative writers. He is on the side of the Bloomsbury mindset, because writing for him has to be 'moulding shapes' from a very individual experience. This view would seem to exclude writers, such as Agatha Christie, Dorothy L. Sayers (1893–1957), Stella Gibbon (1902–1989), Daphne du Maurier (1907–1989) and others, from being classed as 'literature' or 'creative writers'. For instance, du Maurier wrote a short story called *The Escort* (1945) in which she has to produce a thriller, narrating as a British naval officer in the setting of the Second World War. Her ability to write empathically as well as with a high level of linguistic ability would exclude her, in Hoggart's thinking, from being a creative writer.

The world has changed in this respect, but something else has to be added to explain the over-simplicity of Hoggart's thinking. This is a point about Virginia Woolf's writing life. She was of the school of writers who saw writing as a high art, something to be not only discussed but praised, kept and treasured after a valuation. But she also wrote in the shallows of the marketplace. In an essay on 'Virginia Woolf and the Magazines', author Dean R. Baldwin makes this assertion:

> Her letters and diaries are peppered with references to her need for money. Nor can she be accused of focusing exclusively on her novels, for she produced reams of essays, reviews and other literary

> journalism, the writing of which she frequently rejected for its hard work, low pay and frequent rejection ...

The fact is that in these interwar years, there was a massive growth in the numbers of those who aspired to be creative writers – be that writers of common *shlock* or delicate poets writing about their inner angst. In a 1937 competition for writing a novel, restricted only to teachers in Britain, there were 8,000 entries. The writing courses were beginning to appear, with familiar advertising with statements such as 'Do your friends say' you ought to write a novel when you tell them an anecdote? Or 'A guide to the telling phrase and the happy metaphor.'

If creative writing is going to be a 'subject' on a *curriculum* or even a concept entailing a one-off or short series of workshops and talks, then a look at its social history makes it clear that in most cases, there is room for all three of Hoggart's writers: the high culture practitioner, the writer of popular fantasy and the in-betweener middlebrow who hooks into realism and writes of ordinary people. The classes in writing throughout *c.*1900 and the 1940s show definite contrasts: in 1912 there was a workshop run at Harvard University in the United States by George Baker (1879–1951) but in Britain during these years, the gradual emergence of such courses was by correspondence in most cases.

They turned out creative writers and we have to ask the basic question: did they all want to write for literary journals or produce fiction and poetry for niche markets? Of course not. Publishing was booming, and a scan of most of the women writers discussed in this volume shows that most learned by doing and dealing with negotiations themselves. Between the product of the imagination and the white page covered in text there lies a mass of factors directing at success; following that, there are another cluster of topics awaiting the writer's attention, from editing to knowing the right contacts.

Nurses and Others

Some of the landmark works of the immediate post-First World War years after the 1918 Armistice give the reader some hints about the situation for the talented new wave of women in the arts, business and culture. One of these works was Lytton Strachey's (1880–1932) classic, *Eminent Victorians* (1918). Just when women had proved, in their bold and essential nursing activities behind the trenches, that they were equal to men and to some seasoned professionals in the profession, out comes this cheeky, radical and revisionist work of popular history by a key member of the Bloomsbury Group, and the book has plenty of negativity regarding the 'Lady with the Lamp' – a model for so many 'advanced women' of the preceding generations who had been inspired.

Strachey succeeds in somehow trying to make Florence Nightingale's (1820–1910) noble intentions appear distasteful and misguided: 'But no! She would think of nothing but how to satisfy that singular craving of hers to be *doing* something. As if there was not plenty to do in any case, in the ordinary way, at home. There was the china to look after ...' The sarcasm comes over as ambiguous and doubtful in its aims. Strachey even manages to cast a dark shadow on the roots of the famous nurse's unease: 'Why was even her vision of Heaven itself filled with suffering patients to whom she was being useful? So she dreamed and wondered and, taking out her diary, she poured into it the agitations of her soul.' Here we have that Bloomsbury attitude of undermining efforts by those immersed in life once again: fine for Strachey to sit in his armchair and write about those who worked to change the world for the better.

In his novel *Lord Jim* (1900) Joseph Conrad (1857–1924) had made his theme: 'In the destructive element immerse' and in E.M. Forster's *Howard's End* (1910) here were writers suggesting to the world that communication, social assistance and public service had to be integral to human success as the technology of modernity began to change life for the better, and here is Strachey, undermining and playfully poking fun at a woman whose course of life and achievement must have symbolised the new woman's desire to follow such heroines. Nevertheless, nurses and others became templates for the kind of liberation on the perceived horizon for a generation of young women.

There is one novel from the 1890s that gives a great deal of insight into these aspiring women writers: *New Grub Street* (1891) by George Gissing (1857–1903). In the character of Marian Yule, Gissing gives the kind of impression and comment that would not be available elsewhere. In one scene, set in the British Museum Reading Room, Marian is researching for her father, Alfred. Gissing explains, 'Alfred Yule had made a recognizable name among the critical writers of the day; seeing him in the title-lists of the periodicals, most people knew what to expect, but not a few forebore [*sic*] the cutting open of the pages he occupied.' Now, Marian, he sees, 'had merit quite distinct from anything of which he was capable ...' But is Marian in any way fulfilled? Gissing leaves the reader in no doubts about this: 'When she made a show of resuming work, every now and then it was evident that ... She could no longer apply herself as before. Every now and then she glanced at ... People who were passing; she was tired, and she even had a slight headache ...' Marian is working at a lower level, aiding the work and career of an older man – one who is established at no more than the situation of a literary hack.

The beginnings of the revolution in this area of writing may be mapped out by reference to certain events, publications or even influential people. One very engaging and meaningful instance of this is an essay by Christina Anto, who had written about a novel called *The Frantic Misfortunes of a Nurse, or, The Probationer* (1910) by A.M. Irvine (1866–1950). Anto notes the continuance of the novel's popularity beyond the Edwardian era, and she points out that 'An Edwardian romance novel contained features of both prescribed Victorian propriety and the reinterpretation of femininity and womanhood in the war years and modernity.' Anto also notes that the heroine, Agnes, is '*the femme incomprise*' of romance fiction, 'identifiable and pitiable' in the genre; these are part of the barriers in the way of her journey to love, but of course she is a nurse, and the substantial literature of the experience of nurses during the First World War asserts and confirms the fact that in the figure of the nurse it is plain that much of her presence and nature relate to aspects of the 'new woman' about to emerge.

In other words, what trailed behind the banner, as it were, of the proclamation of the new woman – a capable, professional, assertive person who knew the paths she chose to her personal success – was the notice to male readers that women writers could and did create female characters who were in the texts to provoke thought and to show that the reality could seep into the mythology when it came to the changing landscape of the feminine in society.

Publishers were quick to see the significance of the nurse in this changing society. A typical example of this is in *War and Women: From Experience in the*

Balkans and Elsewhere (1913) by Mabel St Clair Stobart (1862–1954), which is on 'the experience in the Balkans and elsewhere' and relates the author's trek to the Balkans with the Convoy Corps. This group was linked to the Red Cross. She was powerfully behind her pacifist beliefs and expressed her views with strident assertions, prefacing her books with 'If these governments have made up their minds that it is virtuous to kill their enemies – in accordance with the Mohammedan rather than the Christian faith – it would be more consistent if they abolished Red Cross work.' St Clair Stobart also explained much of the impetus behind the 'idea of service', which stands as a foundation for this aspect of social change: 'For if woman desired to share in the government of the country, it seemed plain to me that they must share in the responsibility of defending the country.' Her conclusion explains the basis of the nurse as the exemplar of 'The Probationer' who has passed the tests and become equal:

> He who wishes to cling to the old that ages must leave behind him the old that ages. May I then ... ask those who base their opposition to woman's participation in the more active work of the outer world, and who cling to their time-worn fetish 'a woman's sphere is in the home' to remember that the women who desire to serve their country are not the women who neglect – they are on the contrary, the women who would defend their homes ...

Of course, the popular prints, ephemera and publications all supported the general drive to make the figure of the nurse, both in the First World War and in the following flu epidemic, a figure who was always on the verge of being a symbolic representation of the femininity being shaped by circumstance.

There was also another source of writing from the Edwardian and Victorian years: the governess. Not only had the character of the governess inspired such books as *Jane Eyre* (1847) by Charlotte Brontë (1816–1855): it was also an element in social history that had writers in the heart of its institutions abroad, such as the English governesses working in Russia. Harvey Pitcher (*b.*1936), writing in the 1970s, when he interviewed women who had done that work, discovered such women as Mary Russell Brown, who wrote about her Russian experience. Pitcher notes, 'Miss Brown was later to become quite a successful writer of stories and serials for women's magazines, and in the early 1930s wrote a lively account which was never published, of her two jobs as a governess in Russia before 1914.' Her works are now in an archive: the Leeds Russian Archive, and she is one of many women writers who stand behind the successful travel writers of the interwar years.

Women were beginning to stand on their own feet, to be truly independent, and one only has to glance at the experiences of women in the proliferation of clerical work to see how capable these new versions of women workers were. Not only had they kept the munitions factories running and the nursing facilities alive, but they were also crucial to the office work in the expanding metropolis and the growing regional towns and cities. In her Lord Peter Wimsey novel, *Strong Poison* (1930), Dorothy L. Sayers has two very competent office workers play important roles in the storyline – one of the most thrilling of Sayers's concoctions as the novel is about Wimsey's desperate attempts to save Harriet Vane, whom he wishes to marry, from the noose. In one of the most tense scenes in the novel, Miss Murchison, who has been 'planted' in a solicitor's office to try to ascertain evidence that the lawman stands to gain by the will of an old lady relative.

Not only does Miss Murchison have to learn how to pick a lock, tutored by an ace burglar, but she then has to open and inspect some personal files in the lawyer's office, while arranging for some time to work between observation from other staff. Then, following this, Miss Climpson is given the task of entering the home of the old lady with the money to be left in the will, and infiltrating the home to find similar evidence.

Strong Poison not only has the character of Harriet Vane, a crime writer more successful than the male character, whose death is suspicious; she is arguably the epitome of the new version of the commercially successful woman writer (like Sayers herself of course). In a skilfully extended scene of tittle-tattle about the possible fate of Vane, we have this:

> Yes, but what made her do it – if she did do it?
>
> 'Oh she did it all right. Sheer, beastly spite and jealousy, that's all there was to it. Just because she couldn't write anything but tripe herself, Harriet Vane's got the bug all these damned women have got – fancy they can do things. They hate a man and they hate his work.

> You'd think it would have been enough for her to help and look after a genius like Phil [the deceased victim] wouldn't you?'

At another point in the novel, a man is asked, 'You wouldn't want a wife who wrote books, would you?' Sayers puts a strong vein of interest through the entire novel relating to the writing life of a successful woman writer such as Harriet Vane; Sayers also adds the contemporary interest relating to the more obscure and risky fiction of the victim, Philip Boyes, compared to Vane's work. Boyes is the *avant-garde*: 'All these literary works were of what is sometimes called the advanced type. They preached doctrines which may seem to some of us immoral or seditious, such as atheism and anarchy, and what is known as "free love".'

The women writers had arrived as the post-First World War years struggled on through all the trials one would expect at the end of a global conflict, which has given every person in Britain a series of tough trials and demands. But the opportunities for the writers, from Dorothy L. Sayers to Daphne du Maurier and from Winifred Holtby to Agatha Christie, were there, and visible. For many they were also attainable.

Chapter 1

The New Freedoms and Celebrity

'Dear G.,
Will you please bring a tube for Kate's front wheel, she thinks she had better have a new one, as this one seems to be punctured everywhere and all around the valve ...'

An anonymous letter
to a friend in Oxford
dated 1907

In 1919, fortune smacked Britain in the face, just as the First World War was ending, the flu raged and people died in their thousands. But it had some compensations, and one of these was specifically for women: the Sex Disqualification (Removal) Act 1919. This was a massive step towards the kinds of lives and freedoms that intelligent, highly-motivated and creative women wanted, and needed. One fruitful way to see this influence is in the professional clubs; there had been clubs for women since the mid-Victorian period, but now they were a new breed. In fact, they were exactly what women writers needed, and we can see this if we look at Marie Belloc Lowndes (1868–1947), along with the new women's professional clubs.

The 1919 Act followed on from The Representation of the People Act (1918), which had given the vote to a proportion of the female adult population, but there was still work to be done. The 1919 Act made a professional life and career a possibility for women; in Section 1 we have 'A person shall not be disqualified by sex or marriage from the exercise of any public function, or from being appointed to or holding any civil or judicial post ...' In other words, women could now be lawyers, administrators, businesswomen and officers in the criminal justice system. They could sit on juries, and in 1921 there was the first instance of women being on a jury in a murder trial.

Writing, of course, had always been the kind of occupation a woman could pursue with no resources except what she had at home. She needed only pen and paper to make a start. But of course, there were all the other elements involved in the pursuit of a career as a creative writer, such as agents, publishers, editing, promotion and advertising. None of this includes that real necessity of course: learning the skills of a writer. Today there are hundreds of courses, online and in education, concerned with the practical skills of creative writing; back in *c*.1900 the concept was not there.

Celebrity and Fame: The Influence of George Meredith

George Meredith's (1828–1909) writing – particularly *The Egoist* (1879) had a strong appeal to women; the reason is not hard to find, as the book deals with the consequences of a man's arrogance, and Meredith uses a very entertaining irony and a satirical bite to make the wealthy men all rather ridiculous, and the nature of marriage as being little more than a series of restraints on woman. He was read, admired and written about for decades after his death in 1903. His impact on women writers cannot be underestimated, and his career needs explaining here.

When the 'new woman' of the 1890s – the mostly bourgeois adventuress into the cultural world of the arts who perhaps wore bloomers and travelled independently – aspired to become a writer, it was a case of not only learning the skills but also being noticed. The notion of networking arrived. Many years before this there had been the phenomenon of 'puffing' as employed by critics, when the poems of James Montgomery (1771–1854) had been published and then energetically promoted. In the *fin de siècle* years, the notion of celebrity in writers' work and standing was well established. James Milne, writing in 1934 and looking back on the late Victorian and Edwardian years, explains what was happening:

> Back in those years, authors who thought it not wrong to help their books … Along, after having written them, were called 'boomsters'. Today they would be embraced by their publishers and envied by their rivals, for undoubtedly, the element of pushfulness, which can

> be not only practical but commercial, is more alive, more active, a more definite force in the world of books than used to be the case ...

Celebrity, being known, having one's books known about, was part of the deal, then as now. To see a perfect example of this, the case of George Meredith illustrates the phenomenon. In January 1887, Anton Chekhov (1860–1904) wrote to his uncle, Mirofan, 'My stories are read out at evening parties, everywhere I go people point me out, I have so many acquaintances I cannot cope with them all ...' He was experiencing something he grew to hate: literary celebrity. Some writers cope admirably with renown, and other drown in it, engulfed by praise and the demands of flattery. But for Meredith, being a celebrity was something he could handle with both alacrity and delight.

When I first read him, back in the 1970s, it was not difficult to find his work. Author Ioan Williams (*b*.1941) came to my university in Wales to talk about Meredith, and I recall going away to search out the books. As I came to see later, the Meredith personality was in the way. A search through some background books led to a photograph of the great sage of Box Hill in his bath chair, in which he clutched a little dog as his donkey, Picnic, who is straining to pull him along, and this was in James Milne's *The Memoirs of a Bookman* (1934). Milne's words were the first I came across explaining the special status of Meredith in the late Victorian and Edwardian years. Milne quoted J.M. Barrie at Meredith's funeral in 1909: 'When a great man dies, and this was one of the greatest save Shakespeare, the immortals await him at the top.' That funeral, and the obituaries of 1909, made it perfectly clear that not just a great writer, but a major celebrity, had died. Thomas Hardy (1840–1928) wrote a poem for his old friend and mentor in May 1909, ending with the lines:

> ... Further and further still
> Through the world's vaporous vitiate air
> His words wing on – as live words will.

The words did indeed 'wing on'. Siegfried Sassoon (1886–1967) published a book-length study; E.M. Forster expressed his admiration, and when

Meredith later became a Penguin paperback author with *The Tragic Comedians* (1880) the blurb added something different from the celebrity and sage image: 'he had fought hard and long. Not until his sixtieth year did recognition come, and what the world calls success.' The 'success' was an understatement, and ironically, in that paperback novel, the opening chapters concern a man – Alvan – who is undoubtedly a celebrity: 'She heard things related of Alvan by the underbreath [*sic*]. That circle below her own, the literary and artistic, idolized him.' Meredith as a sage and a teacher was apparently a wonderful entertainer; he was the guest you wanted at dinner. Joseph Balen, writing in 1960, commented on his hero: 'immense physical and mental vitality, a penchant for collecting friendships from all classes, and a love of dazzling an audience with spirited conversation.' His novels are full of dinners and high talk, often sprinkled with Latin quotes and ambitious similes; his status as the sage of Box Hill has been fully established. A certain J.P. Collins visited him in 1912 and on the day after the meeting, Collins wrote, 'The intoxication and the sense of privilege were beginning to wear off.' A year ago I began to re-read him, and I asked myself the question, why and how was such a reputation made? Reports mostly agreed that he was staggeringly original and 'modern' and, of course, the words most often attached to his name are 'Modern Love', the words of the title of his most remarkable achievement some might say, in his role of poet, for Meredith was poet as well as novelist. This point has added to the difficulties of appraising Meredith, as J.I.M. Stewart (1906–1994) put it in his 1970 edition of Thomas Hardy's short stories, coupling the two authors:

> It is interesting that these are the only two major English writers to defy classification in one important regard: neither can be confidently called a novelist who wrote poetry ... Long after their death, critical opinion is divided as to where the chief importance of Meredith and Hardy lies.

It is not difficult to argue that Meredith's impact on his younger contemporaries in the 1890s was profound. Our best evidence for this lies in the autobiography by Diana Cooper (*b*.1940), who recalled that 'Meredith was in high repute in those Oxford days so we all knew *Love in the Valley* [1851] by heart.' Her name came from her mother's admiration for *Diana of the Crossways* (1885), and Meredith bothered to reply when Cooper wrote to him on his birthday. Cooper was at the great man's funeral and she wrote, 'accompanied by Podgie and carrying a treasure-armful of purple irises, we took the train to Golders Green and I saw to my sickening horror George Meredith carried in a small casket by his daughter.' Still thinking about that giant reputation, comparing him in my imagination to Walt Whitman (1819–1892) or Charles Dickens (1812–1870) in this respect, I noted that such was the quality of Meredith's writing that back in 1851, at only 23, Meredith sent a copy of his first poetry collection to Alfred Tennyson (1809–1892), and surprisingly, received a reply. According to biographer Robert Bernard Martin (1918–1999), Tennyson rarely troubled himself to respond to such gifts.

Then came the impact of reading Meredith with the key question in my mind: why was this man such a celebrity? My first reading – an attempt to read *The Egoist* – created a puzzled response. After a few chapters, I had the sense that intense verbiage and a succession of clusters of complex metaphors had blocked my understanding. Fiction entails a bond and a trust; this concerns a sharing of the fabricated narrative. The words were impressive, and certain images stood out with the sharpness and shock of a metaphysical lyric from John Donne (1572–1631). I had to try again, and the result was a profound realisation that here was a Victorian novel (published in 1879) that was peculiarly modern: it had whimsicality, playfulness, metafictional awareness; in reading it, one is aware of an impressive array of intertextual influence, from echoes of Jane Austen (1775–1817) to extended scenes in the fashion of Meredith's father-in-law, Thomas Love Peacock (1785–1866).

The novel has Wildean wit; it is saturated with commentary on 'We English' and on class, manners, young and old, and most of all, a dwelling on a fundamental and radical appraisal of the 'modern marriage' and all its rituals, trials and strains. Overlying the novel, like a threatening cloud, in the Married Woman's Property Act (1882) and the revisions of the property of wives and the retention of what is theirs.

When I came across this, I knew that I was in contact with a writer of true vision as well as multi-layered and intellectual humour: 'He saw none but Clara, hated none, loved none, save the intolerable woman. What logic was in him deduced her to be individual and most distinctive from the circumstance that only she had ever wrought those pangs.' I could be reading D.H. Lawrence, I reflected. Yes, there were heavy Homeric similes, ambitious mixed metaphors, images pulled out so far that their material ripped the fabric of the thought behind. But these are forgiven in a novel of such panache, energy and contemporary urgency, fun and resonant statements. At the final page, one image stuck to me like glue: 'She was aware that she was nailed to her sex.' It was all a matter of matching a very powerful, designed, fabricated orchestration of images, all reflecting the inner states of his main characters: that was the key to his success. Above that there is the sheer delight in showing human folly and self-deception, mainly in the person of Sir Willoughby; there are elements also in Meredith's fiction, which if written today would very likely cause offence, such as statements on Jewish characters or on potential abuse of weaker characters, but these are, of course, interwoven in the narratives of their time and place.

Staggering response number two came with the poetry. One line from *Modern Love* (1862) has been shooting around my mind ever since I first read the first of those sixteen-line sonnets: 'By this he knew she wept with waking eyes.' It is an opening guaranteed to astonish and create the effect of the ancient mariner being in your path, as you wait for the story. Other lines assault the senses: 'I claim a phantom-woman in the past.' Surely, something Thomas Hardy read and also the startling attack on the senses in so many other poems, such as 'He drops the silver chain of sound' in *The Lark Ascending* (1881).

I have become convinced that beneath the image of the ailing, ageing George Meredith lies a very talented writer, whose constant flow of imagery made him the kind of poet we might find in Emily Brontë (1818–1848) or in Walt Whitman: writers of any category or genre who find that poetic expression is as instinct in their nature as their own breath. My reading discerns two figures: the man who perhaps provides the modern template of the literary celebrity, and the genuine creative artist beneath. Meredith wrote to Thomas Carlyle (1795–1881), after being advised to write non-fiction: 'Truth I take to be the broad heaven above the petty doings of mankind which we call facts.' If we open up the enquiry to ask what we learn about literary celebrity from Meredith as a case study, then perhaps the first answer is that such a phenomenon, though not new in 1890, reinforces the view that the identities of artists and writers had undergone a radical change long before (some scholars argue that the early eighteenth century was a formative period); when *noms de plumes* came along, and when writers existed behind the extensions of their personalities into public creations, as in the case of Lord Byron (1788–1824), it became possible to play games with one's readership. The expansion of popular publishing throughout the nineteenth century meant that Charles Dickens the public speaker revealed a figure who was usually eclipsed from view, demonstrated to the industry that book sales and writers could be yoked together with a profit in mind.

There is no doubt that Meredith relished an audience, and he would talk for hours to writers as well as to those curious souls who walked to Box Hill and took in as a tourist sight his flint cottage. But my principal discovery was that all this was one thing, one activity, for Meredith. What occurs repeatedly is his awareness of 'the young'. Diana Cooper saw this, along with her intellectual peers; essentially, all this was the same activity as the circulation of love poems in the early Stuart circles, but now, with Smiths, Mudies and the railways, celebrities could be fashioned and then visited, quizzed and even sought out at home. As Meredith was pulled around in his bath chair, *The Strand* magazine was running a series headed, 'Portraits of Celebrities at Different Times of their Lives'.

My feeling is that Meredith was not the first truly notable literary celebrity (there is Lord Byron of course) but the scale of his influence on other writers surely matches that of James Joyce or Gustave Flaubert (1821–1880), but Meredith had an influence that went way beyond the books and poems. He has come to seem, to my mind, the celebrity whose presence overwhelms the mere words in his field of influence.

It is more a case of explaining his influence than seeing him as a celebrity and no more. If we had to look for a more recent instance of this stealthy but profound influence on future writers as well as contemporaries we might suggest Philip Larkin, whose quietly revolutionary voice and set of attitudes found their natural vehicle in the poetry of the melancholy observer. Meredith, by contrast, was staggeringly different. Reading his fiction now, we have to cope with a stance taken in the narration that accepts that the reader will share the stance, and if not, then they will enjoy the work required to fall into step with Meredith's voice.

In his short preface to *The Tragic Comedians* (1880), he starts with a challenging word – 'fantastical' – and he roots out the implications, showing that the modern sensibility embraces the sweetly entertaining slipperiness of the language's word hoard. Surely, although Meredith's image and public notoriety was more than that of a sage; he was one of those rare writers who gauged the set of attitudes to human relationships that were forming a new sensibility, as the century came to an end.

'Journos' and Clubs

There is also one other important foundation in this gradual emergence of the woman writer before the end of the First World War: the opening up of journalism and the skills of typing and shorthand that would definitely assist progress. By 1829, Charles Dickens had mastered shorthand, and he started work as a reporter in the ecclesiastical courts; he had learned the script by working for his uncle, John Henry Barrow (1796–1858), who was working parallel to Hansard in doing parliamentary reporting.

The emergence of Pitman's shorthand was a massive contributor to the establishment of women writers within the spectrum of writing, from journalism to fiction. Sir Isaac Pitman (1813–1897) first made his system generally known in 1837; the skill was at first known as phonography, and it soon became popular in the world of the press and reporting. Running parallel to this were other advances in the creation and support of professional women, such as The Society for Promoting the Employment of Women, founded in 1859 by Jessie Boucherett (1825–1905). In 1858, a publication linked to this society, *The English Woman's Journal*, had already been established. The organisation was the first to include a printing press in women's education, and also classes in shorthand.

There is an insight into the early days of using Pitman's shorthand in the biography of writer and comic singer, George Grossmith Jr (1874–1935). His father, George Grossmith Sr (1847–1912), was an established crime reporter for *The Times*, and one time when his father was away, Grossmith Jr covered the trials at Bow Street. He had to write reports in triplicate, using a primitive form of duplicate paper. Fortunately, things had improved by the last decades of the century.

By the time we reach the first decades of the twentieth century, there is a totally different picture. As historian Dr Nicole Robertson notes, the *Pitman's Shorthand and Typing Yearbook and Diary* (first issued in 1892) is a strong indicator of the popularity and impact of shorthand on women's working lives. She wrote that this guide 'can provide information on a broad set of questions pertinent to this group of non-manual workers including how new technology shaped and influenced the nature of clerical work …' Of course, shorthand also helped many writers broaden the portfolio of what skills they could off on the foot of the ladder when it came to writing and editing.

There was also the similar skill of typing. G.K. Chesterton wrote, 'twenty million young women rose to their feet with the cry "We will not be dictated to" and promptly became stenographers.'

A notably crucial part of the new woman writer's networking and efforts to be known and read, was the professional club. When Marie Belloc Lowndes called in at her Thirty Club in February 1915, she recorded in her diary:

> I sat between Lady Stanley [1807–1895] and Fanny Prothero [1854–1934]. Everyone felt uneasy about the Russian position [regarding the First World War], but not much was said, owing to the presence of the Russian Ambassadress. There was a good deal of talk about the effect of the war on human beings. Marie de Rothschild [1927–1996] told us that she had heard the Germans had a hundred submarines ...

This is a staggeringly important insight into a woman writer's life at that time: there she is, chatting with several celebrities, totally involved in the issues of the day, and completely at home with the context.

Firstly, what were these clubs and how did they emerge in society?

Jack's Reference Book for Home and Office (1930) listed thirteen of these, including the famous Lyceum in Piccadilly and the Albemarle (for ladies and gentlemen) in Dover Street. For Belloc Lowndes, her club was unique, and very modern – it was meant for women working in advertising, along with other professions – known as the Thirty Club. This still exists, and uses Claridge's for its meetings.

Walking in Albion Street, Leeds, when I was a young trainee tax officer in the 1960s, I saw the brass plate, and I had to check out the place. The words proclaimed a 'club' of some kind. In fact it was for 'gentlemen' and in my working class early life in the city I had met no gentlemen at all. The word fascinated me, and so did the notion of a club. After all, the only use of the word I knew was in the 'Stamp Club' at my secondary modern school. The word 'club' suggested to me something secret, special and exclusive. Consequently, later in my life when I became a writer and historian, I was always sensitive to the idea of a club. When the germ of this book was planted, no gentlemen figured in my outline. No, women had clubs too, and they are intriguingly important institutions.

When I learned that there were women sitting in London clubs, reclining on a *chaise longue* perhaps, or sipping tea and discussing politics, my attention was grabbed, and now those women snugly ensconced around the corner from the buzzing heart of the British Empire, as they were in *c.*1920, cried out for their stories to be told. What added to the invitation for a true enquiry into these lives and locations was a second 'club' in my life: the working men's club. Now, this was originally a place offering self-education as well as relaxation, but by *c.*1960 when I first entered one, the various rooms inside were all about fun and leisure, from snooker to 'turns' on stage. But there was an aspect of such boozy places that stirred a sense of revolt: they had a room from which women were forbidden.

Sitting down to write this history then was partly with the aim of showing that women and their professional writing lives deserved a full account, and that those secondary areas of life that always attach themselves to a creative profession, such as networking and promotional work, need to be better known.

If we look for the origins of the word 'club' we start with a simple definition, which seems to embrace all versions of the societies we might think of:

> A society of persons who club together, or form themselves into a knot or lump. In this sense the word was originally applied to persons bound together by a vow (German: *gelubede*).
>
> *Brewer's Dictionary of Phrase and Fable* by E. Cobham Brewer (1870)

There's something bland and comfortable about being in 'a knot or lump', but it's the 'vow' that troubles if we apply it to history.

Clubs, long before they were places for chat and discussion, were potentially dangerous places. Edinburgh, for instance, was always a place of clubs for gentlemen, and they tended to toast. Toasts reinforced ideologies, beliefs, tastes and political stances. A toast to the right man was essential, or even to the right principle. It was 'them and us'. This club believes that ... and this club gathers together because ...

Jenny Uglow (*b.*1947), in her book, *In These Times: Living in Britain Through Napoléon's Wars, 1793–1815* (2015), about Regency Britain, explains: 'Rakes young and old also joined private club and riotously informal drinking societies. A few had their hair cut short, in the revolutionary style, but they still enjoyed the coarse eighteenth-century jokes of bums and farts and tits ...' A person was either in the club set or they were nothing. If you didn't join a radical club or a riotous club, you still had the really fashionable ones. Uglow describes these neatly: 'There were new clubs, fashionable among gamblers, like the Cocoa Tree and Watier's, opened by the Prince of Wales' [later King George IV (1762 –1830)] chef [Jean-Baptiste Watier] and patronised by Beau Brummell [1778–1840] and the dandies.'

In the Georgian years, and more intensively in the Regency, clubs indicated dissent. The coffee house might be for business and for vanity and relaxation, but a 'club' was for radicals. Napoléon threatened across the Channel; kings and queens had been decapitated and there had been riots in the streets over in France. No, a club meant anarchy.

But it wasn't only in the Regency either that clubs were trouble. In the last decades of Queen Victoria's (1819–1901) reign (1837–1901), clubs and societies abounded; the city was a nest of anarchists and terrorists alongside the less openly subversive groups who were trying to change art and aesthetics. A club then might be simply for revolutions in style, design or literary technique; but equally it might be for subverting the social order. Or, as was the case in 1886, the gentlemen's clubs might well be seen as targets for those radicals. In that year, the Social Democratic Federation (a club of socialist aspirations) gathered in Trafalgar Square for speeches and marches. But times were hard, and matters escalated. Almost 40,000 people decided to march on Dod Street police station, and there was a rampage. Thousands entered Pall Mall, and the well-heeled leisured class were in for a hard time. Historian Jerry White (*b.*1949) describes what happened:

> There appears to have been some provocation from one of the Pall Mall Clubs ... But whatever the spark, there was no doubting the blaze. Club Windows the length of Pall Mall and St James's Street were shattered with stones. Shop windows in Piccadilly were smashed and their contents looted as the Stampeding crowd turned it mind to plunder.

What had happened throughout that century was that clubs had developed first as places for the wealthy and the rising middle-class businessmen, but also as places for working men; on the other hand, they had also become political groups. The only common ground was that people were either members or they were not. *Them and us* ruled the day.

By the time of the first women's clubs in mid-nineteenth century, the Victorians had come to see that on a wide spectrum, clubs for the discontented were frightening, disturbing places, and in complete contrast were the clubs for the rich, at the heart of London's theatrical and diplomatic square mile, where wealthy men gathered to enjoy the charms of their cultural richness. Colonel Frederick Wellesley (1844–1931), great-nephew of the Duke of Wellington (1769–1852), gives an instance of this dichotomy, as he accounts for the pleasure of leaving his clubland to venture into a 'Night House' in the Haymarket area. Not only did he and his friends go to brothels and even to see executions; they had a club porter to arrange these visits.

The transition, then, was one of the word 'club' itself undergoing a number of identities, all male-centred, and so when the women first planned their clubs, they obviously wanted something different. The men in their clubs had often treated them as retreats, caves, escapes to oblivion where the pressures of time and work could be left behind. One story laughs at this:

> A lady called at Brooks and asked the hall porter if Mr X was at the club.
> 'I can't say, madam' said the porter.
> 'Please find out, and if he is, say his wife wants him.'
> 'Sorry madam, but members of Brooks don't have wives.'

By the twentieth century, it is clear that women's clubs were mostly concerned with not only offering relaxation and good talk, but also in purposeful activity. Take The Efficiency Club, for instance, created by Lady Rhondda (1883–1958) in 1919. She gave a lecture on the reason for the club's existence at Westminster Central Hall, and she noted the aim of promoting and encouraging improvements in the worlds of professional women in business and other areas. Susannah Stapleton, in her admirable biographical work on 'Lady Detective' Maud West, explains further:

> The membership included representatives from many large-scale employers of women, such as Selfridge's and Lyons' Corner House, as well as doctors, dentists, aviators, lawyers, headmistresses, editors, saddlers, builders, artists, musicians, engineers, and of course, one private detective. It claimed to be the first organisation of its kind in the world.

Stapleton goes on to explain that they had 'informal members' nights to share tips on day-to-day business practices.' It is impossible to imagine this happening at the men's clubs such as the Savage or the Beefsteak.

'Club' was to lose the connotations of radicalism or elitism for many in the twentieth century, as the wealthy people who were rich through estates were joined by the *nouveaux riches* from the world of commerce and industry. Yet still, being a member of a club was to have its practical reasons, matters not really related to style and prestige. In other words, they provided an overnight stay or a place for a group of friends to arrange to have a lunch undisturbed, and where they did not have to clock-watch.

On 23 June 1915, Marie Belloc Lowndes, sister to Hilaire Belloc, noted in her diary that a friend had telephoned her and told her that a sea battle was in progress on the Dogger Bank. Later, her friend rang again and said that the news was confirmed by the Admiralty. Belloc Lowndes 'telephoned Freddie. He said that nothing of the kind had reached *The Times* office.'

Here was a woman who needed to be informed. She was a successful novelist, and just before the First World War her novel, *The Lodger* (1913), had been adapted for the screen, directed by Alfred Hitchcock (1899–1980). Her father was a French lawyer, Louis Belloc, and her mother was Bessie

Parkes (1829–1925), feminist and editor of the first real feminist periodical, *The English Woman's Journal*, who had thought of the idea of such a club back in 1857.

She was the new woman in every sense: she had made a huge success of her writing career, and could multi-task, schmooze and communicate with people from all backgrounds and social class. She was wanted for panels, discussions, committees and, of course, in clubs and societies. She was only too happy to oblige when asked along to take part in cultural affairs, and she was valued and respected in a range of contexts across the metropolis.

Belloc Lowndes came from a family that liked to keep the mind alive, stay informed on current affairs, and generally be involved in the arts and in society. She had been married for nineteen years when she made that diary entry, and she had a widening circle of literary and political friends. Of course, she wrote a great deal, and she networked when she could, but what did she need in addition to all this – something that would give her opportunities such as advanced news about naval battles and perhaps the latest hot debates in Westminster? She needed a club. She found one: The Thirty Club.

The Thirty Club was established in 1905 simply as a dining club. Men were involved then, and members came from the world of media and advertising; they made contacts over the pond and in New York they found kindred souls in the Advertising Club. When Belloc Lowndes called in for lunch and a chat in 1915 it was not exclusively for women, but in 1923 the Women's Advertising Club of London was formed. There had been a revolution in the lives and aspirations of both wealthy women and educated middle-class women: the Sex Disqualification (Removal) Act 1919. All kinds of doors opened for the fresh generation of educated women who had gained degrees or achieved high status in their occupation, or who were simply aspirational people with a circle of influential and well-heeled friends.

Yet, even before the Thirty Club had its women's arm, Belloc Lowndes had some very pleasant times (in spite of the war) with her female friends, such as her meeting with Marie de Rothschild and Lady Stanley at which they discussed Russia's place in the war.

The position referred to was diplomatic, not sexual, but in years to come, the clubs would move away from such serious matters. Belloc Lowndes was moving in high circles. She used her diary to let loose her feelings about the current situation on returning home from these conversations: 'No, I do not believe in Zeppelins or an invasion ... They are very fragile. They have not even ventured to send them into France.' How wrong can you be? On 2 November 1915, she was describing the horrors of a Zeppelin raid.

What Belloc Lowndes was doing, however, at her club, was enjoying a cultural pursuit that had been envisioned sixty years before and had arrived in considerable numbers by the turn of the century. The 'new woman', as well as demanding the vote and riding bicycles, wanted a rich and independent cultural life of her own, away from her husband, where she could enjoy the company of like-minded women friends.

By 1930, there were twelve such exclusively female clubs in London, listed in *Jack's Reference Book for Home and Office*, from the sheer intellectualism of the University Club in Audley Square to the clubs, which appealed more to the chatters and shoppers, close to Oxford Street and away from Piccadilly where the traditional men's clubs were mostly found.

Belloc Lowndes was typical of the successful woman writer of her time. The 1890s had brought about an acceleration in the need for serialised fiction in the numerous new periodicals such as *The Strand*, *The Idler* and *Pearson's Weekly*. Along with these came the women's magazines, and as always happens, with publishing comes the gathering society of reviewers, journalists, agents and others, who work alongside. Since the seventeenth century, the assemblies of such folk had been in coffee houses and pubs of course, but a club was a very different thing.

Women wanted rest and recreation. If our image of a men's club is one of a deep armchair, a whisky-soaked old raconteur and a long-suffering servant, then nothing could be further from the typical scene where the women gathered. The first club that might be called modern was the Ladies' Institute, which lasted from 1860 to 1867, had a reading room and a dining room. It was open until 10.30 pm at night. For a subscription fee of just 1 guinea the facilities were yours. But a really telling coda to that is the fact that the governess class could avail themselves of the club's rooms for only half the cost.

Belloc Lowndes, as a thoroughly modern woman, would have appreciated the situation in the United States. There they had a General Federation of Women's Clubs by 1890. There were reasons for the high tone of the core of the United States clubs, such as the emergence of women lawyers in most states by the 1880s, and the opportunities for women in all kinds of professions. After all, the first woman detective was in the Pinkerton way back in the 1860s: Kate Warne (1833–1868), whose work saved Abraham Lincoln (1809–1865) in an earlier assassination attempt.

From the beginning, there was a mix of attractions, and these may be reduced to two: conversation and shopping. But that is not meant as a trivial comment. The conversation in the Victorian clubs was mostly of a very sophisticated and intellectual level. There is a wonderful satisfaction in the offering of a professional club. Dr Johnson's comment on the institution was, 'Sir, the great chair of a full and pleasant town club is, perhaps, the throne of human felicity.' The author of a handbook on clubs, produced by the Whitbread group in 1950, expressed the Colonel Blimp attitude to Belloc Lowndes's cultural treats: 'There is something essentially masculine about a club; or, if one dared say it, perhaps something essentially non-clubbable about a woman.' How wrong can a man be? Strangely, attitudes of men-only conservatism hung on for some time. The Junior Constitutional Club had a prominent notice in the vestibule: 'Notice. Lady visitors are requested to use the lift and not descend by the staircase.' One might think the women carried some kind of plague.

The truth is that, in the Edwardian boom years of clubs of all kinds, the men's places were more often than not places where business was conducted, and that was anathema to women. We have to feel sorry for the harassed and flustered men such as the lawyer-entertainer Corney Grain (1844–1895), who wrote a hurried note from his Beefsteak Club in 1889 to a Mrs Robertson who had booked him for a family party:

> Dear Mrs Robertson,
>
> I could come February 15th 1890. Would the train due at Broxbourne at 7.36 [pm] do? It would give me time to get something to eat after my work ...

There was no room for any such rush and sweat in Belloc Lowndes's world of club and conversation. Men had it all wrong: the old coffee house tradition of doing business and making deals inside the comfort of a club was just not on.

Some coxcombs had tried to argue that a club made a man better husband material: 'Clubs induce habits of economy, temperance, refinement, regularity, and good order; and as men in general are not content with their condition as long as it can be improved, it is a natural step from the comforts of a club to those of matrimony ...' Which world was the author, a Mr Walker, inhabiting? He wasn't going to fool anyone.

Marie Belloc Lowndes and Friends

Returning to Marie Belloc Lowndes, if we ask the question: what type of woman needed the new clubs in their first flowering, in the *fin de siècle* literary world? Belloc Lowndes provides the answer. She was that variety of writer who appears to be everywhere, available for comment on any issue in the news. In a feature on women and marriage in one periodical she said, 'I do not think it proper for a wife to be put in the same position as a housekeeper.' She was usually reported as an example of the new women who had a brain and used it. One reporter defined her as 'a clever journalist who specialises in the *Almanac de Gotha* [a directory of European royalty] and is inexhaustible in details about subjects like royal wedding cake and the Prince of Wales' baby-linen.' She was certainly noticed as a writer, and her books were widely reviewed. When her novel in dialogue *The Philosophy of the Marquise* (1899) was reviewed in every branch of literary reportage one could imagine; that was gratifying to her no doubt, as when she was first noticed it was as 'a woman gliding about in her own quiet way' at a glitterati party.

Most of all, Belloc Lowndes was a celebrity and a personality. She was a celebrity *with* a personality in fact – far more than simple the brother of Hilaire Belloc. She was best known for her novel, *The Lodger*, printed in the 1911 *McClure's Magazine* and published in book form in 1913, then later filmed by Alfred Hitchcock in 1927. When one writer produced a Christmas piece on who was walking around London looking for gifts and drinks, she was there among such luminaries as 'The Hon. Mrs Henniker ... President of the Society of Women Journalists ...' and 'Mr David Murray, surrounded by a circle of appreciative friends.' When she made her first social impact, in the late 1890s, she was singled out as a clubbable type, and on one occasion a feature headed 'Women Writers at Dinner' we have a glimpse of her in her element:

> Fifteen years ago a handful of women writers dined, drank and smoked together and, undiverted by the fascinating presence of men, so appreciated each other's company that their numbers each year have multiplied to one hundred and ninety-six who on Monday dined at the Criterion. Miss Beatrice Harraden was in the chair, and the vice-chairs were filled by Mrs Steel, Miss Netta Syrett, Mrs J.R. Grove, Mrs W.K. Clifford, Mrs Walford, Mrs Violet Hunt and Miss Marie Belloc-Lowndes.

What did they do? They toasted the royalty and indulged in some memories, and then Beatrice Webb gave a talk on economics. This was the future. This was what the women's clubs were destined to be: a sorority with a workable mix of activities from personal to universal. They were determined to keep up with the modern world but still inhabit a 'woman's world' in terms of their emotions, affiliations and shared involvement in life.

It was entirely fitting that Beatrice Webb gave the talk. She had written, memorably, in her autobiography, that in the nineteenth century there had been a transference of 'the idea of service from God to man.'

Belloc Lowndes, even in her first years as a successful writer and city personality, had grasped the essential fact that success in one's art and craft came along with a presence in the media. A century before our world of computers and mobile phones, tweeting and websites, she saw that a 'social presence' was necessary. Deals were done face to face. Contacts were made at parties and conferences. The women's club was the obvious extension of the notion of the 'old boys' network which oiled the wheels of the British Empire and allowed families to keep everything that they wanted to preserve 'in the family'.

In that microcosm, Belloc Lowndes was a 'natural'. She also saw the appeal to readers of the notion of a club for women to her readers. In the early years of the twentieth century, there was a scandal in the national papers about gambling clubs, and Belloc Lowndes made the most of this and of women in clubs in *The Lodger*, in this scene:

> 'I wonder if *M'Sieur* would care to become a member of the club' he said in a low voice, 'I do not press *M'Sieur* to do so, but you see both Madame Bailey and her friends are members of the Club ... I fear it is no use our going to the Playing Rooms downstairs.'
>
> 'The Playing Rooms?' Sylvia a member of a Club? And – for Chester's quick legal mind had leapt on the fact – 'of a gambling club!'

When Belloc Lowndes walked into her club in Audley Street she was doing something as thoroughly modern as possible. Good gracious – men realised that women even *smoked* in them! Belloc Lowndes may well have done. She knew all about the men's clubs, where most members appear to have smoked. A memoir by Cyril Clemens (1902–1999) notes that Belloc Lowndes met some 'Lions in their dens' as *The Idler* magazine referred to literary celebrities. Cyril recalls,

> Yet another memory of Mrs Belloc Lowndes' youth is that of having met Mark Twain [1835–1910] during more than one of his sojourns in England. Some wonderful gatherings were held in his honour, and at a dinner given by an institution entitled The Vagabonds' Club he made what she believed to have been one of the best speeches in his life ...

Belloc Lowndes rubbed shoulders with rich, famous, poor and struggling then. She could talk to anyone and maintain interest. What is really interesting is to consider the fact that the women like Belloc Lowndes who relished the new clubs for their sex seemed to know quite well what the men's clubs were like – and they wanted something different.

What women wanted to avoid was the triviality and fussiness of the men's clubs where, notoriously, the curmudgeons, the opinionated and the over-indulged old bachelors were set in their ways and could ossify if left undisturbed. One story from Douglas Sutherland (1919–1995) raises a smile on this:

> Every club has its complaints book where gentlemen can air their grievances. Thus one gentleman may complain that another snores too loudly in the smoking room, or consistently fails to raise the lavatory seat. A gentleman of my acquaintance resigned in a huff when three of his fellow members complained that he was helping himself too liberally to the milk pudding.

It is not difficult to see in the earnest statements of aims and objectives women gave when the new clubs were announced and described. They wanted to stay clear of these kinds of trivial happenings. Perhaps such thoughts led to a too serious attitude, but they clearly understood that aiming too high meant that a fall could still lead to high standards. Aiming too low could mean a dip of far too extreme a nature.

The groundwork for the cultural revolution after 1919 may be seen in the Edwardian years of course. Life-writing specialist Claire Tomalin (*b.*1933), in her biography of Katherine Mansfield, points out that the arts 'were in a ... state of eruption' with 'New magazines, edited and written by new men and women, and read by an intelligentsia no longer confined to the middle classes, were appearing.' She also points out that the editor of the *English Review*, Ford Madox Hueffer (1873–1939), 'had a declared policy of seeking working-class writers.' It is clear that well before the emergence of the women writers who began their efforts to be published and noticed after the First World War, there were plenty of women active in the arts and working individually to be seen, heard, read and listened to. In the world of music and the theatre, for instance, in brochures issued by an agent in the provinces the female presence is considerably notable. In the brochure, giving 'a list of artistes' the entrepreneur has 180 women singers on his books, and can offer clients in search of entertainers The Euterpean Ladies' Orchestra, directed by Emilie and Annie Scott, alongside such talents as Nellie Ganthony who presents 'humorous, musical and emotional sketches.'

Chapter 2

Becoming a Woman Writer

'During my pregnancy I wrote a great number of these novelettes at a guinea a thousand ...'
Ethel Mannin (1900–1984)

By 1917, we may see, in a prominent advert placed in the papers by Mills & Boon, just how much presence there was on the verge of the interwar years, of women writers. Together with their publication of the works of Jack London (1876–1916), the famous publishers of romance had on their books, I.A.R. Wylie (1885–1959), whose new novel *The Shining Heights* (1917) was foregrounded in the advert, and the book was described as 'A long, powerful and absorbing novel by one of Britain's most popular novelists.' There was also *Kris-Girl* (1917) by Beatrice Grimshaw (1870–1953) 'an exciting story of the South Seas' and *Love* (1917) by W.B. Trites. They even published poetry and non-fiction and the women were there also, with *The Experiences of a Woman Doctor in Siberia* (1917) by Dr Caroline Matthews (1877–1927) and *The Doll's Day* (1918) by Carine Cadby (1864–1957).

Business was booming. The publishers even had their Pam Ayres (*b.*1947), in the shape of Janet Begbie (1897–1953), author of *Morning Mist* (1916), and they also published Eden Phillpotts (1862–1960), who was to be a formative influence on the success of Agatha Christie. The traditional married woman writer was still there in their lists, such as Mrs George de Horne Vaizey (1857–1917), who had several works in the advert, including *The Adventures of Billie Belshaw* (1912) and Mary L. Moreland (1859–1918).

The popular women writers often conformed to the racy and compelling images of them in the media. Mills & Boon's star, I.A.R. Wylie for instance, lived the life of a romantic heroine. She was Ida Wylie, born in 1885; she was Australian, born in Melbourne, but with a Scottish family connection. Her father was in constant turmoil, escaping financial difficulties and failing in a political career. Wylie, though she experienced finishing school was largely educated at home, and like Agatha Christie and the Brontës, she invented all kinds of stories. She was so clever and receptive that she gleaned masses of material from an Indian friend, enough to provide the basis and people for novels set in India.

She was then an active Suffragette, and her home was a retreat for the unfortunate women who had been arrested and imprisoned under the Prisoners' (Temporary Discharge for Ill-Health) Act 1913, known as the 'Cat and Mouse Act', which led to prison force-feeding. Wylie was part of the editing group of *The Suffragette* and came to know Christabel Pankhurst (1880–1958).

But Mills & Boon knew they had a major figure on their books. Her novels were often the basis of Hollywood films. John Ford (1894–1973) made *Four Sons* (1928) and perhaps her most famous product – *Keeper of the Flame* (1942) – was directed by George Cukor (1899–1983). Wylie was fond of women and wrote in her autobiography that 'I have always liked women better than men. I am more at ease with them and more amused with them.' Her life was remarkably singular and at times sensational, and in between all the activity she published over forty novels.

Storm Jameson knew her, and at one time they met and talked, and Jameson reported: 'We had been friendly for many years, and she asked me how much I had put aside against an imminent old age. "Not a penny" I told her. She was sincerely horrified. Having made a great deal of money, far more than I ever earned, she had a terrible fear of losing it ...'

The new world of the woman author who lived a life accurately described as 'dashing' had arrived; there is no doubt that, as press reports show through the interwar years, there was a public of readers hungry for the biographies behind the writings of many romantic novelists, and some of the really successful ones (such as Agatha Christie, Daphne du Maurier and Storm Jameson) were intrepid travellers and brave co-equals with the inhabitants of the male world of action and adventure. Of course, the women in this advert were not all surrounded by high drama and excitement: there was Janet Begbie, daughter of the writer Harold Begbie (1871–1929), for instance, who was renowned for his financing of socialist and charitable schemes. Janet Begbie worked away quietly, writing fiction as Elizabeth Croly and poetry: the latter made her reputation.

The Struggle: Help From Sir Philip Gibbs

Every writer knows a great deal about rejection. In the days before the internet and e-mail, the rejection letters dropped through the letter box along with the heavy manuscript. Trying to succeed as a writer entails trying to understand what publishing is all about and what might make an editor interested in one's work. This struggle is neatly exemplified in some letters from Sir Philip Gibbs (1877–1962) at the end of the Second World War, written to a writer who had sent him a manuscript. Gibbs had experienced just about everything involved in the literary business, and had written several books in both fiction and non-fiction. He was born in 1877, and his first taste of writing was in working for the *Daily Chronicle* in the 1890s; this was followed by his first book and then came his work as a reporter in the First World War.

He joined the ranks of the writers of reportage when 'darkest England' became a dominant theme in the 1930s. By the 1940s, he was a grand old man of letters, having known publishers and editors in all kinds of areas, and some of his correspondence with would-be writers has survived. The following is a summary of one of these cases. The author in question, as far as is known, never made it into print. The first stage in this writing was brief. It begins with 'I'm very sorry but I can't decipher your English ... I am very glad to know you had some pleasure in reading my books. I am sorry I can't help you about *The Pageant of the Years* [1946] as it is out of print, and I am afraid there is no prospect of a cheap edition.' This was the beginning: compliments on his writing. Then came his work as an agent, and he responded with a polite 'I look forward to reading your book' and a batch of publishers' letters. The next stage was an overall summary:

> Dear Miss ...
>
> I enclose a letter with your typescript sent by registered post but omitted to refer to your postscript about indicating passages to cut. I think it would be much better if you performed this operation, omitting those paragraphs or pages which you don't consider essential. I think perhaps the story of your childhood is a little too

> long. To my mind the interest of the narrative increases when you become a nurse …

After this, Gibbs is ill, but does offer something:

> Dear Miss ...
>
> Many thanks for your kind letter. I am a bit better in health since last I wrote to you. I return your 'Retrospect' and do hope you will have luck with it, in spite of my somewhat gloomy remarks. Some of my pages broke away from the fastening and I adjusted a few of them. As I told you before I have found your book very interesting, and pleasant reading, and it is only the condition of publishing today which is weighted against it ...

The writing goes on, however, and the next letter really addresses both the typescript and the market. His remarks offer some thought that are familiar to any writer who has been the subject of that kind of comfort that tends to make the task seem even more impossible than it was when the work was first submitted:

> Dear Miss ...
>
> I have been handicapped in sending your typescript by feeling very unwell, and being in the doctor's hands. But I have read a great deal of it, and would like to keep it a few days longer. I have read enough, however, to form an opinion about it. I have found it very pleasant and interesting reading, but I fear very much that the story you tell of your own life is not sufficiently unusual or enthralling to appeal to a publisher who is out to make a profit on a fairly large scale – as any publisher is, especially at the present time when he can't afford to take a risk owing to the high cost of producing a book. Now, if you were a famous film star or singer, or lady of exalted rank, or a wicked and notorious woman, there would be a clamour for this book of yours, and the publishers would fight each other for it! But as you

> are unknown to fame, they will, I very much fear, turn down a book like yours however pleasant and amusing. That is a severe indictment of modern conditions and taste, but there it is – frustrating to the unknown writers. I only wish I could be more encouraging but it is best to tell the truth as I see it. On the other hand, I would not suggest giving up all effort to get it published, and it might be worth your while sending it to Hutchinson ... They produce more books than anyone and have subsidiary companies like Jarrolds etc. I have one minor criticism, not of great importance. Some of your parentheses between brackets are unduly long and tend to destroy the rules of grammar and syntax. Also, I believe the book would be better if you cut it down rather ruthlessly here and there ...

The hapless writer certainly gets advice here, and the account of the publishing industry is uncannily modern to today's reader. What Gibbs does show is that the range of such advice does not change radically through the years: the determining factor is the market, and what is bought from the bookshops by the good British public. The other point here is that Gibbs was a professional, but clearly a freelance: his critique was largely from a writer's experience rather than from the study.

The Chaos of Creation and Being Read

Choose any point in British history and try to find out what was actually demanded of the woman who set out to be a writer. Until the twentieth century, the Becher's Brook of the track towards print was the notion of a fitting subject. Rich women and aristocrats might have plenty of educative travels to recall; true rascals and tearaways might travel alone even, through dangerous territory – as Diana Mayo, heroine of *The Sheik* (1919) by E.M. Hull (1880–1947) does; then of course there are the moral tales and Christian works for children and the national schools of the Victorian years. But the original writer – a woman essentially comparing with a man in terms of the trajectory of her life – was a rarity.

When the Augustan and Romantic ages brought definite changes in this (between *c.*1770 and 1830s) then, as Jane Austen's career proves, new genres brought more opportunities. A scan of the women writers in that period who made it into print shows two particular trends: firstly, that non-fiction, such as diaries and journals, was always a possibility if a person had backing and status, and secondly, that in popular genres and conventions, women could then hide behind their *noms de plumes* as the Brontës or George Eliot (1819–1880) did, and in many cases they wrote, as Mrs Humphry Ward did, with no female first name evident.

The obstacles were largely the same for would-be writers of the lower-middle class or working class, but in the nineteenth century there was a new readership in the population of the new towns and cities established during the long process of the Industrial Revolution and the expansion of circulating libraries. There was also the practice of heading towards print by appealing for subscriptions, as John Clare (1793–1864) notably did, as a working man whose poems were backed by middle class gents. For equivalent women writers, there were similar openings, and also the Christian readership.

In terms of how the serious literary press considered women writers, something may be gleaned from the first issue of *The Times Literary Supplement* in 1902; the truth is that the esteemed periodical ignored them. The first three pages (small print) featured Edward FitzGerald (1809–1883), Scottish life and letters, Napoléon's campaign in Poland, Leigh Hunt (1784–1859), the Chinese intellect and an indictment of our Indian administration. By page four things look up a little, as under the verse reviews we have Katherine Tynan (1859–1931) and Mary Robinson (1757–1800) noticed; the main fiction reviews concern two male writers' work, and two pages of material on drama are solely concerned with male writers. The two women authors shared a sentence: 'The former is one of the most genuine productions of the modern Irish muse; the latter, of which the sentiment ranges over England, France and Italy, over the present and the past contains much delicate imagination, much reflection, and much grace of phrase.'

Still, there was a revolution going on in the world of workaday authors who saw their life in terms of business rather than high art, as the Society of Authors had been established in 1884, and from their prospectus of 1912 it is clear that a number of women writers were involved in the work of the council of that society: Lady Lugard (1852–1929), Mrs Humphry Ward, Marie Belloc Lowndes, Edith Nesbit, Mrs Alec Tweedie (1862–1940), Cicely

Hamilton (1872–1952) and Miss E. Simmonds. The group had around 2,000 members and their publication had a monthly circulation of 2,500. There had been battles to establish proper copyright protection, on both sides of the Atlantic, and a primary aim of the Society of Authors was protection in the context of the legal implications of contracts. Their primary aims were in this area, and they listed advice in their prospectus, the first two statements of this were:

> Not to sign an agreement of which the alleged cost of production forms an integral part.
>
> Not to enter into correspondence with publishers who are not recommended by friends or by the Society [of Authors].

This has certainly been a great success story, when one reflects that the idea began in the Savile Club in 1883, when a working party began it. Alfred Tennyson was the first president.

Still, in most cases, aspiring women writers had to do what they have always done when trying to be noticed and to be read. Established authors worked as readers for the publishers, and before the 1920s, the situation was largely unchanged since the first work of the writers who grafted for the circulating libraries and the three-volume railway novel. On the plus side, there were lots of publishers, some small and some powerful.

A useful case study in this context is the publisher of the bestsellers by George and Weedon Grossmith (1847–1912) and Jerome K. Jerome (1859–1927), *The Diary of a Nobody* (1888) and *Three Men in a Boat* (1889) respectively. They also published Anthony Hope's (1863–1933) *The Prisoner of Zenda* (1894). The firm was Arrowsmith, and they were founded by Isaac Arrowsmith (1802–1871) who began by printing timetables of steam packet trips. After he died in 1871, James Williams Arrowsmith (1839–1913) took over, and he was the one with an eye to bestsellers.

This shows how a small company could flourish at that time. He may not have published women writers, but there was a lesson to be learned by others in his trajectory. In contrast, and very much as an enlightening factor in women's success into print, there is the case of the powerful publishers such as Isaac Pitman. In their catalogue for 1910 they include in their fiction list Frances M. Brookfield's (*c.*1858–1926) *My Lord of Essex* (1907) ('the romantic episode of Cadiz') along with *Anne of Green Gables* (1908) and *Anne of Avonlea* (1909) by L.M. Montgomery (1874–1942), and *The Glory of the Conquered* (1909) by Susan Glaspell (1879–1948). Biography was also an option for the women, as on the list there are: *The Cambridge Apostles* (1907) by Mrs Charles Brookfield (Frances M. Brookfield) and *Mrs Gaskell: Haunts, Homes and Stories* (1910) by Mrs Ellis H. Chadwick (1882–1928) and *The Countess of Huntingdon and her Circle* (1907) by Sarah Tytler (1827–1914).

If one studies the arrivals into print of some prominent women writers immediately post-First World War, then what strikes one is the web of influence, some of it literary and some of it autobiographical and personal. Virginia Woolf's essay 'Modern Fiction' charged the main group of influential Victorian novelists with materialism, and she explained this as being a fiction of constraint, something held in a restricting template: 'The writer seems constrained, not by his own free will but by some powerful and unscrupulous tyrant who has him in thrall, to provide a plot, to provide comedy, tragedy, love interest and an air of probability embalming the whole ...'

Now, if one looks at, say, the writing of Daphne du Maurier, in her first phase, leading to her debut novel, *The Loving Spirit* (1931), one finds, in the writing process, something entirely typical of the beginning novelist.

Du Maurier wrote *The Loving Spirit* in sections, conceiving a generational and rather epic novel; she thought there were flaws, and indeed Margaret Forster (1938–2016), du Maurier's biographer, notes the possible weaknesses as it was first written regarding its structure. The most marked influences on her style and voice were William Somerset Maugham (1874–1965) and Katherine Mansfield, and so du Maurier's work makes an excellent case study in looking at Virginia Woolf's point about the limitations of the solid Victorian novel. Mansfield followed the Bloomsbury mindset in applying impressionist and soul-searching journeys into selfhood; Maugham took a sound objective view of humanity, embedded in circumstance and social process. Du Maurier could do both.

Woolf saw the novel she inherited as constraining but also something of a weight, a force for atrophy. In the most famous of her explanations of how fiction should be written, in contrast to this former convention, she becomes poetic: 'Examine for a moment an ordinary mind on an ordinary day. The mind receives a myriad impressions – trivial, fantastic, evanescent, or engraved in the sharpness of steel. From all sides they come, an incessant shower of innumerable atoms ...' This is all very fitting for a literature of interiority – of writing that is interested only in the internal, self-reflection within human life. But what Woolf described as materialistic is in fact a view that persists.

Popular fiction from *c.*1919 was expressed in a range of genres, most of them showing no similarity to Woolf's demonstration of her definition of what authentic fiction should be. In Woolf's novel, *Mrs Dalloway*, she showed how her theory could be executed. In her opening she has Clarissa Dalloway thinking of a man: 'he would be back from India one of these days, June or July, she forgot which, for his letters were awfully dull. It was his sayings one remembered; his eyes, his pocket-knife ...' She thinks this as she contemplates the morning and about the forthcoming arrival of workmen. Yes, this is how the human mind functions: preoccupied, random, undisciplined. But why is this superior to the external realism of Arnold Bennett's townspeople in *Anna of the Five Towns* (1902) or Joseph Conrad's mariners sitting around a table in Deptford?

Homo sapiens may be understood by inspection of the exterior – what is actually seen and sensed – and by imagining what is being constructed by the brain inside our wonderfully constructed bodies.

The emerging women novelists surely exemplify the variety of paths taken, after the Victorian solidity and materialistic fictional worlds. Du Maurier and Mansfield represent varieties of the writer who has innate ability and a deep desire to create fictional worlds. Their works show examples from a wide spectrum of the possibilities of writing technique from Woolf's interiors to the absolute 'surface writing' of the documentary forms my following chapters will examine. Du Maurier was a natural in the sense that she simply wrote something, as a girl: poems, playlets and stories; Mansfield did much the same. Whereas Mansfield made voices for narrative that leaned towards Woolf's preferences, du Maurier worked hard towards the entire picture of people in context. She established a routine of regular writing: 'She settled down at a table feeling the weather was symbolic of the kind of book she wanted to write – a story about a seafaring family in which atmosphere and a sense of place would dominate ...'

Margaret Forster explains that with an eye to describing how instinctive was the storytelling in du Maurier's character. Her more mature work shows just how much interiority may be in fictional characters without the deep scrutiny of *Mrs Dalloway*'s inner thoughts and feelings.

In fact, this leads one to reflect that Woolf's critique of the Victorian materialist fiction is really a point about the degree of *fabrication* in narrative; all fiction is largely invented, but some fiction is more invented than others. Hence, the 'materialist' writing is all in a frame of invention, she implies, whereas modernist narrative somehow should be closer to authentic living, the true sense of a being from deep inside. But arguably, there is as much fabrication in imagining the inner voice as there is in writing the dialogue uttered by the spoken voice.

Nuts and Bolts

This is all by way of a preface to the questions about how women learned the art and craft of writing in these years. In the 1920s, representative works show the variety, the range of options, and these each demanded specific skills. But there was of course the commercial angle also. Du Maurier lived in the midst of a wealthy, artistically inclined family: her father – Gerald du Maurier (1873–1934) – was a famous actor and her grandfather – George du Maurier (1834–1896) – was an author of novels, including *Trilby* (1894), which was a *succès d'estime* in its day. More than that, her uncle, Willie, was a literary agent, and he helped her into print when she began writing short stories, as he also edited a magazine called *The Bystander*. But she began with a taste of the real world of the struggling first-time author, as she had written a number of stories and was thinking of trying to publish a collection as a full-length book. She sent her work to the agent, A.P. Watt, and did what every aspiring author has to do: wait nervously for an opinion.

A.P. Watt had been founded in 1875, and is generally regarded as the first genuine literary agency. A.P. Watt was the firm that handled much of Arthur Conan Doyle's work, starting in 1891 when A.P. Watt sent a story, *The Voice of Science* to *The Strand* magazine, and the Sherlock Holmes stories followed.

Archives contain material, which shows how much A.P. Watt did for Conan Doyle, and in one letter, the Sherlock Holmes author wrote to his agent: 'I am always content with the prices that you get.' A.P. Watt is notable as the agent who clearly defined the role and nature of an agent. It was founded by Alexander Pollock Watt (1834–1914).

Du Maurier had no immediate success with the stories but then her uncle, Willie, stepped in, gave her a high profile in his magazine, and later, she wrote the first novel, and that was taken by Michael Joseph (1897–1958), but the new writer then had a familiar task: some re-writing. Although it went to Heinemann, and they liked it, there was work to do. Margaret Forster explains: 'There were really two novels here, determinedly lashed into one, with romanticism drifting into realism and both suffering from confusion.' But she had arrived. Her first professional steps into being an author were taken after the usual learning curve, from working on the idea in its kernel form, through to a finished draft and then a re-writing of parts. In contrast, Mansfield had also started by writing short stories, and had kept to the form, first publishing in magazines, and then gradually, after meeting and learning from other writers, she perfected the form to the best of her ability. Where du Maurier had to have a plot-driven tale in addition to the depth of character, Mansfield could take Woolf's approach and 'dig deep' into her people.

In the early 1920s, though, the markets were opening out. There was a hunger for modern fiction, with its themes relating to the rapidly changing ideologies and the challenges to established and settled values and opinions. Popular genre had centre stage. A 1928 newspaper feature discussed popular novelists in terms of league tables and basic borrowing statistics. It reported that 'Sheila Kaye-Smith [1887–1956] and John Galsworthy [1867–1933] are the two most widely read present-day woman and man novelists in this country.' One speaker from a library group added, 'In our several hundred branches we find [H.G.] Wells [1866–1946] is down the list some distance ... there is not anything like the demand for [Joseph] Conrad's works that there was.' In terms of women writers, the feature went on, 'the order of popularity of present-day women novelists was given as Shelia Kaye-Smith, Rose Macaulay [1881–1958], May Sinclair and G.B. Stern [1890–1973].' But as usually happens in such surveys, there are odd surprises: 'Quite the success of the publishing season has been a book by an American dealing with Old Peru.' The range of choices for novelists was widening at the time, and media attention growing. One talk on contemporary novelists noted that there were 'great men and competent women' and added,

> But we may say, both of Rose Macaulay and Virginia Woolf, that they are women of original mind: that they have penetrated below the surface of life, have criticised life, either directly or by implication, that they are able to tell us something about human life ... that we did not know before.

Originality was still being prized here; the impact of the Bloomsbury mindset was evident. But the speaker, Louis Wilkinson (1881–1966), had one important reservation about Woolf: 'that *Orlando* was the only one of her books that the general reader would be able to read with patience.' It may be summarised: by *c*.1920, the public had become well aware that women writers existed and were mediated widely, and that anyone aspiring to join their ranks could choose a place on that spectrum from the novel which 'had something to tell us about human life' to the merely entertaining narrative.

Writers 'took side' on this question of whether to write for the general reader or to write for the elite who saw fiction as an art to be aligned with the visual and musical arts which were playing a part in the aesthetic movement that attracted the literati. One writer who made his aims as a writer utterly explicit was J.B. Priestley (1894–1984), who surely spoke for so many of the women writers of realistic social fiction. In one of his essays written for his *Delight* (1949) collection he wrote, explaining an encounter with a young man who complained that Priestley's writing was 'simple':

> There was now revealed to us the gulf between his generation and mine. He and his lot, who matured in the early thirties, wanted literature to be difficult. They grew up in revolt against the Mass Communication antics of their age. They did not want to share anything with the crowd. Writing that was hard to understand was like a password to their secret society. A good writer to them was one who made his readers toil and sweat. They admired extreme cleverness and solemnity ... A genuine author, an artist, as distinct

> from the hacks who tried to please the mob, began with some simple thoughts and impressions and then proceeded to complicate his account of them ... Difficulty was demanded ...

He developed his argument with, 'But then I am not impressed by this view of literature as a cerebral activity. Some contemporary critics would be better occupied solving chess problems ... They are no customers of mine.' He concludes his essay with the assertion that it is possible to explain the basic work of Carl Jung (1875–1961) in thirteen and a half minutes, and he adds that he had done just that, when he gave a birthday tribute to the great psychologist. When he had achieved that task, Priestley notes, he 'felt like honey in the rock.' In other words, his essay explains a difficult and admirable talent: to write with simplicity without distorting or misrepresenting the subject.

One suspects that many of the women writers *c.*1930 were of Priestley's attitude of mind. The aim of his writing was to entertain, but also to inform; yet that informing process was what the novel genre had always done, since Daniel Defoe (1660–1731) in 1720: to write for the general reader who has the curiosity and intelligence of the kind of person whom the Victorians would have defined as an 'artisan'. This was the middle rank with qualifications and work above the labouring class; their 1920 equivalent were the typist, the administrator, the middle manager, the sales rep and the clerk. The novel had always been a means of creating stories for people who wanted to hear that their experience was not only universal, but individually valuable; they also wanted to be reminded in their fiction that there were common purposes in society, and that these related to a moral geography of their nation. After all, what had that first war against Germany been all about?

This is not to say that cerebral fiction has no value; it is simply about readership and taste, and about where readers wished to belong in the midst of that upheaval in British life between the death of Queen Victoria in the early 1900s and the imminent threats from fascism in the late 1930s.

Reading and Influence

Now the topic of reading and writing as a woman comes into prominence. Theorists have produced several theories about the differences between male and female writers, but what presses most strongly on the present focus is that the women writers of the First World War generation – those beginning to write in the *c.*1915 to 1920 period – is that they inherited the Victorian and Edwardian prejudices about women. There is no doubt that women starting out as a writer around that early Georgian age were well aware of the radicalism and dissent around them. The gendered writing coming from this may be seen in the work of many of the writers figuring later in these pages, but there is also a wider issue.

This concerns the increasing preoccupation of many women with the male sex and 'maleness'. In some cases there is the establishment of female gay writing, as in Radclyffe Hall, but this theme seeps into all kinds of related writing; Daphne du Maurier had a manly side to her, and she loved male company (platonic as well as sexual); in *The Sheik* the heroine, Diana Mayo, is more masculine than other figures around her, and her feminine element is latent, awaiting the man who can bring out her sensuality.

Writers' reading and influence become prominent here. The writers often read something of the adventure genre when young, and were aware of the female travellers who were writing about an unknown distant world. This filters through into, for instance, Dorothy L. Sayers's character Harriet Vane, who is as tough and capable in a male convention, whereas the detective, Lord Peter Wimsey, is articulate, sensitive, and has a strong sense of empathy in his social world.

What the initial phase of engendering a book is exactly needs a different approach. In my experience, most of this first phase is about troubled thoughts and mental explorations. One's mind fastens onto the kernel of the book and then frets. I worry about the genre, the market, the originality, the voice, the tone and the authenticity *ad infinitum*. I find that there is no avoiding this worry. Then a day comes in which everything seems right to embark on that opening sentence. By that time, one has thought hard and long enough about the voice and the opening scene or mental 'moment' of the teller. After that it is all about trial and error until everything comes together and, in most cases, this never happens.

Back to the beginning now, it might be asked, when someone starts out as an aspiring writer, where does the confidence come from? There is confidence in the characters, confidence in the factual basis and confidence in the sheer pretence of fabricating a narrative. Maybe when there is enough self-belief behind all these, what could just happen is that the writer might find confidence in him or herself.

Writers are always asked about who or what influences their work. The answers seem to be readily available, but often the line of thought is simply about perhaps one major influence in the form of a single book or a single author. All creative artists know that the matter of influence on the work is a complicated case of thousands of different currents filling the one pool of 'material' and 'imagination' rather than one strong, dominant flow of some presiding genius overshadowing the words appearing on your screen.

The heart of the matter for me is that constantly and eternally fascinating subject of the pre-verbal and the verbal. That is, somewhere in my brain a collection of words and images exist in a form different from words or images. There is a melange, a confusion of perhaps several dozen feelings, blurred memories and a few sounds, all reclaimed from something somewhere deep in there, where the germ of what might be a poem or a story lies.

Influences change; they come and go. As we change, so do the influences. When I was 20, I adored Thomas Hardy's work and once referred to him as the greatest novelist who ever put pen to paper. That opinion is very far from me now. Also, I never use the word 'greatest' or 'best' when writing or speaking about art any more. The words mean nothing.

I had been writing for around ten years before I fully realised that being influenced by another writer or artist was possibly not a good thing for one's reputation. I also realised that, in order to avoid the facile criticism that one's work is nothing more than a melange of other voices, a special understanding was needed about the effects of the influential forces at work. In Alfred Brendel's (*b.*1931) long conversations with Martin Meyer (1928–2019) in the book, *Me of All People: Alfred Brendel in Conversation with Martin Meyer* (2002), I found a perfect example of a person who is fully acquainted with influences on his art. Brendel is, of course, known primarily as a pianist, but he also has poetry collections to his name.

When Brendel was asked, after mentioning a host of favourite artists and poets, 'What might be at the root of all these varied influences?' His answer was:

> Perhaps my predilection for comedy, for [William] Shakespeare [1564–1616], for [Johann] Nestroy [1801–1862]; a lightness of touch which [Italo] Calvino [1923–1985] writes so beautifully about in the first of his *Memos for the Millennium* [*Six Memos for the Next Millennium* (1988)] ... and something that corresponds to the Dadaist Raoul Hausmann [1886–1971]. Statement that Dadaists loathed stupidity and loved nonsense.

When I first read these remarks, I thought that this was evidence of a confused mind, swimming in other art, but after reading the book, I came to see that Brendel had thought long and hard about what strands worked into his own art. I saw that he had seen the necessity of an artist to understand the presence of others' work in one's own words or images.

One of the most exhaustive accounts in this area of women's writing comes from Ethel Mannin in her part-autobiographical work, *Confessions and Impressions* (1936). She includes a chapter headed 'Apprenticeship' and included in this are details of her reading, notably in political ideas as well as in serious literature, and she makes it clear that she was writing at the same time:

> I was under the literary influence of the early Gilbert Frankau [1884–1952] ... so it was full of adjectives and amours ... Then I made a second effort which I called Road to Romance. It was all about a girl who walked out of the suburbs 'into the sun' ... I had also just read Richard Le Gallienne's [1866–1947] *Quest of the Golden Girl* [1896]. Herbert Jenkins declared this second attempt to be better, but said it wanted a lot of altering ...

She was in a maelstrom of reading and writing trying at learning by doing. But then some luck and persistence came her way.

Mannin was only in her teens when the editor and publisher Charles Higham (1931–2012) asked her to 'get out' an issue of his magazine; she did exactly that, and proved herself. Then came a magazine called *The Pelican* and she wrote for that. She took stock of what she had done after *The Pelican* folded in 1919:

> During the three years I had been with Higham I had written hundreds of articles, short stories and advertisements. I had published a few articles, stories and poems in the various newspapers and magazines, and written hundreds of thousands of words on every subject, from commercial vehicles to gramophone records; I had written articles on oil power, the Better Spirit in business, the Future of British Trade, window-dressing, the art of salesmanship ... I wrote critiques of plays I had never seen ...

Yet Mannin managed to write four books in these years, and her learning phase began to include the fashionable socialism of her time. A close friend, referred to as J.S., helped and guided in the reading and activities. 'We worshipped at the Shavian shrine, and I read Socialism and Superior Brains, Man and Super-man and John Bull's Other Island.' She also became an ardent reader of William Morris (1834–1896) and also was attracted to the works of Oscar Wilde (1854–1900). Overall, in Mannin, we have the absolute opposite of the Bloomsbury approach to writing. She learned by being immersed in the hurly-burly of the commercial side of writing and she was happy to learn how to edit and re-write, putting in all available hours in between her travel and other paid work.

Modernism brought many things to the table when it comes to our attempts to understand the literary life; one of these was the general understanding about originality. Of course, modernists and later post-modernists borrowed, referenced, appropriated and inter-textualised at random, because the new awakening about creativity was related to notions of there being nothing new under the sun. This led later to the 1960s poets and some American poets playing around with the pleasures of random shuffling of 'found' language, and these concoctions could be very entertaining in performance, but in the end I would argue that true, meaningful influence in literature is all about the presence – often invisible – of other tones and attitudes, or even vocabulary, in the work being created. There had to be an organic whole made, with language generated afresh, in the new work. It is the verbal equivalent of a shadow walking beside one, a guide or a mentor, maybe metaphorically at one's shoulder, but nevertheless firmly there, and now a part of oneself.

A useful metaphor might be that of a pastoral landscape. Take a rural landscape painted in *c.*1880 and there will be the presence of John Constable (1776–1837) or Nicolas Poussin (1594–1665) and others, but more as a sense than as a shape or intentional element in the composition.

Looking at the women writers under scrutiny here, what strikes the reader about their influences is that the exterior world of politics and challenging social change is always there. The immediate pressures and demands of the world of responsibility are always near, and when documentary fiction began to boom, their experiences found a natural home.

There is also the major question of the range of work needed by writers, embracing the actual skills of writing in every aspect. Today, a writer is expected to write a draft, do copy editing and structural editing, spend time on social media, network, perhaps give talks, write on their work for magazines and spend a great deal of time on research. In addition, there is the necessity to read extensively and constantly; in most cases, as we learn from memoirs, aspiring writers grow up surrounded by books and read randomly, as Sir Walter Scott (1771–1832) describes his hero in *Waverley* (1814), and in women's writing, a perfect example of this exists in Colette's (1873–1954) book, *My Mother's House* (1922): 'If I bent over the fascinating abysses of terror that opened in many a romance, there swarmed there plenty of classically white ghosts, sorcerers, shadows, and malevolent monsters, but the denizens of that world could never climb up my long plaits to get at me ...' But Colette was fortunate in that she had a mother who understood the nature of reading, and how all experiences have their useful place: 'But after all ... you must learn to use your judgement. You've got enough sense to keep it to yourself if you understand too much, and perhaps there are no such things as harmful books.' Agatha Christie explains what today might be called the culture of reading in her childhood, and that process of the discovery of stories is central to the notion of becoming a novelist of course: 'Grannie sat either at the table or in a huge leather-backed carver's chair ... The tables, sofa and some of the chairs were taken up with books, books that were meant to be there and books escaping out of loosely tied-up parcels ...' Christie discovered the appeal of the *Bible* stories, children's books, and many miserable tales that she read 'with great satisfaction'. Then, as she worked surrounded by poisons, the idea of a detective tale arose in her imagination. This introduces the more substantial element in reading for a writer: the notion of influence. Christie started to conceive her detective: 'not like Sherlock Holmes of course. I must invent one of my own.' In the context of the First World War, she was familiar with the sight of Belgian refugees and so the question arrived: 'why not make my detective a Belgian?'

In Christie's beginnings as a writer, we see the challenge of mastering the skills and the secondary work behind a book: 'I finished the last half of the book ... during my fortnight's holiday. Of course that was not the end. I then had to re-write a great part of it – mostly the over-complicated middle.' Many women writers were extremely widely read, and read far more than popular fiction or the 'set books' in their education; a biographical scan of these lives shows very clearly how intelligence and perception was applied to influential reading. In the case of Winifred Holtby and Vera Brittain, they studied at the University of Oxford, but although they read scholarly and serious classics, they read far more. Brittain explains: 'Even when this correspondence began in 1920, Winifred [Holtby] understood very clearly the difference between first-rate and second-rate literature. The fact that she could not yet write well herself only gave her the greater reverence for those who did.' Holtby read English classics but also contemporary writing, and Brittain refers to John Masefield (1878–1867), Rudyard Kipling, Walter de la Mare (1873–1956) and W.B. Yeats when she writes about influences on her friend.

The new women writers soon learned the required abilities and disciplines of the literary life, but as always, there were flippant and humorous features in the press which continued the false impressions of the public who often think that successful writers produce genre works at the rate of one a week. One such feature (from the 1930s) headed 'Hint for Novelists' has this tongue-in-cheek advice: 'In last year's book titles were one hundred and thirty one beginning with "mystery"; eighty four with "death"; and eighty three with "murder".' The piece also claimed that twenty years earlier only five had 'death' or 'murder' as the words. The conclusion is that: 'All things considered, the murder-mystery motif is distinctly more popular. So the proper ingredients of the title having been fixed, all that remains for the author to do is to write up to it.'

In the social context of the 1900–1920s period in particular, there is the question of writing in the life of the 'domestic goddess' imagined as the traditional mother and wife – the *Hausfrau* in the sociology of gender. In one now obscure piece of fiction we have this:

> A while after my first book came out and I realised suddenly what it meant to have plenty of money. I wrote another book, and another and another. Then one day it occurred to me that I need not work any more [*sic*]. I was a successful woman and I wasn't happy ... don't do what I did. There's only one chance in a thousand that you'll be a really successful woman ...

Of course, this puts together the notion of 'easy money' and the morality of the accepted norm of female behaviour. The writing of novels could be a challenge to the norm. But it had also invited comment, as the form became possible in the higher culture, of a more heightened and exclusive attitude. In a feature by Andrew Lang (1844–1912), written in the 1890s, there is more to be said about the prospect of writing a novel than the popular opinions often imply. Lang was reviewing a book on how to write a novel, and the author, Mrs Macquoid, insists that the true novelist has a quality she calls 'vision'. Lang stresses the basic skills and stamina involved in the art, and tackles the subject with a description that would fit the 1920s aspiring writers: 'A few tests may be easily put to himself by the neophyte. First, why does he think of beginning at all? If it is because he has nothing better to do, or because other people do it, or because he may possibly make some money, then he had better save himself trouble.' Whatever the successful quality of the novelist is, Lang concedes, it could be called vision but even that is not satisfactory; the vision may come from hard work, as well as a natural gift. His conclusion seems to answer the difficult question about how the writer succeeds: 'The born story writer will "find himself" and his method. The others are only taking trouble in vain and giving trouble to publishers' readers. On the whole, a warning not to begin writing a novel at all is the only sound advice for ninety-nine aspirants in a hundred.' Forty years later, when there had been massive changes in the various contexts in which novels were produced, there are features such as this on the Scottish playwright Betty McCabe, who worked as a housemaid in London and wrote under a *nom de plume*. She told the media in 1934:

> Betty [McCabe] came to London to work as a maid, inspired by a speaker who said that we in England could not produce such good film scenarios as the Americans ... Now she is well on the way to becoming a successful writer, as she has written film scenes and dialogues, has reviewed books and has many plays and one thriller being reviewed by a prominent film mogul ...

The Life of the Mind and the Life of Material Being

If the historian of women's writing has to introduce a case study that shows the ultimate dilemma of the woman writing at home, in the midst of family ties, it is surely the work of French writer Alba de Céspedes (1911–1997). Her *Forbidden Notebook* (1952 and reprinted 2023) is a classic, and in a review of this, Clare Pettit explains, referring to the character of Valeria: 'Terrified that her husband or children will discover the notebook, she moves it on from place to place: the ragbag, an old trunk, a cardboard suitcase, an empty biscuit tin.'

The new woman writer, if she was not living with servants and cleaners, and did not have unearned income, had to exist somewhat in the manner of de Céspedes. Between the end of the First World War and the cultural climate of the Second World War, many women, like Ethel Mannin and Agatha Christie, had been doing hard work, either physical or subsidiary to managers in business, and writing in whatever time they could make for the typewriter or the notebook.

Bloomsbury and related attitudes took the notion of literature as a concept existing in the same category as religion or philosophy. The life of the mind was paramount: literature dealt with ideas and personality, with the complexity of the inner selfhood; the other fiction existed is the realm of the working world, the domestic milieu and the setting of production, where topics such as readership and the marketplace existed. A very interesting instance of this is to be found in an essay written by the editor of *The Countryman*, J.W. Robertson Scott (1866–1962), in 1941. He had been asked to reflect on the life of a writer, and this was his summing-up of his profession in terms of how he related to it:

> Nor, even after a lifetime's practice, do I reckon myself really good at writing. I have sighed when I have seen the book MSS of a well-known friend of mine, written in a clear hand, with hardly a scratch, in exercise books, like a good scholar's work ... I certainly do not write with ease. Writing a book is, for me, from start to finish, heavy labour. This is due ... partly to a lack of skill and partly to lack of aptitude. It is owing also, to compunctious visitings [*sic*]. So much of my life has been given to the overhauling of that easy writing which makes such hard reading that I would not willingly add to the sum of it.

Robertson Scott explains well the arduous and demanding nature of writing a book. The creative process he depicts in his contrast with his friend's work, could be a template for understanding the difference between the notion of writing a book with total confidence and writing a book in the manner of a craftsperson who knows and suffers every stage of the work. Obviously, his account of the hard labour behind the more engaging process of creative writing is something applying to every writer, and it figures in many of the memoirs written by women. Naturally, in the vast majority of cases, the relationship of writer and editor was as significant for the nature of the finished work then as it is now. Also, as is the case today, progress in all the skills involved was learned by doing. This is all material often obscured in memoirs and essays, as discussion centred so much on the imagination at work behind the writing.

If we contrast this with, say, Edith Olivier's (1872–1948) account of writing a book, in her memoir, *Without Knowing Mr Walkley* (1938), the oppositions are very marked. In a chapter on 'Writing Books' she describes an opposite practice to *The Countryman* editor's; for Olivier it is a matter of the speed of thought and the mass of material: 'My mind works so fast that the hands cannot follow it, and if the instrument lags behind, the whole thing is spoilt.' Therefore, she learned what many do today – 'I therefore trained myself to compose on a typewriter.' The impression one derives from this chapter is that Olivier had the ability to handle a treatment of a literary subject with ease, and also with the freedom to write to her own interests. When, for instance, she was asked to write a short biography for a series by publisher Christopher Davies, she chose Mary Magdalene, and she confesses that her book 'was not really a biography at all but a work built up from a number of the beautiful imaginative and poetic lives of the Saint written during the Middle Ages.'

Becoming a woman writer then, in the interwar years, entailed a mix of talents and skills, with plenty of hard work; but the arena was splitting by the time the women with no 'room of their own' started writing at the kitchen table in between family duties: some saw writing as an important place in the life of the mind, whereas others saw the skills of writing as matters tied to the readership in this new world in which the Representation of the People (Equal Franchise) Act 1928 had given the vote to all women over the age of 21, with no reference to property ownership.

The rarefied microcosm of discussion about books and writers considered by an elite of well-read folk with high culture in their veins and thoughts was entrenched in its round of reviews, publishers' parties, book launches and literary awards. By its side was the world of Ethel Mannin, Agatha Christie, E.M. Hull and Angela Thirkell, with their desire to share a story, take it close to the reader's senses and experience, and either entertain them or offer imaginative escape. Somewhere in the middle in this scene were the writers such as Daphne du Maurier and Stella Gibbons (1902–1989), or Dorothy L. Sayers and Hilda Vaughan (1892–1985), who ploughed a seam close by, but who went their own way.

It is interesting to note that a figure such as D.H. Lawrence, who was at times on the fringes of the Bloomsbury mindset, and who fictionalised Katherine Mansfield in his work, sat uneasily somewhere without hooks into any great liner sailing by in the oceans of literature. Yet, his belief in something beyond the life of ideas never sits easily with his impassioned and supposedly enlightened sexual and existential themes.

Most women writers of this period seemingly never had a reason to place themselves in any literary 'schools' or elites. But it was an age of friendships, travel, exciting openings of the spirit and the senses. The novel, since its creation, always had a major part to play in this process of self-revelation, and that process happened, both in Bloomsbury and elsewhere. What strikes a modern reader is the tendency for women writers to make friendships with their staff at publishers, and sometimes with the publishers themselves. Up to a period as recent as the 1980s, the current Mr Boon at Mills & Boon usually took his authors out to lunch when there was a reason to have a chat. The talk was no doubt a mix of business and humour, and that social convention now reads like a very ancient piece of literary history.

Chapter 3

More than Bloomsbury

'She was struggling with her sentences, those long sentences that had to be so exactly carried out.'

Gertrude Stein (1874–1946)

There are a number of ways of looking at the radical changes in fiction during the Edwardian years and into the 1920s. One way is to see the now 'modern classics', which the works of Virginia Woolf, James Joyce, T.S. Eliot and others have become as somehow formative; another perspective is to see that in the period itself, they had very little impact on general writers and readers. Of course, what we now call modernism with its challenge to accepted narrative genres and conventions passed by so many of the writers of that period who were often in print and who produced what their publishers wanted from them.

Winifred Holtby, for instance, was well aware of the challenges being made to the traditional Victorian fiction. Her friend Vera Brittain, in her memoir *Testament of Friendship* (1940), writes this:

> We compromised with the tutorial opinion which deplored our inexplicable preference for popular forms of literature by promising to collaborate in a work of historical research which we thankfully abandoned as soon as we discovered how unfavourable were its chances of making any impression.

She adds to this another kind of avoidance of anything smacking of the elitism of literary coteries: 'In the autumn of 1923 we moved into a spacious mansion flat in Maida Vale, without in the least realising that we were exchanging the choice habitation of intellectual Bloomsbury for a district with quite another reputation ...'

The Novelist as a 'Higher' Artist

At the end of the First World War, after the horrendous shock of the flu epidemic and the social upheaval, the 1920s brought extremes of circumstances in many ways: there was the General Strike of 1926 and the Wall Street Crash three years later, but it was on the human, individual level that the suffering and deprivation had set in. This raises the question as to how much we may glean about the malaise in a civilization from its response to the appeal of a 'live for today' view of life as opposed to the discipline of religious belief and practice, which tends to advise deferred gratification, with eyes on future beatific peace and rewards in the world to come.

In the writing and stories around popular culture there was certainly a strong appeal: that of the pull of sensual, escapist and self-rewarding lifestyle so often depicted as a post-First World War response to the lifting of threats to peace and an end to the long succession of deaths of loved ones in such a horrendous theatre of war as the trenches on the Western Front.

There may have been the literary elites who could understand the difficult references to classics and modern languages, and to the self-referential knowledge holding the coteries together, but there was also the middlebrow writer on the scene, and these writers perpetuated and indeed advanced their genres. One may argue that a genre narrative comforts and entertains, and offers only predictable storylines, but that is to ignore the subtlety with which popular cultural narratives handle important elements in the meta-narrative of a social context or period. In other words, 'serious' literature may deal head on with important themes, but their readership is usually small; on the other hand, popular genres may have equally important themes, but their readership is large.

To understand how literature and creative writing, or any of the arts, may rise to the status of being a version of a religious life, perhaps the object is more visible in the world of music. It is hard to find a more tangible example of a life dedicated to art and creativity than Clara Schumann (1819–1896). Her father, Friedrich Wieck (1785–1873), was a man obsessed with music and the life of music from performance to study. His Clara was going to be a phenomenon: a pianist of the very highest order, and so he set about creating his family genius. At the age of 5, Schumann started taking formal lessons in piano; she then gave private concerts in Dresden when she was 11, followed by concert tours across the German states. When she married composer Robert Schumann (1810–1856) in 1840 her life as both pianist and wife to another musical genius began.

Hers was a life dedicated to her art. She had children and she had a social circle of friends, but her playing and composing were central to her spiritual life and her intense romantic and impassioned art. After Robert Schumann's death, she was a close friend of Johannes Brahms (1833–1897), yet another composer and pianist who put music at the heart of his life: he never married, and he and Schumann had what was almost certainly a platonic relationship.

The last two paragraphs could be about Virginia Woolf, born Virginia Stephen in an intensely literary household, with cultural life and high ideals of art; she also lived to create, in spite of her repeated sufferings with mental illness, and she eventually took her own life. Both Schumann and Woolf must have thought of art and little else, as they were driven to achieve, to be noticed and to be adored. If the modern reader understands this, then the circle of friends referred to as 'Bloomsbury' becomes comprehensible. Around Lady Ottoline Morrell (1873–1938) at her Garsington home and in highbrow London, 'Bloomsbury' was gradually created by the commentators, and it became a frame of mind, an aesthetic and an attitude to life and art which permeated the higher culture of metropolitan life after the First World War and into the advancement of modernism.

The interest in the present context for all this comes from the lines of thought explained by John Carey in his book *The Intellectuals and the Masses: Pride and Prejudice Among the Literary Intelligentsia, 1880–1939* (1992). In a review of the book, Donald N. McCloskey summed up the argument: 'Carey's wider point ... is that the *avant garde* was ... fleeing its bourgeois origins and keeping clear of the proletariat masses. It was making itself ... into a new aristocracy ...' The reviewer quotes Carey: 'The intellectuals could not, of course, prevent the masses from attaining literacy. But they could prevent them from reading literature by making it too difficult for them to understand ...' Anyone who has taught T.S. Eliot, Virginia Woolf or James Joyce at a secondary school in Britain will understand what kind of truth there is in Carey's words. Equally, anyone who has taught those texts in any working-class context will know the truth they state. In other words, the Bloomsbury attitudes, though never a written credo or a formulated manifesto, caused a rift in literature and creative writing, which has persisted.

This massive oppositional situation is evident everywhere in our society in any cultural context. For instance, the book review pages in broadsheet papers and in review periodicals do not include romantic fiction, western fiction or any genre considered to be popular, meaning that the writers and publishers involved are aiming at readers who do not wish to be given fiction with philosophical dimensions, esoteric themes or Latinate vocabulary. There are readers who want relaxation, to share a compelling story, and there are readers who want a narrative complexity when they read a novel, along with demands on their brains. The novels entered for the Man Booker Award every year reflect this; only very rarely do the media concern themselves with noticing 'lightweight' fiction as it is considered.

Carey's book isolated a worrying line in modern literary history, and the women writers who began to be in print between the first Bloomsbury Group books through to the second wave of modernism up to the Second World War, were fully aware of the two routes that fiction was taking: a novel either supplied an imaginative adventure or it provoked the reader to think about ideas, issues and psychological themes.

Women writers and their work began to be a presence, and many of them set out to create a stir and to equal men in their need to travel, take risks and be willing to cause a scandal. During the First World War, the middlebrow woman writer was already attracting attention. The *Hull Daily Mail*, for instance, reported on Charlotte Cameron (*c.*1872–1946), with the headline: 'The Spell of the Black Woman – A Remarkable Novel'. The paper began with 'For the very first time in literary history, a woman novelist has utilised the Cameroons as a background for a remarkable story.'

Cameron was a Fellow of the Royal Geographical Society and had been called 'The Modern Mary Kingsley' as she was a seasoned traveller. She was interviewed, and said, 'I have limned the life in Togoland [German Empire in West Africa] as it really is, with the aim of appealing to the colonising instincts of the Englishwoman.' The place was a German colony, and although Cameron perpetuated imperial bias, and she was in favour of colonialism, the point is that the subject of her novel was typical of the innovative ideals, as well as the new status, of a woman writer.

Biographies make it clear that most women writers starting out were well informed regarding the Bloomsbury route to publication. A writer of special interest here is Katherine Mansfield, who submitted stories in most cases to editors she knew, and their contacts would often open up more outlets for her. But her career, becoming friendly with Virginia Woolf and marrying John Middleton Murry, as well as knowing D.H. Lawrence well, is not her whole story. She knew the importance of the marketplace and knowing readers, but essentially she wrote what she wanted, and often her work did not progress. She tried to write plays, and some were destroyed or never succeeded; she wrote poetry and non-fiction, but it says a great deal about her that her journal attracted publishers and has remained full of interest.

In a scholarly study of women writers and their journals, Judy Simons pinpoints not only the reason for this interest in memoir and personal writing, but something much wider: 'Katherine Mansfield's retrospective vision marks her both as a modernist, in the vanguard of literary experiment ... and as a woman, drawing on essentially feminine modes of thought to establish her unique perspective on experience.' This provokes some thought on the true importance of the flowering of women's writing after 1919: that it is concerned with a fundamental difference in the perception of reality and of the self between male and female. This point makes a workable platform for understanding why there was this flowering, and what it was that made women of the middlebrow background take such a prominent role in this revolution.

For it was a revolution. Middlebrow people are not commonly associated with revolutions. They might comment and assess, but history shows us that the proletariat and the students (intellectuals) occupy the vanguard in violent social change. When Fyodor Dostoevsky (1821–1881) was blindfolded and faced a firing squad for his dissenting radical views of the tsarist Russian state, he was one of many intellectuals. Where were the 'people of the middle'? They were keeping the essential work up to date; they were feeding, cleaning, instructing, doing quotidian tasks, unnoticed. Well, when creative writing and journalism became options for them, they had a lot to say.

The Loneliness of the Writer – And the Adventures

Naturally, writing is a solitary occupation. Writers have often included in their memoirs some accounts of the search for the perfect place to write. Today, a 'writers' retreat' is offered by arts organisations in the belief that one may 'get that book written' at last with the peace of a rural spot well away from other people, work and responsibility. Virginia Woolf's 'room of one's own' was naturally appealing but the line of thought relates more to the 'kitchen table' writer who yearns for writing space. This relates also to Cyril Connolly's (1903–1974) famous adage, 'There is no more sombre enemy of good art than the pram in the hallway.'

The myth of the solitary creative soul communing with nature might be no more than a fantasy, but surely the point is about time for concentration and for clear thought, away from distractions. In that case, writers' spaces for writing take on a new perspective when we place the writer in the context of the interwar years, when women were still largely seen as the 'angels in the house' and sacred as family generators, the 'weaker vessels'.

Travel and adventure were far more desired and revered at this time. The arrival of such things as the Imperial Airways aircraft and the cruise liner, with the popularity of coach travel around the British Isles and railway travel in Europe, meant that the supposed solitary writer could actually be very much on the move, researching and people watching as E.M. Forster shows in his character of Miss Lavish, who 'proceeded through the streets of the city of Florence, short, fidgety, and playful as a kitten ... It was a treat for the girl to be with anyone so clever and so cheerful.'

Storm Jameson had definite views on this important point. She was interviewed in 1928 on 'clever women and immoral women' and she was puffed up into a celebrity by the reporter: 'one of the most successful of that band of young women novelists whose originality and activity constitute a striking feature of literary life in London – who, by the way, is only 31 – when invited to express herself on the subject of careers for married women ...' Storm said 'I don't say that it is impossible for a married woman with children successfully to run a separate career ... but I do say that it is practically so.' She did not approve of childcare to allow a woman to write, undisturbed; she also thought that the 'average Englishman' didn't agree with careers for married women. She had reflected on 'clever women' and concluded that such people become so obsessed by their efficiency that their imaginative faculty suffers. She wanted women who did far more than shopping and becoming 'hopelessly domesticated' as this made for dullness. More to the point for the age she lived in, Storm added that 'I think that chastity has been deleted from the tables of virtues.' She also said 'A girl who has sex adventures today certainly does not look upon herself as fallen.'

Another general contrast that has to be made is that so often, a trend may be observed: the women writers who wrote genre and popular stories tended to work very much alone, not domestic and family oriented or as the word was used then, 'spinsters'. That is to say, the independent woman was increasingly choosing the kind of life that the more singular and extraordinary Victorian female travellers and amateur historians were living. Agatha Christie went out to archaeological digs in the Middle East, and Dorothy Carrington (1910–2002) wrote about such places as Corsica. In 1930, as a newspaper headline proclaimed, Mrs Rosita Forbes (1890–1967) was reported as typical of this: 'A Woman Novelist's Desert Ordeal.'

She had been interviewed after journeying for 8,000 miles across stretches of what was then Persia, where she was taking time away from the typewriter to work in first aid support.

Forbes told the press that at times, she had been a lonely wanderer, and at other times she had been part of a donkey caravan. She said 'I was going around Persia in lorries ... Comfort wasn't in it, but I managed along quite well. In one lorry there were some pilgrims from Baluchistan going to the city of Meshed. On that occasion we drove along roads but also went on old rough tracks.' She saw women walking with both babies and rifles on their shoulders, and went within earshot of Russian guns. She 'spent an exciting eleven days among sporadic battles.' Her worst time was when she spent three days in the desert with no water. She was eventually rescued by a caravan of donkeys.

There was also much opposition and prejudice. The only benefit of this is that adverse comments tend to provoke replies, and the replies tend to bring out worthwhile points. In 1935, for instance, the Welfare of Youth Convener of the Presbyterian Church was reported in the press when he expressed criticisms: 'He dared to say that he knew two or three girls who had gained fame by writing novels but who could not spell and knew nothing about punctuation.' The response was impassioned. Helen Simpson said this was nonsense and Angela Thirkell kept to 'unfortunate'. The convener had asserted that 'A surprising quantity of nearly illiterate work appears every season.'

The writer's comments, on reporting this speech, prompts the reader to reflect on the reputation of women writers at the time, as he wrote: 'He is the rash man who spoke slighting [*sic*] of feminine fictionists.' A factor in this attitude of the press to women writers is also the general attitude in British cultural history; the habit of reading, in addition to the business of writing books, had always been alien to the working-class culture and to the middlebrow mindset. Part of this lies in the regard that writers were held here, as contrasted with, say, France, Russia or in the Austro-Hungarian Empire and the German states. Most visible in Russia is the view that creative writers were expected to contribute to debates on social change, and to be respected social figures who were asked for their opinions on political and social affairs. The women writers of the interwar years were often concerned with that 'idea of service' that Beatrice Webb wrote of, and when the 1930s in particular brought the aftermath of economic turmoil along with the rise of fascist states, writers and artists increasingly brought those issues into their writing and looked for imaginative ways to explore them.

While the Bloomsbury mindset was constantly concerned with the work of art and the process of creation, the middlebrows wanted narratives made around new freedoms, fresh and revisionary views of such institutions as the family, religious belief and challenges to social values. Behind the new fiction – even in genre writing – there was often an exploration of those formerly fixed Victorian values and conventions, which had seemed, before 1914 and the movement for the liberation of women, ineradicable.

The readers of the new middlebrow writing hardly needed to give much time to high level offerings on the crumbling ideologies of the last generation, such as may be found after long study of *The Waste Land* (1922) or *Ulysses* (1920); neither did they have any urgent need to understand the complex changes going on around psychoanalysis and our comprehension of the self and identity. But what those readers could – and did – do was place such issues and questions inside the popular plot-driven stories, in the plays and poetry of the troubled decades following the First World War. If the idea of service 'had transferred from God to man' as Webb asserted, then creative writing could play a significant part in the stirring of ideas, relationships and the erosion of established values holding society together.

The middlebrow reader wanted to reflect on social issues; they wanted to know the wider world through travel and through fiction that included depictions of faraway locations; they also wanted to know why there were changing opinions on the nature and value of art, culture and literature.

As a background to all this, there were the political changes; the Labour Party, between *c.*1900 and 1940, had attained a respectable status, and it had governed; socialist ideas permeated much of social debate; the First World War had nurtured pacifism as well as experiment and innovation, and Wormwood Scrubs had been the home of such figures as Bertrand Russell (1872–1970), Fred Copeman (1907–1983), Plaid Cymru activists and Basil Bunting (1900–1985). The significance here is that from 1919 the spectrum of writers, covering all political persuasions, was broadening; as a 1960s song has it, 'Build high, build wide your prison walls so there may be room for all' because radicalism was now covering a much more diverse ground, and stable government could never be assumed.

Much of this change at the very base of art and culture became visible in the Spanish Civil War. Dannie Abse (1923–2014), in his autobiography, *Goodbye, Twentieth Century* (2001), puts the impact of that war on British writers very strongly: 'For me Guernica meant Cornford dead, Lorca dead, Caudwell dead, Fox dead. Heroes dead, dead, dead.' When he lists some of the dead poets he is aware, as so many were, of the many women who had been involved, such as Gamel Woolsey (1895–1968) and Carlota O'Neill (1905–2000). Scholarship has revealed many more women writers (American and British) who were in that conflict, as will be seen in a later chapter.

After all, what was it about the Bloomsbury mindset that set it apart and form a rather difficult room to find in the great mansion of British literature in its time? First, there was the appeal of a secret, exclusive club; the mindset was built on hundreds of studies and memoirs, and these writings are packed with disagreements, dislike, exclusivity and often passing quarrels on anything from aesthetics to the wrong decor. Second, there is the feeling in those who are set apart from that exclusive club that they are missing something, being left outside. Finally, with a wider sweep of reference, it is useful to consider the theme at the heart of E.M. Forster's modern classic of the early twentieth century, *Howard's End*.

In this novel of two Englands, Forster places the character of Leonard Bast, the clerk who aspires to be part of the higher culture. Forster gives the two sisters whose cultural lives Bast reveres and wishes to join the name of Schlegel, perhaps from the brothers Schlegel who were somewhere in the area of either polymaths or dilettantes, so wide were their literary and philosophical interests. But Bast represents the new arrival on the cultural scene – the person who thinks there is something wonderfully enlightening about social and aesthetic gurus such as John Ruskin (1819–1900), whose book *The Stones of Venice* (1851) has enthralled Bast. Ruskin also campaigned, wrote and spoke about the working man being potentially part of the new arts, crafts and creativity in the last years of Queen Victoria's reign. E.M. Forster gives the man the role of the struggler, outside the circle, striving to be a part of what he thinks is something that will form him, shape his own ideals and aspirations.

The quote in *Howard's End*, 'only connect between prose and verse' is a metaphor which, in itself, assumes the existence of a higher and lower duality: the verse is the higher order of living and being, while the prose is the material, lower and less aware life of work, earning money and being partly shut out from any deeper understanding of what the Schlegels and Bloomsbury concern themselves with.

Sigmund Freud's words from *Civilisation and its Discontents* (1930) come to mind again: 'Our present sense of self is thus only a sunken residue of a far more comprehensive, indeed all-embracing feeling ...'

Hence, so much of modernist writing of the period is related to an indefinable yearning, an awareness of something more, something better. This division between the acceptance of the 'lower' middlebrow aesthetic of Bast against the Bloomsbury mindset persists through to our own times. It is there in the play and film *Educating Rita* (1983) by Willy Russell (*b.*1946), in which Rita, a working-class young woman, sits in a family pub sing-song and feels a melancholy sense of sadness and frustration, explaining later that she wants to 'sing a better song'. The keynote is aspiration – the Bast position in life. It is also the position made available to so many after the Education

Act 1944 and the later arrival of grants for working class people to study for a degree at university.

Bast might stand for a growing urge in the lower-middle classes to have their share of the alluring culture they see in the 'higher' life of the professionals who live amongst an interchange of aesthetic ideas and theories. Forster here is accessing a common image running through the literature of this time: the brutality and material-based crassness of the male in the lower reaches of society. Katherine Mansfield, in her story *The Little Governess* (1915) makes much of this in a scene on board a train in Europe as the governess travels to her work in Munich, Germany. A band of young men, noisy and intrusive, are rude to her and frighten her as she sits alone in a reserved carriage. There is no doubt that the male in this fiction, post-First World War, is usually created in a series of contradictions, and the fact that Forster makes Bast a sympathetic figure, while at the same time concentrating on the two extremes of Mrs Wilcox's world of *Howard's End* against the modern scramble for money and status.

However, if, as Forster makes clear in his portrait of the Wilcox family and ethos – making money and gathering wealth – works against his pleas of 'only connect between prose and verse' then we might not expect the high cultural worshippers at the shrine of 'art for art's sake' to be concerned with cash and the practicalities of writing as a trade. But this is Virginia Woolf, writing in her diary in 1930: 'When we made our six months accounts we found I had made about £3,020 last year – the salary of a civil servant, a surprise to me, who was content with £200 for many years. But I shall drop very heavily I think. *The Waves* [1931] won't sell more than about 2,000 copies.'

Similarly, Sir Harold Nicolson (1886–1968), who had married Vita Sackville-West (1892–1962), had these concerns:

> Discuss finance. Vita [Sackville-West] keeps on saying that we have got enough to go on with. But when one goes into it, that represents only two months. I must get a job. Yet all the jobs which pay humiliate. And the decent jobs do not pay. Come back to Long Barn. Arrange my books sadly ... Vita thinks I should make £2,000 by writing a novel ...

From all this social and historical background, it is plain that the emerging women writers were participants in this middlebrow revolution in which the Bloomsbury view of literature was out of focus with their own view of the literary world and indeed the world of workaday reality which became their subject in some genres. Virginia Woolf insisted that the woman writer needed 'a room of her own' but in this glimpse of Winifred Holtby by Vera Brittain we have something else: 'I can still picture her with an armful of books, wandering around the house in search of a quiet corner for uninterrupted work.'

Chapter 4

Discover Yourself

'I gave my entire self to the task of saving my entire self.'
Jean-Paul Sartre (1905–1980)

In the first phase of the interwar years, there are a number of factors that gave women reasons to write, and most of these are nothing to do with earning a living. Of all the fundamental questions about why we write, the satisfaction, mixed with a dash of vanity is at the heart of it. George Orwell (1903–1950), in his essay 'Why I Write', uses the term 'aesthetic enthusiasm' and has this to say in explanation: 'Desire to share an experience which one feels is valuable and ought not to be missed.'

For the women writers at this time, there was clearly a set of reasons for writing, most around various versions of politics, but the sharing of experiences in the world – after such a cataclysm as 1914 to 1918, creates the bedrock.

Understanding the state of Britain when it finally came up and began to see a new normality, facing economic hardship instead of bullets and gas, is important in seeing things as women writers saw them. For instance, men had brought that terrible war. Not only had they found reasons to kill thousands of young people across Europe: they had also faced internal struggles regarding a range of issues relating to citizenship and individual freedoms. Then, by the 1920s there were still huge problems to face: housing, unemployment, public health and education. In all these areas, women were beginning to be a presence; as the decade progressed, the country saw the first woman member of Parliament – Nancy Astor (1879–1964), the first women fully in the criminal justice system, and women in business and industry. Men had formerly been central to these but now they were facing challenges to their comfortable norms in life. The radical changes seeped into cultural life and recreation, sport and the arts, administration and local politics.

Men had brought wars; men had led and given most of the orders; they had also been, since Victorian ideologies took pride of place regarding woman's place in home and work, little more than repressive and domineering. Now there were oppositions to this. One of the driving forces to the opposition was the written word. By the late 1930s, the media had reacted to this presence in a remarkable way. In an issue of the *Daily Express* for 1938 there are these headings to main features: 'Actress Claims right to Box a Man's Ears', 'Seeks Man she hit with Bridal Cake', and 'Runaway Bride Hides from Sister in Locked Hotel Room'. The front page of the issue proclaims a special shopping issue, and by page three the reader is faced with a full-page feature on fur coats for sale from bankrupt stock. The men have their sports pages, but life is happening, the sub-text says, where the women are immersed in action and vigour.

In such a context, it is no surprise to find that men in the creative writing, and notably in the fiction of these years, are subject to the scrutiny of the female looking-glass. In addition to this material setting, the world behind these writers had become familiar with the ideas of Sigmund Freud and others under his influence. British writers not only looked into the domestic relationships in the changing sexual politics of the new world: they also looked abroad, to Paris, Berlin and the United States. Travel writing boomed, and most of the writers tended to travel in search of subjects and themes; the Americans opened up the aesthetic pleasures of Paris, where Sylvia Beach's bookshop was to publish James Joyce's *Ulysses*; Berlin, with its homosexual openness and gay cultural life, was reported on by Christopher Isherwood, Stephen Spender (1909–1995) and W.H. Auden (1907–1973) in fact and fiction.

In the popular fiction of these decades, much of the light fiction offered the familiar triangle of *woman in search of herself – brutal and insensitive male – cultured and sensitive male*. This is seen in a novel typical of the sub-genre such as *A Late Lark Singing* (1953) by Naomi Jacob (1884–1964). The blurb has this: 'The reader will be deeply moved by the story of Ann's search for knowledge and a fuller life and for her courageous attempt to remain to a husband she can no longer love.' In fact, the hero, a Yorkshire farmer, is dangerously violent, in the mould of Heathcliff, and he commits homicide, narrowly escaping the noose. Ann is hungry for learning and literature, and a friendly bookseller acts as her personal librarian for a small fee. She reads the classics, attracts the cultured and sensitive man, and eventually is happy.

The men in this branch of fiction were often varieties of Heathcliff, Rochester and Lockwood from the major Brontë novels *Jane Eyre* and *Wuthering Heights* (1847), and Ann explains her desire to lift herself from farmer's wife to something else in this context; the bookseller, Brattle, says, as Ann notes the Brontë novel: 'Keep hold of that book, Mrs Power. That will bring you in a great deal more than you paid for it – one day.' In the microcosm of writing and art, men were far more than the romantic hero; their ideologies and their sense of hierarchy were exposed to the microscope of the most ingenious novelistic ploys and styles. For men, the problems persisted; into the 1930s, over 600,000 ex-servicemen were depending on pensions; there were the 'hunger marches' of the poor and unemployed, and the streets had their drifters and beggars, as depicted by W.H. Davies (1871–1940) and George Orwell. More than this, the governmental chaos continued: the Conservatives won in 1922 but by 1923 a minority government was being formed by Ramsey MacDonald (1866–1937). A long dispute with the miners made all this worse, and then the General Strike of the early months of 1926 was the nadir of all the social chaos.

At this point, of course, male characters were firmly in place within the romance genre, and here we need to check on the nomenclature involved, because through the Victorian and into the Edwardian years, the term 'romance' was applied to varieties of fiction, which today would be called 'male adventure' or even 'works of dramatic interest'. The words 'romance was extended throughout these years into other genres'. Even in true crime volumes it was used, as in R. Storry Deans's (1868–1938) *Notable Trials: Romances of the Law Courts* (1906), which is in the true crime slot on the shelves. This was the age of H. Rider Haggard's *King Solomon's Mines* (1885) and the masculine heroes such as Sherlock Holmes, Raffles and the dashing military types of such works as *The Four Feathers* (1902). All these works prolonged the long-standing conventions of the alpha male, out in the world, seeking tests of his manhood.

Taking up this point, it may be noted that in much of the writing by men after the First World War there was a sense of their having missed their chance of proving themselves in the masculine world. Understanding this helps to grasp the male characters of the women writing through the interwar years. Christopher Isherwood (1904–1986) provides the clearest example of this. His father, Frank (1869–1915), died in the First World War, and Isherwood wrote extensively about what he termed 'the test'. In his autobiographical work, *Lions and Shadows* (1938), he explains this: 'I myself had been to public school. But here we enter upon further complications. I knew, or had known while I was there, that public-school life wasn't, in my heroic sense, a "test". It was a test, if you like, of social flexibility, of a capacity for "getting on"...' But the 'test' of manhood was there as well for his generation:

> Like most of my generation, I was obsessed by a complex of terrors and longings connected with the idea 'War'. War, in this purely neurotic sense, meant The Test. The Test of your courage, of your maturity, of your sexual prowess. 'Are you really a man?' Subconsciously, I longed to be subjected to this test ...

Before the advent of modernism and Virginia Woolf's notions of the interiority of ourselves, men, for women who observed them or had to live with them or work with them, must have seemed very one dimensional. Their writings delineate a world in which communication and everyday talk are limited to what linguists call 'phatic communion' – that is, the language we use to bond, to mark a point of inter-relationship. It is any wonder that, given this minimal effort at relationships, women's writing should excel at depicting communication? The consequence of men's limitations (and here we have to use Woolf's point about the materialistic fictional universe of H.G. Wells, Arnold Bennett, John Galsworthy) is that they will enter the arena in women's fiction as one-sided minds avoiding the examination of selfhood which takes centre stage in modernist writing and art.

Men and women, and their very separate emotional composition, have always been at the heart of the novel of course; the more the novel became a form capable of delving deeper into these differences, the more interest was generated, but even more significant has been the breakdown of the 'separate spheres' ideology of man the breadwinner and woman the domestic and family ruler. In the interwar years, as women characters in much fiction were created with these new subtleties and depths, the potential for fiction of more emotional complexity emerged. In Elizabeth Bowen's (1899–1973) novel *The Death of the Heart* (1938) the novel begins with a long conversation by a man and a woman, their talk concerning a young woman called Portia, and the tenor of the talk moves around opinions and judgements of the subject in question. A theme steadily emerges, and at one point there is a statement of the explorations to come: 'In this airy vivacious house, all mirrors and polish, there was no place where shadows lodged, no point where feeling could thicken. The rooms were set for strangers' intimacy, or else for exhausted solitary retreat.' In some ways this theme of the essentially inward-turned nature of the self and the inevitable solitariness of existence, impinges on both the modernist preoccupation with the difficulty of knowing others, and also, it is almost anticipatory of the 1950s literature of class and social division through the necessity of giving part of one's self-conceptions. Bowen writes: 'But a man must live. Not for nothing do we invest so much of ourselves in other people's lives ... It cuts both ways: the happy group inside the lighted window, the figure in long grass in the orchard seen from the train stay and support us in our dark hours.' She states her conclusion boldly: 'Illusions are art, for the feeling person, and it is by art that we live, if we do.'

There is a European feel to the narrative voices she makes – a sensibility often hidden in the chaos of living. In this she is close in many ways to the work of Christopher Isherwood and Graham Greene (1904–1991).

However, what persists most strongly in respect of the separate worlds of men and women, placed in this new world of business, careers and more social and moral freedom, is the assertion that women (as the First War had shown) are totally equal to men in the hard work and learning curve of writing for a living. Creative writing, and more specifically writing for a defined reader, as in popular genres, requires an attitude far removed from any notion of 'art for art's sake'.

This subject is prominent in a novel of 1933: *High Rising*, by Angela Thirkell. Here, Thirkell sets up an opposition of two writers. Laura Morland writes light, popular fiction, while George Knox (1841–1927) is a serious writer of serious biographies. Laura's first impetus to write stems from the need for an income: 'Laura [Morland] had written for magazines for some years past, in a desultory way, but now the problem of earning money was serious ...' A character called Miss Todd expresses a defence of the popular which offers a demarcation of the world beyond Bloomsbury:

> 'Mrs Morland,' she said impressively, 'they save my life. That's why I read all your books. I don't care for good literature, but when I read about clothes, it's like taking opium. I forget all about Mother, and death and dividends, and I Revel. I know I couldn't wear them. I'm not the type, even if I could afford them. But they mean a lot to me, and your books have been an awful help to me ...'

Laura Morland has a publisher, Adrian, and he is the human face of the industry, being a close friend to her. In their first conversation in the book, Laura explains her standpoint as a writer, anticipating George Orwell's essay 'Good Bad Books' (1945): Adrian asks for an explanation of the term and she responds with, 'Yes, not very good books. You know, but good of a second-rate kind. That's all I could do' she said gravely.' Adrian sees her talent, however: 'Adrian's only complaint about Laura was that she was too unconscious of her own worth ...'

When Orwell appears, a learned but amusing discussion about uncles in history, as Orwell's current book is on Edward VI (1537–1553). Thirkell makes his subject humorous, and he speaks like a chirpy, very modern don, in a tutorial: 'It is delightful, dearest Laura, to hear all about your book ... we shall have a long talk and you shall tell me everything.' Morland is depicted as the absolute tyro at the writing profession; she struggles to change a ribbon on her typewriter, and when it comes business, there is this: to this novel view of a literary agent's functions, Adrian could say nothing. So Morland went on, 'Nonsense, Adrian. You send me a contract, and I'll get George Knox to read it, and he will say a hundred per cent too little, and that will give me a pretty good idea that your terms are all right.'

High Rising puts the writing profession in a whimsical frame of fun, friendship and the old contrast of the ditsy woman and the professional man, but she does so in such a way that the reader might forget that actually, Laura is the contemporary writer, able to spin the yarns that contemporaries want to read. A biography of Edward VI is *very niche*, as a modern publisher might put it. Orwell's verdict on the contrast Thirkell presents shows some sympathy with this contrast: 'All one can say is that while literature remains such that one needs distraction ... light literature has its appointed place; also that there is such a thing as sheer skill, or native grace, which may have more survival value than erudition or intellectual power.'

Women writers were not always welcomed by male writers either, as there were still oppositions, including such catty and petty responses as this by James Agate (1877–1947): 'Let women writers write on subjects they know about. I do not want to read some Wimbledon spinster's views on the amours of a Spanish bull-fighter any more than I want to hear from a Spanish miss about the love-life of an Arsenal centre-forward.'

Such attitudes were still in the air, and the implication here is that there should be restrictions on a woman's imagination. It seems as though Agate is implying that women cannot extend their empathy and research knowledge into worthwhile narrative. It is therefore no wonder that writers such as Angela Thirkell depicted her character of George as noisily self-concerned, while Louisa felt constantly second – best as a writer.

The Story in Two Fabrications

In the writings of the Bloomsbury mindset and in the narratives of the popular genres for women readers (primarily) we find two broad conceptions of a story. Since the first writings in English, in Geoffery Chaucer's (*c.*1340s–1400) time in the fourteenth century, the aim of a story (usually spoken aloud in the case of Chaucer and other poets) was to share a story, as a smoothly constructed narrative: a share in a created world, a world of imagination but one which relates to the world of the teller and the tale. Since that time, as the form of the novel arrived, in the early eighteenth century with Daniel Defoe's *Robinson Crusoe* (1719) and other works, the scope and subtlety expanded, but still, by the Victorian years, the main driving impetus behind the writing of a novel was to share a story, known to be invented, and separate from the writer, in spite of the fact that such novels as *Jane Eyre* were supposedly, as a fictional device, autobiographical. The point is that the novel (with a few exceptions such as *The Life and Times of Tristram Shandy, Gentleman*, 1759) presented a fictional world and the reader suspended disbelief, as Coleridge said humans did when entering a theatre or reading poetical tales.

Now, with modernist ideas, here was a situation in which the writing of the story could be part of the story; something we now call *metafiction* became part of the scene. Here, both reader and writer allow the present reality of the time of reading to enter into the pretence of the act of telling the story. One of the clearest examples of this is in a Katherine Mansfield story, *Je ne Parle Pas Francais* (*c*.1920), in which we have, early in the story when the narrator is establishing the locus of the tale, this: 'Do you believe that every place has its hour of the day when it really does come alive? There does seem to be a moment when ... Everything is arranged for you ...' This direct address to the reader is a plain creation of metafiction. It might as well be a signpost saying: *the story is this way. I made it up*. Two pages later we have an appeal to the reader's mind: 'That's rather nice don't you think, that bit about the virgin? It comes from the pen so gently; it has such a 'dying fall'. I thought so at the time and decided to make a note of it ...'

Literature has become a word game here, not simply a different way of telling a story. It implies that the reader is being asked to be complicit in a fabrication, and to see the fabrication in process. This is directly opposite to the traditional realist story in which both reader and writer tacitly agree to immerse themselves in a fictional world they share until the last page and the closure.

Viginia Woolf's insistence that our lives have to be depicted as 'moments of being' inside our subconscious, revealed in the process of a story developing, may be one element in the special relationship of writer and reader, but the opposite views go further. There is a resistance in us to the acceptance of the view that the artifice of art has to be transparent. Yes, we enjoy a story being put together, but in popular narrative, the plot drives the story that will keep us in the sharing pleasure of the tale. In a Bloomsbury narrative, there is a massive assumption that interest in the *artifice* will always dominate. If there is a community in which art itself is the centre of all conscious attachment to living, then that art will be in every area of life. When Christopher Isherwood wrote an essay on Virginia Woolf after her death, he explained this very strongly:

> The Bloomsbury family held together by consanguinity of talent. That you could express yourself artistically, through the medium of writing, painting, or music, was taken for granted. This was the real business of life: it would have been indecent, almost, to refer to it. Artistic integrity was the family religion; and in its best days it could proudly boast that it did not harbour a single prostitute, pot-boiler or hack ...

After the First World War, storytelling lost its innocence whenever it was discussed in the study, over dinner or in offices wherever the literati gathered. Their theory was most likely valid, and their thinking has turned out to be part of the basis of much modern literary theory, but literary theory is not popular writing: that is a very different concept.

When, in the early phase of the years covered in the present work, writers such as Agatha Christie, Daphne du Maurier and Winifred Holtby sat down to write a novel, no sense of breaking the fictional worlds they were making ever entered their craft. In years gone by – as in Charlotte Brontë for instance – there had been brief metafictional elements such as 'Dear reader' and the famous phrase from *Jane Eyre* – 'Reader, I married him.' But these scraps of metafiction simply say *look, we have been enmeshed in this story, and you know the heroine like a friend, but it is ending well ...*

There are writers in these years who saw fiction as a mimetic reflection of the material world before them. Ethel Mannin's tremendous output shows her constant preoccupation with the world of power, politics, relationships and emotional ties. There is no room for reflections out of the university tutorial room. Agatha Christie's notion of a detective novel was a narrative that would involve her readers' minds in logical deduction, character assessment and the solving of a puzzle, but these were embedded in a realistic context. Readers would soon conceive of what an English village was, what a vicarage was like, and how people spoke in conversations when there were things to be hidden.

There was a literary revolution happening in 1919 when the First World War ended, but it was happening at a level only acknowledged in the literary reviews and periodicals; as far as popular culture was concerned, novels primarily meant (as they do today) either a story to fill some leisure time or a story to draw attention to some aspect of life, moral dilemmas and important issues about the way people live together.

There was plenty in life to escape from when the women writers began to write new fiction that would deal with society and its difficulties, or people with the strain and sufferings of a post-First World War society in which deaths and casualties had been immense. A very interesting case in this context is the life and writing career of Dorothy Edwards (1903–1934), whose only two books, *Rhapsody* (1927) and *Winter Sonata* (1928) show a fascinating example of someone who was, in life, attached to Bloomsbury (she worked for John Middleton Murry) but very much a writer with her individual talent. Christopher Meredith explains that she was an outside all her life but she was 'an intellectual who could pass for posh in South Wales ... but wasn't part of the working class at perhaps its toughest moment. But she certainly didn't pass as a *bourgeoise* in Bloomsbury, and her stories are full of outsiders ...'

Edwards, who took her own life in 1934, dying at only 31 years of age, presents little worlds in which strangers arrive, encounters happen, music and the artistic impulse make for the real positive in a dull milieu, but nothing changes and the outsider leaves. It is as if the stories all come together as a large metaphor for the existential angst of the artist who has only one joy and delight: a creative escape which is ephemeral, set against engulfing responsibilities and duties from the world around. In her story *The Conquered* (1926) there is an attempt at a general insight: 'It seems to me now that the world is made up of gay people and sad people, and however charming and beautiful the gay people are, their souls can never really meet the souls of those who are born for suffering and melancholy, simply because they are made in a different mould.'

The stories in *Rhapsody* celebrate the fleeting moment of the coming together of people through a short sharing of artistic beauty, and a heightening of consciousness. But this is always unsatisfactory in any socially healing way. But also, the people in the stories are subservient to the works of art. They sit by the works, mainly musical composition, and they try to achieve the realisation of the feelings from the paper or from the notes produced by their instruments. Yet there is always disappointment. One might suspect that the stories are a critique of a Bloomsbury attitude to art.

It is hard to resist the traditional attitude to stories as healers, melders and reminders that bind society together. That is, basic stories, when tribal or communal, do not individualise: they bring together. The Anglo-Saxon poem *Beowulf* is about heroism and sacrifice; it deals with the virtues and values of a warrior society that has to be so because of exterior threats and for social cohesion. A society needing to stay together in these ways has to make uniting stories, and stories that promote shared values. Conversely, modern stories, after the modernist challenges and re-thinking of all this, recognise the complexity of selfhood. The individual, one might argue, is a negative force in a society that desperately needs uniformity. In the world of the 1914 to 1918 conflict, uniformity of thought was essential from the viewpoint of the generals and the German haters.

For the Edwardians, there had been a curiosity about the women novelists, which lasted into the Georgian years: the periodicals took an interest in them and treated them as 'news'. *The Idler*, in the 1890s, had dealt with the question of *how women novelists work*. In fact, common sense could have answered that question: they work in much the same way as male novelists. Yet the curiosity was there, and it had to be answered. Anyone could have predicted the view that writing a novel, for a woman, was a question of what we would now call *issues*. Women have lives, the argument went, in which there are thoughts and preoccupations beyond the province such authors as Joseph Conrad and Anthony Trollope (1815–1882). But, of course, the male writers had tried hard to create women characters. The only conclusion was that there were special insights, especially in a world in which there was a readership with a fresh sense of what a woman could achieve. What lay beneath the question was what George Orwell was to state in 1940: 'When one says that a writer is fashionable one practically always means that he is admired by people under thirty.'

The readers of fiction at the time when *The Idler* presented its findings on the matter, was largely one of that rising class of commuters who were being directed into the new social world of bikes and bloomers, river trips and country hiking, and who saw the expansion of the mind as being as important as the expansion of the horizon. In other words, they were the Basts again. There was such a thing as recreation for the clerks and shop-girls, the stenographers and the charabanc travellers; in fact, modernist notions of literature were coming at just the right time, but they would be noticed only by the people who wanted to be pushed and advised in those corners of modern life in which one might 'better oneself' and have opportunities to show it.

When women did enter the literary business, in everything from editing to networking, they certainly did it with zest and resolve. Winifred Holtby toiled ceaselessly, even when her illness became severe, at all the chores loaded on the lone writer, working to make a mark. D.J. Taylor, biographer of George Orwell and chronicler of the 'Bright Young People' in these years, shows this type of women perfectly in an essay on Inez Holden (1903–1974), who was a close friend of Orwell's and who represents that tireless application to work we find across the board in the women's lives; Taylor writes of her 'backstory', saying that she appears in Evelyn Waugh's (1903–1966) diary,

> when the two tyro journalists were briefly employed by the *Daily Express* [together with] the early novels published by Duckworth; part-time work as a columnist on society magazines; and infinitely mysterious mid[-]1930s period when she may or may not have been a member of the Communist party.

The same kind of dedication to work with books, writing and publishing is evident in the biographies of Ethel Mannin, Storm Jameson and Virginia Woolf, and we must add to that the incredibly large number of hours required to write popular fiction for a growing market. Naomi Jacob's later novels have a list included of previous works, and this list in *c.*1950 included thirty-six novels, two plays and ten works of autobiography. Angela Thirkell's Barsetshire novels series numbers twenty-nine volumes, along with three volumes of non-fiction; Gladys Mitchell (1901–1983) produced sixty-six mystery novels.

The Persistence of Two Unreal Worlds: Mansfield and *The Sheik*

Threat and Freedom might be the keywords of much women's fiction in this period. These notions take all kinds of forms, but they are visible, intriguing and informative wherever they appear. Yet we also have a transition period: in the years 1918 to 1919, the list of women writers beginning to come through into notice and review are a mix of middlebrow and highbrow. That is, because modernist ideas and practice had started to show an exciting new ideology for narratives of a fresh realism, the excitement, along with the implicit invitation to join in the new spirit, appeared alongside the established genres.

Katherine Mansfield provides a perfect case study here. Her first work was *In a German Pension*; she had stayed in Germany and the experience of that culture faced her with the temptation of a powerful satire against the nation who were already by that stage, rivals in imperial ambitions to Britain. Mansfield did not want this reprinted, when pressed by the publishers, Constable, to do so. She had moved on from an openly grotesque and positively Swiftian repugnance at the humanity under scrutiny, to something quite different. This description of *Herr* Hoffman will show the technique:

> 'If I drink a great deal of M*ü*nchen beer I sweat so' said *Herr* Hoffman.
> 'When I am here, in the fields or before my baths, I sweat, but I enjoy
> it; but in the town
> It is not at all the same thing.'
> Prompted by the thought, he wiped his neck and face with his dinner
> napkin and carefully cleaned his ears.

A few years later, when Germanophobia swept the land and Germans in Britain were interned in camps, the book would have been a bestseller, and it did well commercially when finally reprinted. But Mansfield was a very different writer by 1918. She had fallen under the influence of Virginia Woolf, but there are notable differences in their work also. Claire Tomalin highlights this in her biography of Mansfield: 'Both Virginia and Katherine made the fragility of feeling, of happiness and life itself into their subject; both felt a degree of antagonism for the male world ... both turned to their childhoods and their dead to nourish their imaginations.' Yet there is much more in the nature of their differences.

In the years around 1920 to 1925 both depicted the inner lives of their main characters, and both were concerned with 'the fragility of feeling, of happiness and life itself' but at her most individual, Mansfield was metafictional: she stepped into the reader's engagement with the fiction being created, in order to stress that making a story was not only a shared enterprise, but was also something that was desired by both: the writer hungered to make an authentic fictional world, and the reader desired to step into it and be led towards a resolution, a closure, a deep satisfaction about the fictional place or the created 'human' at play in make believe.

This is boldly apparent in much of the fiction in *Bliss and Other Stores* (1920). In *Je ne Parle pas Francais*, as already noted, the aim is to take on board the Freudian dimension – to incorporate a sickness of the mind and sensibilities by integrating a formative shock. The narrator, Raoul Duquette (1879–1962), introduces himself to the reader and then quickly steers the reader into the important trauma: 'When I was about ten our laundress was an African woman ... when she came to our house she always took particular notice of me, and when the clothes had been taken out of the basket she would lift me up into it ...' Then this follows:

> One day when I was standing at the door, watching her go, she turned around and beckoned to me, nodding and smiling in a secret way. I never thought of not following. She took me into a little outhouse at the end of the passage, caught me up in her arms and began kissing me. Ah, those kisses! Especially those kisses inside my ears that nearly deafened me.

This may or may not be some kind of assault, but it is intimate, and in a context of real feeling being difficult of expression; the stories are inhabited by those who aim to relish life, stretch themselves into ultimate sensual experience in every sense, often in an interior world, or at least a tightly domestic one. The modernist fiction is acutely concerned with the spectrum of acute feelings, and the longed-for enjoyment of the material world. In her story *Psychology* (1920) Katherine Mansfield provides a template example: 'Roll your eyes if you can and taste it on the breath. It's not a sandwich from the hatter's bag – it's a kind of cake that might have been mentioned in the Book of *Genesis* ... And God said: "Let there be cake. And there was cake. And God saw that it was good."' There are footnotes to the understanding of Mansfield in relation to Woolf and the Bloomsbury ethos. One of these is found in Woolf's diary in January 1941. She is writing about James Joyce's *Ulysses*:

> I remember Miss Weaver, in wool gloves, bringing Ulysses in typescript to our tea-table at Hogarth House ... Would we devote our lives to printing it? The indecent pages looked so incongruous ... and the pages reeled with indecency. I put it in the drawer of the inlaid cabinet. One day Katherine Mansfield came, and I had it out. She began to read, ridiculing; then suddenly said But there's something in this, a scene that should figure I suppose in the history of Literature ...

Does Mansfield appraise the book with any sense and judicial thinking? No, her mocking is possibly about something she cannot see was 'writing' in her own sense. But then she says something hagiographic, almost as if she wants to be seen toeing the party line about what is genius and what is not.

As Claire Tomalin noted, the male world is under scrutiny too, and this world is often threatening, either on the equilibrium of an ordered life or against the female wish for individuality. This theme is vivid and powerful in *The Little Governess* in which the woman in question has to travel by boat and train from England to Munich. The journey is frightening, and made so by men. Some young rowdies disturb and threaten her tranquillity in a 'woman only' carriage, and then an aged but reserved man sits in the carriage after the notice has been torn down: 'He put his thumb-nail under the label *Dames Seules* and tore it right off and then stood squinting at her while an old man wrapped in a plaid cape climbed up the high step.' The old man befriends and helps her; he seems harmless, and indeed acts as a guide and companion in Munich, but after taking up his invitation to go to his apartment, this happens: 'It wasn't the same old man at all. Ah, how horrible! The little governess stared at him in terror. "No, no, no!" she stammered, struggling out of his hands "one little kiss. Just a kiss, dear little Fraulein. A kiss!"'

Katherine Mansfield, while writing her last collection of stories, was seriously ill, but she was able to work with determination and purpose, and the world she creates is somehow an intense personal vision of that need for the self to be acknowledged and to be social, to be defined somehow within relationships, when it is clear from the narrative voices in the stories that such integration is very hard for all of us.

In complete contrast is the huge bestseller, *The Sheik*, which created the desert romance – a sub-genre still very much alive today from publishers Mills & Boon. The novel made a truly successful film and made Rudolf Valentino (1895–1926) into a mega-star of the cinema in its early years. Hull was the daughter of an American ship owner. She was wealthy, of course, and consequently travelled a great deal. When she saw Algeria, she had the beginnings of a favourite setting for her fiction; her novel stayed in the top-selling lists for two years, selling 1.2 million copies across the globe. Diana Mayo, the heroine, is more macho than most males, and plans a journey into the deserted, unescorted, apart from a native guide. Her story is given with a strong and impassioned voice, with a poetic tone and a rhetorical attitude to romance. The word 'romance' in its setting *c.*1920 was something very different from the use of the word to denote a type of popular fiction as existed in Georgian and Victorian Britain. Here, as it existed in periodicals and serials, it was an exotic, adventurous narrative of female affections in encounters with alpha males.

Hull gives the reader some help in coping with the man at the heart of the tale:

> To Diana before she had come to Africa the life of an Arab sheik in his native desert had been a very visionary affair. The term sheik was itself a very visionary affair. She had been shown sheiks in Biskra who drove hard bargains to hire out mangy camels and sore-covered donkeys for trips into the interior. Her own faithless caravan-leader had called himself 'Sheik' but she had also heard of other and different sheiks who lived far away across the shimmering sand ...

There is, naturally, a series of obstacles and a battle of wills, but once the true sheik has exerted his will, the romance genre finds its central focus: surrender and sensual fulfilment: 'Holding her look with the mesmerism that he could exert when he chose he read in her face her final surrender, and knew that while it pleased him to keep her he had broken her utterly to his hand.'

The first third of the novel is very much concerned with Diana's hard, male toughness; she knows no fear, and she is handy with a revolver and a skilled horse rider. The wilderness has no fears for her. But, of course, the romance genre is a test as well as a route into understanding the woes and sufferings of a woman caught in the traps of normality. If one thinks of the great and classic romance novels such as *Jane Eyre*, *Rebecca* (1938) or *Brief Encounter: A Novel* (1975), then certain domestic claims on the heroine's nature crop up, like fences at Aintree racecourse. These might be called the Dolly Messiter factor. When the heroine and her doctor beau meet for the very last time in the station buffet, in Alec Waugh's (1898–1981) *Brief Encounter: A Novel*, just as they are welling up with emotion, and the heroine has said she does not wish to live, in comes the chatty and shopping-laden Dolly Messiter, to talk about trivia.

Dolly Messiter is the normality factor in romance. She represents the quotidian, the repeated words and actions of the entrapment of the prefigured life. In most cases, that entrapped life is marriage. Madame Bovary did everything to escape any Dolly Messiter; Jane Eyre even had a marriage proposal who offered such a fate in imperial India.

All this is the block to romance, and in a strange way, both Katherine Mansfield and E.M. Hull wrote much about the hurdles created by normality, routine and set relationships. There are ways of escape from the life of the kitchen and the sitting room, listening to the *Light Programme* BBC radio broadcast, in *c.*1930, but if there are too many people like Dolly Messiter, there is always the bookshop and the romance shelf.

Natural Ability and the Marketplace

When Georgette Heyer (1902–1974) was only 15 years of age, her first novel was published. This was in 1921, and was followed by eleven more works of fiction between that date and 1930. She had arrived, and very young. Her life as a writer provides us with a proper template for the successful women 'earner' of the time in the literary world. She earned enough to finance a small shop in the country run by her husband and her brother. But she had also had the trials of married life, travelling abroad to Africa and Macedonia with her mining engineer husband, Ronald Rougier (1900–1976). Heyer defines that version of the creative writer who has immense personal talent, and this disposition relates to an inward-turned selfhood, which is sustained by the imagination. She is to be aligned with Emily Brontë and Emily Dickinson (1830–1868) in this respect. One might suggest that her exact opposite at the time was Ethel Mannin, in whose largely autobiographical work, *Confessions and Impressions* we have what might be the crusading manifesto of so many writers of the time:

> Most people are dead, for all they move about the face of the earth. The women for the most part are not merely dead like the men, but buried as well. See the rushing to buy the banned book, to get hold of it by hook or by crook, to see the risqué play, the substitute for the sexual satisfaction they have never known.

This Lawrentian outburst somehow proclaims one of the creeds of the writers who came along to stir in the world of both sexual politics and relational politics.

But for Heyer, the satisfactions of the creative in one's self were deep in some internal pool, awaiting form and expression. But at Jane Aiken Hodge (1917–2009) reflects, referring to a sequence of early Heyer novels, 'All four novels show Georgette Heyer preoccupied with the class structure of English society.' She may have written mostly historical novels, but Heyer was using ways other than the strongly explicit as we find in the Mannin corpus.

Class was indeed a theme at the very core of writing. The extensive writing about the effects on the class hierarchy caused by the First World War has become a large body of work, showing for sure that the conditions in the trenches did a great deal to make the various members of the British class structures see themselves more objectively. Men from different echelons of class status were shoulder to shoulder, and the result was a stealthy process of revelation for many. In Wilfred Owen's poetry this is clearly seen. In his poem *Miners* (1918) for instance, his closing lines use the pronoun 'we' so that a very proletarian title has opened out to a vision of all humanity, overriding 'class':

> The centuries will burn rich loads
> With which we groaned,

Whose warmth shall lull their dreaming lids,
While songs are crooned.
But they will not dream of us poor lads
Lost in the ground.

An interesting case study in respect of 'natural ability' is that of Stella Gibbons, who is remembered now for her comic classic, *Cold Comfort Farm* (1932). She wrote several other books but this is quirky, strongly individual and probably unique. Lynne Truss (*b.*1955), who of course produced books in this very difficult genre that aims to amuse, explained a key event in Gibbons's life; her father Telford Gibbons was a depressive, and was clearly a torment for his family:

> Telford [Gibbons] was threatening suicide; Maudie was begging Stella [Gibbons] to persuade him not to do it; and in the midst of the drama Stella noticed that her father was hiding a smile. It was a turning point. Once she realised that misery could be enjoyed, and used as a tool of family oppression, she rejected it.

What Gibbons illustrates in her treatment of the wonderful humour of *Cold Comfort Farm* is something that occurs in other works of the 1930s – the striking and compelling power of comic character. Charles Dickens's statement about building the novel *The Pickwick Papers* (1836) from the concept of Mr Pickwick applies here: Christopher Isherwood achieved it in *Mr Norris Changes Trains* (1935); P.G. Wodehouse (1881–1975) achieved in multiple contexts with Jeeves, and Pamela Hansford Johnson (1912–1981) with *This Bed Thy Centre* (1935) and even more powerfully with *The Unspeakable Skipton* (1959).

Gibbons found her natural ability to be in that rare blend of satire and pastiche that works so well in the novel's setting in Howling and it mix of Mary Webb (1881–1927) derived characters. When she wrote about the book in a 1966 essay, her explanation was, as Lynne Truss summarises, 'she likened *Cold Comfort Farm* to some unignorable old uncle, to whom you have to be grateful because he makes you a handsome allowance, but who is often an embarrassment and a bore ...'

Gibbons found that vein in her creative make-up that led to such a successful product, and the marketplace was not something that was aimed at; she simply wrote with a structure and a fictional voice that worked like a new and piquant recipe. However, there is a strand in the novel which may be pointed out as an acute pastiche of the popular documentary method in fact and fiction. This is with the writing used to send up a male writer, Mr Mybug. Flora asks about the book he is writing and the response is this: 'Yes, it's going to be dam' good ... it's a psychological study of course, and I've got a lot of new matter, including three letters he wrote to an aunt in Ireland, Mrs Prunty, during the period when he was working on *Wuthering Heights*.' He goes on to say that 'no woman could have written that' (referring to *Wuthering Heights*), but he gets no reaction of shock from Flora. He progresses to say about woman: 'woman ... the eternal unsolvable and unfindable X ... All we have left of this fragile, wonderfully delicate relationship between the older woman and the young man are these three passionate letters ...' This view is thoroughly askew and unsupported, of course, but what Gibbons is doing is showing how a 'woman writer' is supposed to write, and that she cannot write like a man. The entire enterprise of *Cold Comfort Farm* is that the expected delicate 'Robert Poste's child', Flora, will not be able to cope, yet she does so admirably, and even more extreme with regard to Mr Mybug's bizarre thinking is the fact that Flora deals admirably with a male world.

Chapter 5

The Other Englands

'Writers should be willing to go and live for a long enough time at one of the points of departure of the new society.'

Storm Jameson

There is no doubt that, after 1918 gradually the awareness of the 'other England' beyond the southern middle class consciousness, became an issue. In fact, it became essential to acknowledge it. So many of the returning servicemen came home to a version of England that had become exposed during the First World War. In the trenches, officers had been close up to working men, labourers from town and country, and this experience was written about, painted and described. A similar thing was to happen in the late 1930s when men left for Spain to fight against Francisco Franco (1892–1975).

There was 'another England' and it had previously been consigned to the footnotes of history. The myth making of the country writers had allowed this place to exist either in idyllic contexts (as in Thomas Hardy's more pastoral than tragic novels) or in melodramatic or sentimental modes. Looking back at this working class history it appears obvious that our general awareness of this class comes most significantly when they play a part if great historical events such as the Peasants' Revolt of 1381 or the Pilgrimage of Grace in 1536. But in the 1920s and after, it was impossible to ignore the labouring classes, and also it was essential to validate and understand them. Their men had marched off to war in the pals' regiments; their miners had built the trench works, their nurses had tended the sick, and their railwaymen had made supply lines effective.

The women writers either knew of the working class from close-up (like Phyllis E. Bentley in Calderdale) or they knew about them through education and reading; these mysterious people who kept the coal supplied and the fish on the table were beginning to be seen and acknowledged. The landmark documentary film on fishermen, *Drifters* (1929), by John Grierson (1898–1972), is typical of the new interest in work, and in writing it appears notably in such works as *Down and Out in Paris and London*.

There was plenty of gritty real life and tough working conditions in the post-First World War Britain, after that three or four years of readjustment between the Armistice and the General Strike of 1926. Historian David Cannadine (*b*.1950) has studied the nature of class in Britain across the centuries, and in his remarks on this period he writes:

> On the one side, there was a continued decline in the number of small workshops and an unprecedented growth in large-scale factories, often associated with new industries, as with the motor car production lines at Longbridge and Cowley. The 1920s also witnessed a succession of mergers and consolidations, which meant that giant new businesses were formed, such as the 'big four' railway companies which were created after the aftermath of the First World War, and ICI [Imperial Chemical Industries] in 1926. This simultaneous expansion in the scale of production and business organisation inevitably undermined the localised, paternal world where the owners, the managers and the workers had been part of the same close-knit factory communities.

That was only one side of the coin. There was the shift in notions of the hierarchy of British class society was; after the suffrage reforms between 1867 and 1928 it was clear to everyone that, in the famous words of one member of Parliament: 'Now we must educate our masters.' The Independent Labour Party, the Fabian movement and the various left-wing smaller groups all pressed for more reform and for the leftist government to arrive. The Liberals and David Lloyd George (1863–1945) had overseen the war effort and had taken some steps to placate the growing working class voting body. But after the 1917 and 1918, revolutions in Russia and Germany had engendered fears and apprehensions about violent social change in the establishment. The trade unions were the focus for a great deal of radical unrest; David Carradine notes that 'In 1914, there were 4.1 million members [of unions]; by 1920 there were 8.3 million, representing almost half of the total workforce.'

The 'other England' had made the world of literature and art seem like some cardboard child's theatre, in which those who painted the walls, ploughed the land and dug out the coal were painted into the back-drop, never moving around in the action of the play. George Orwell did a great deal to put this right, with his books dealing with the lives of café workers, miners and factory workers; there was also W.H. Davies, whose *Autobiography of a Supertramp* (1908) had opened up the lives of people drifting from doss house to hostel across the land. George Bernard Shaw wrote a glowing preface, and explained the narrative voice: 'I have read it through from beginning to end, and would have read more ... It is a placid narrative, unexciting in matter and unvarnished in manner, of the commonplaces of a tramp's life.' The women played a part in this revelation also. One cannot overlook Flora Thompson's (1876–1947) *Lark Rise to Candleford* (1945), which not only explains rural work and village life, but provides a guide to the slaughter of pigs, for anyone starting out as a smallholder. There is a genre entirely distinct in these decades, placed along with Thompson's books. The genre reveals village life – or small town life – in a manner that explains the diurnal and routine as something quintessential, comic and packed with an understanding of British working lives. John Moore's (1907–1967) *Portrait of Elmbury* (1945) gives this treatment to a fictional shadow of Tewkesbury; the tradition carried on into later decades with Ronald Blyth's (1922–2023) *Akenfield* (1969) and even in the Larkin tales of H.E. Bates (1905–1974). But in the women writers, the substance of this subject is often there in the provincial fiction. A perfect example is *The Rich House* (1941) by Stella Gibbons. Here, what is established for the reader is provincial and seaside – something entirely British: 'Mrs Pask sighed. A wild night by the sea had always excited her, ever since her girlhood in this very town fifty years ago …' and we also sense an intimate geography of the place, as cosy and normal as the drawings and descriptions in Agatha Christie's Miss Marple novel. In *The Murder at the Vicarage* (1930) the reader son sees the compactness of the story's topography. Miss Marple lives right next to the vicarage, and the artist's studio where a torrid affair takes place is a stone's throw from both the vicarage and the old hall.

In the late 1920s, the media discovered the pleasures and rewards of 'documenting' life as it is lived. The need to present the facts, edited and directed of course, became a feature of all the arts and writing as the 1930s went on. The women writers played a part in this, as they of course were part of what was increasingly seen as a voiceless and unseen England – the culture that had been pressing on regardless when the British Empire, war and diplomacy had had to carry on, run by men. Now, when strikes and divisions seemed to be tearing life apart, artists as well as politicians began to see the value of shining a light into the dark corners, and try to understand what the Victorians had called 'the underclass' and the 'labouring poor'.

In the first decade of the interwar years, between the Conservative victory in 1918 to the second Labour government of 1929, there were massive tests and demands made on the British population, which obviously impacted on writers and artists everywhere. Between 1922 and 1926 efforts were made to do something about the post-First World War crisis in employment and housing. There were also issues relating to pensions and in 1925 there was the establishment of old age and widows' pensions. Then came the General Strike of May 1926. With all this in mind, it is obvious that such living conditions and social crisis would have an impact on the women writers.

The first Labour government under Ramsay MacDonald followed by their decline in 1924, added to the steady decline of the Liberal Party as well, and the consequences of all this upheaval at the heart of government meant that an era emerged in which there was a distinct rise in the voices of the workers, and along with this came the appearance of what many refer to as the proletarian writer. What was happening was a growing awareness of the ordinary working people – the ones who kept the country moving, such as the transport workers, the miners and the labourers.

George Orwell, in his essay 'Down the Mine' put this very powerfully: 'In the metabolism of the western world the coal-miner is second in importance only to the man who ploughs the soil. He is a sort of caryatid upon whose shoulders nearly everything that is grimy is supported.'

In 1926, the media had made the more well-off and perhaps even the upper classes actually noticed who cleaned their kitchens and swept the yard. In the special edition of *The British Worker* during the strike, a piece was printed headed 'One Slice or Two? How the coal struggle looks to a miner's wife …' and this we have a writing style that was to become standard in much new writing:

> No section of the community is carrying a heavier burden than the miner's wife. At the best of times her toil is hard. She has not only all the work of other housewives; the conditions of the mining industry and the housing in colliery villages make her task specially heavy ... Nowhere is housing worse. Sometimes she has little better than a one-room hovel without any of the ordinary comforts of life, and not even a scrap of garden around it ...

What was to emerge was documentary writing. In the work of James Hanley, whose novel *Boy* (1931) was to cause a stir, may be seen the power of a documentary approach to storytelling. Writers such as Winifred Holtby needed to have a weight of fact and reality in the foundations of their stories.

This aspect of writing also becomes apparent in the sidelines of writing. In 1936, Nora K. Smith (1889–1961) – daughter of a very popular Lancashire writer, John Ackworth (1854–1917) – entered novel-writing competition. This was run by publishers Hodder & Stoughton, and Smith won, gaining the massive sum of £1,000. The competition was open only to teachers, but even so, there were 8,000 entries. Her winning novel was *A Stranger and a Sojourner* (1937), and the blurb has this: 'The ugliness of poverty is here as well as the beauty of the hills; and on every page is stamped the personality of Zillah Bowker, drawing her inspiration, her joy and her sorrow from the Lord.' Smith had one more book published, and she died in 1961.

Hanley showed the way in many respects. He was of a working class background in Liverpool and he started writing in the 1920s after fighting in the First World War. By the time he was settled as a writer, and living in rural Wales, he was with his wife, who wrote as Timothy Hanley, the author of three novels and plenty of short fiction.

In the immediate pre-Second World War world of strikes, appeasement, the growth of fascism and the challenge of left-wing thought, Hanley's aims as a writer were to be tested; fortune was on his side, because the age of documentary – in fact and in fiction – had arrived. When Hanley's contemporaries looked around for the most prominent and 'modern' documentary subjects, they found it in work, the worker and of course, in the major industries of coal, iron, steel and fishing. In the late 1920s, film had been used alongside literature to experiment with documentary, and if we include the new medium of radio also, then the richness and potential of the new media for writing in general, then it is easy to understand why so many Welsh writers became involved in BBC work and in related reportage for the new *avant-garde* magazines.

In this new context, highbrow writers and their works and attitudes began to mix with the equally new breed of socialist writers, many of the latter being 'blooded' in voluntary experience in Spain during the Spanish Civil War of the middle of the decade. A perfect example of this new confrontation with material reality, through labour and the working class, is W.H. Auden's experience with the GPO Film Unit in 1936. The unit was managed by film-maker John Grierson, and Auden's comment about the now famous Post Office project *Night Mail* (1936) explains much about what Hanley was to face at the time, with Wales as his subject: 'We were experimenting to see whether poetry could be used in films, and I think it showed we could.' In Hanley's case, the mid-1930s context for his documentary writing was Wales, but it was not the Wales he knew in the north of the principality; the nation's attention was on the coalfield in South Wales, and writers and the media descended on the Valleys for 'material to back up the new socialistic impetus of revealing their own country to the British. An editorial in the left-wing journal *Fact* explains the attitude:

> Suppose, instead of going to work one day without reflecting on what was before you, you were to watch and listen, to observe the buildings the dress, the habits, the conversation, the food and the taboos of your fellows as conscientiously as if you were walking into an African village. What would you see? What would you, a new Dr Livingstone, think could be made of this tribe?

In that same issue of *Fact*, Hanley's story 'Episode' was published, and the company he was in as a contributor fixes him firmly on the left of contemporary politics: Fred Urquhart (1911–2002), Stephen Spender, Storm Jameson and Leslie Halward (1905–1976).

A later issue of *Fact* for November 1937, consisted almost entirely of Philip Massey's book, *Portrait of a Mining Town* (1937) – about the town of Nantyglo, and on the back cover we have this: '*Grey Children*: a study in humbug and misery, by James Hanley. This is the stark truth about the distressed mining villages of South Wales. James Hanley knows all about the HUMBUG and the MISERY and he does not mince his words.'

Storm Jameson was very much involved in this left-wing writing that brought the land and people out into view in this way, as 'the new Dr Livingstones.' The industrial unrest and the 1920s slump had made working class Britain a subject in the process of being revealed.

Storm Jameson

Jameson was one of the contributing editors of *Fact* magazine and she explained the documentary impetus of many writers in an editorial: 'The instinct that drives a writer to go and see for himself may be sound ... he must go for the sake of the fact, as a medical student carries out a dissection, and to equip himself, not to satisfy his conscience or to see what effect it has on him.' Some of the effects of this focus on including a factual, informative basis in a novel may be noted in a review of Winifred Holtby's *South Riding* (1936) by Seán Ó'Faoláin (1900–1991). The reviewer enjoyed the novel, but made one criticism:

> The local government material – the secondary stories of Alderman Snaith and Alderman Huggins, the Sawdons, the Mitchells, the Hubbards and the rest, have given us a far wider landscape, an extremely interesting and real background but the test of their value to the essential composition of the picture is – what would they have been without Sarah Burton's love story?

There was Holtby, trying her best to give the love story a substantial setting in which the reader learned a lot about local government and the social interactions around Sarah Burton. The documentary value escaped the Irish reviewer somehow.

The emphasis of this strand in 1930s writing was about giving the reader a sense of immediacy – of 'being there' where work was going on and where hard life applied its trials to self and family; a typical feature in 1934 was 'hardship and courage on the Clydeside' with the familiar first-paragraph impact:

> I and my wife and my family of five children have got a total income of 33s 3d a week. Ten bob goes in rent and another half a crown for coal and after we've paid for insurance and light we have about half a crown a day for food and clothes for the seven of us ... That's a problem for my wife, and God knows how she solves it ...

Storm Jameson and the *Fact* ethos is explained in an editorial in 1937, which explains the thinking behind what was to be a documentary method in writing, or at times, a subject to handle with the discovery of the working class in mind:

> we have been encouraged to take on a responsibility which normally would normally only be assumed by a university fund ... It is nothing less than to begin a social and anthropological survey of typical parts of Britain. You have read, no doubt, plenty of statistical and economic accounts of this or that area or this or that industry. But have you ever considered the place in which you live and the trade in which you work, with the impartial and distant eye of an anthropologist? Suppose, instead of going to work one day without reflecting on what was before you, you were to watch and listen, to observe the buildings, the dress, the habits, the conversation, the food and the taboos of your fellows as conscientiously as if you were walking for the first time into an African village?

The implications of this statement for creative writing and for the practice of fiction or memoir are enormous. Behind it lies the thinking relating to the new discovery of the working class. Where had they been, in the literature from Geoffrey Chaucer to Thomas Hardy? They had been there in the texts as stock figures, stereotypes, such as Hodge the countryman or Jane the skivvy; they had been the servants in Jane Austen's fiction and the dairy workers in Thomas Hardy. In the Victorian novel, as in say Elizabeth Gaskell's (1810–1865) *Ruth*, which features a seamstress, they were there to be seduced by the rich young men.

Now, here was a left-wing magazine prompting its 1930s readers to become followers of David Livingstone (1813–1873) and enter into 'darkest

England' to discover the underclass. Around the first years of the twentieth century, there had been a series of features on 'the child slaves of Britain' by Robert H. Sherard (1861–1943), and he had, in some ways, prefigured this line of thought. His style would have impressed Storm Jameson: 'I never set foot in Manchester without a shrinking of the heart – an instinctive and irrepressible feeling of pale terror. It is an account of an almost perennial gloom, it is because I am familiar with the dreadful squalor and surpassing misery of its slums ...'

This appeared in the 1904 edition of *The London Magazine*, and was tantamount to being a report of 'white slavery' – something which also filtered into the periodical press at the time and throughout the Edwardian years.

In the issue of *Fact* following the manifesto of Jameson's leader piece, the fiction and features included *Colliery Disaster* (a documentary piece) by J.E. Samuel, along with *Sweat* by Fred Urquhart, *The Deserter* by Stephen Spender and *The Cobbler and the Machine* by Mulk Raj Anand (1905–2004). Jameson was the only female contributor. She had arrived in this situation, leading the mediation of documentary and socialist debate, through a life pathway that illustrates most of the central aspects of the woman writer's route to success in literature. In her two-volume autobiography, *Journey from the North* (1969), she recounts in great detail her journey from birth in Whitby, North Yorkshire to a sea captain's family, through early motherhood, phases of desperate poverty and endless job-hunting, much of this caused by an anonymous husband referred to as 'K' and her ups and downs surely exemplify the experiences common to so many women in all walks of life whenever they were fired with ambition.

Her writing life began with attempts to write novels, and the story of her first three titles shows an impressive dedication, and a determination to make something of herself. She worked by inspiration and hard work, and her progress is marked by episodes explaining a random and wayward creativity:

> On one of these long nights, a character broke into my mind without any warning, from nowhere, from the darkness outside the weak ring of light. A round-faced, disreputable little man, limping and voluble, called Poskett. I knew all about him: I knew that he had trouble with his wife, and why. I knew his weaknesses, his shocking habits, his

> enduring virtue. I scribbled like a maniac, my face burning. The child woke coughing and was sick. I made him comfortable and went back to Poskett ...

Whoever has struggled to write, in the mode of the fabled 'kitchen table' novelist, knows this situation; there is no doubt that Jameson went through several traumatic experiences, often alone or staying with friends, moving from different temporary accommodation. But when she took her chances in London, a string of literary and bookish experiences introduced her to the strange and difficult world of editors, publishers and the learning curve of the aspiring writer. She found low-paid work with an advertising agency, and her first novel finally made it into print at that time: the title was *The Pot Boils: A Novel* (*c*.1919). From there all kinds of confrontations arrived.

One of these was an interview with publisher Fisher Unwin, after her current novel had been rejected. A suggested deal was given, and it was odd:

> He offered me ... a contract to show him my next six books. Innocent as I was, I saw that this committed him to nothing, and me to an appalling number of novels on the off chance that he would approve of them.

On the way out, he handed her a book: this was *The Way of an Eagle* (1920) by Ethel M. Dell (1881–1939) and Unwin said, 'Read this ... it will teach you how a novel should be written.' It's fate was to be thrown from a train window. Yet her learning quickened its pace. She then dined with publishers, and actually gained a small advance from Constable.

The next stage was to work as a copywriter, followed by a significant step forward: she met a man who ran a magazine called *New Commonwealth* and she found herself to be an editor, earning far more than the copywriting. Jameson notes, 'I wrote a great deal of the paper myself; dramatic criticism, political notes, reviews, brief essays – all except the first with a light-hearted indifference to principles.'

After meetings with a number of writers and others in the publishing profession (including Walter de la Mare) Jameson pressed on with the fiction and so, when a remarkably better opportunity came up, she took it. This was to work as a reader with American publisher Alfred A. Knopf. This gave her a profound insight into the way publishing works, and she succeeded.

Finally, as she made it to the opening of her mature style and a definite presence on the British literary scene, she thought more deeply about her abilities and where she was going in her now successful profession. She had a major project brewing: 'It took me three novels to write the life of Mary Hansyke, who became Mary Harvey, from her birth in 1821 to her death in 1923 ...'

The writer who was to write the leader for the issue of *Fact*, the person who was now determined to be a part of the documentary trend and the socialist outlook, had learned and changed with regard to the rough, hard-working North Yorkshire she knew so well. Also, in one of her moves from home to home, she had known a hard, minimal life in Liverpool: at one point she writes of something that would have sat well alongside *The Road to Wigan Pier* (1937):

> The journey from Liverpool to Whitby passes through the corroded valleys of Lancashire and the West Riding of Yorkshire, vast troughs of solid, grimy streets, mills, warehouses, chapels, sluggish canals, factory chimneys, vomiting smoke over hillsides scarred by terraces of squat grey houses ...

'Documentary' is a word that describes a style as well as a content. Most writers in the 1930s were aware of this: the urgent demand to describe and explain the lives and conditions of the working class. For so long these workers had been nothing more than creatures in the background in the novel, and their working days were mysteries to most readers. The books, magazines and periodicals, together with special reports and political enquiries and documentary films, all gathered into a literature of the unnoticed. The metaphor of that *Fact* editorial about comparing such writing to anthropological ventures, was close to the truth, and when the Jarrow Crusade marched through the country to highlight the plight of unemployed manual works, in October 1936, it was noticed.

Novels in that decade began more and more *to reveal*, *to discover* what was there but had been made marginal. Penguin Books joined the trend with their anthologies *Penguin New Writing*, edited by John Lehmann, but in their first issue of 1940 what one notices is that all fourteen contributors are men. The publication was first planned in 1935 and was first published in a different format in 1936 by the Bodley Head. Lehmann's introduction to the 1940 version makes no mention of class or hierarchy, and certainly not of women writers. The subject range is tight – mostly war and work. But in issue 2 there is one woman writer at last: Rosamond Lehmann (1901–1990), the editor's sister. There was very little progress in respect of a female presence by the end of the Second World War. The April 1946 issue has just two women: Edith Sitwell (1887–1964) and Annabel Farjeon (1919–2004).

But this was an important and influential magazine/paperback anthology. Small magazines and the literary press had a presence. However, the later historiography of various literary groupings through the interwar and immediately pre-First World War years have shown this bias. The Dymock Poets – a group of literary intellectuals and poets who lived near the Gloucester village of Dymock, which included Rupert Brooke (1887–1915), Robert Frost (1874–1963) and John Drinkwater (1882–1937), was largely male. Eleanor Farjeon (1881–1965) was there on the fringe. On a larger scale the Poetry Bookshop and J.C. Squire (1884–1958), concerned with what came to be known as the 'Georgian Poets', prompt similar male clusters of writers. The related anthologies of that verse, running between 1911 and 1922, have only one woman writer listed: Vita Sackville-West.

Documentary had several origins. It coalesced into travel books, autobiographies and topography; there were works dealing with the now more acknowledged poverty in the industrial towns and cities; there were also areas of social history that impinged on the genre. J.B. Priestley's *English Journey* (1934) had an impact, as did George Orwell's books on working as a dish-washer in Paris, or a visitor to Wigan Pier. In Orwell's fiction, notably *Keep the Aspidistra Flying* (1936), there is also a focus on the plight of the 'small writer' – the struggling and talented loner, in his creation of Gordon Comstock, author of a volume of poetry, *Mice*, who suffers constant rejection.

An interesting case here is *Yorkshire Tour* (1939) by Ella Pontefract (1896–1943) and Marie Hartley (1905–2006), which was published in 1939 and then reprinted in 2003. The time and place are important. Here was a flowering of regional writing, as the proletarians were there, but also, close by was the rural Englishness, which had spawned such cultural features as the folk song revival and the more widespread interest in dialect. The shire, the provinces and the appeal of the 'local' in national identity, at a time was the country was threatened by fascism of course, all came together as strands in the documentary urge to 'know' and to experience a revelation of cultures and heritage on the verge of oblivion. In this period, regional writers such as Phyllis E. Bentley (1894–1977), Lettice Cooper (1897–1994) and Barbara Taylor Bradford (*b.*1933) began to start writing; there was provincial life itself, as depicted in so many novels by women, such as Naomi Jacob, Kate O'Brien (1897–1974) and Winifred Holtby. Magazines came along with this spirit too, such as *The Yorkshire Dalesman*, which started in 1939 and in its first issue featured Lettice Cooper and Ella Pontefract. In fact, this first issue contains something entirely typical of this mix of genres and categories in the 1930s. After a short piece by Cooper on a memory of a walk in the Yorkshire Dales with a friend, there is a small, close text feature on 'Adult Education in Craven' with this style: 'Expansion work in adult education began in the area eighteen months ago. Pioneer lectures were held in the villages ... The high standard maintained in these lectures ensured that the serious student was attracted ...' *Yorkshire Tour* employed a more direct documentary approach. There is plenty of history and topography of course, but in the chapter on York, for instance, there is the immediacy of the 'report on today' appeal of fresh documentary writing: 'From another part there is the sight of the market where sheep and cattle waiting their turn in the auction mart across the street are folded in pens close under the wall. Black Irish cattle form the main part of the stock ...' In other words, the notion of *reportage* is always prominent. In the 1930s, there was a proliferation of the guide books and reports on social life that was to form a first step towards what became Mass Observation, which was started in 1937 by Tom Harrisson (1911–1976), Charles Madge (1912–1996) and Humphrey Jennings (1907–1950), as they produced a documentary work on a northern town called *Pub and the People: Worktown* (1943), combining words and pictures.

In women's fiction, this spirit of revelation and enquiry found its way into the stories. Such genres as sagas and romances of course, have to give plenty of explanations of settings for plot and characters, and so a gritty realism developed, dealing with a surface impression and perhaps local industry and housing, emerged. But this did not necessarily have to be all concerned with sooty and noisy industrial towns. In the work of Dorothy Una Ratcliffe (1887–1967), for instance, there is an interesting mix of realism, memoir and nostalgia, but there is just as much attention given to manual work, crafts and traditions as in urban fiction. She wrote mostly about North Yorkshire, although she knew the cities of the county too; she had been Lady Mayoress of Leeds during the First World War and had worked in the effort to help the floods of Belgian refugees who came to Britain. Born in 1887, she was always going to be prominent in the arts, but perhaps early on she was marked for a career in music; after finishing schools in Paris and in Germany, she had singing lessons, and a fellow pupil was no less than the great Nellie Melba (1861–1931), outstanding celebrity in the world of opera in Edwardian times.

But she took to writing poems and stories, and also sketches, often of rural life. In her book, *Dale Folk* (1927), she shows the breadth of her abilities and chosen themes, but rural work and physical labour are prominent. In 'Jabe, the Cobbler of Wath' she displays her ability to produce a vignette: 'His cheeks were as red as a Ribston pippin, his beard thick and snowy white, shaven round a firm old mouth, and his peat-coloured eyes held an expression of shrewd friendliness that one so often finds in the eyes of dalesfolk of all ages.' Where, in the 1930s, the documentary approaches would more often tend to include problems and strains, with perhaps some statistics of hardship, Ratcliffe gives plenty of facts but puts individuals first.

In Yorkshire there was a particular growth of writing about the industrial West Riding, and between *c.*1915 and the 1950s there were many novelists and travel writers occupying the regional niche there. Typical of the women writers, as opposed to people such as J.B. Priestley and the new crime writers, was Phyllis E. Bentley. In her autobiography, she gives an account of her growth as a writer, and makes it clear that writing about what was before her eyes and 'in her blood' was her aim. After an early struggle, in which her brother paid for the publication of her first novel, she found success with a two-book deal. She explains her writer's credo in line with the need to have a factual basis and a solid realism:

> Thus it seemed to me that the artist's duty was to present life by means of a pattern, so vividly, so convincingly, so interestingly, and of

> course so truthfully that the reader should – as Defoe remarked when he crossed the Pennines into the strange West Riding textile country – *perceive the reason and nature of the thing.*

Defoe's words are not far from the impetus behind the documentary writing.

Bentley's first attempts, after the failure of that self-published first novel, *The World's Bane* (1918), were the result of continued and massive research; she existed on a number of part-time jobs, from library cataloguing to book reviewing, but in this she was building a portfolio and a *curriculum vitae* that would look good in front of would-be publishers and agents. She had the usual 'almost acceptance' with Sidgwick and Jackson, and then, with Gollanz impressed, she sold them *The Spinner of the Years* (1928). Bentley became one of the foremost regional novelist of the period, and when she spoke of her own favourite novel, *Carr* (1929), she explained, 'But the interesting fact about *Carr* is that it is written exactly in the form of a real biography about a real man ... P.J. [Philip Joseph] Carr was a completely ordinary man ...' The crusade announced by *Fact* was in acknowledgement of the dual aim of the documentary drive: first to show working class life as it really was, and second, to encourage writing with a precise but often lyrical element. Arguably this is seen in essence in this scene from Rosamond Lehmann's story, *A Dream of Winter* (1946), where a workman has come to attend to a bee problem:

> 'Come to take that there swarm. Wrong weather to take a swarm. I don't like the job on a day like this. Bad for 'em. Needs a mild spell. Still, it don't look like breaking and I hadn't nothink [*sic*] else on and you wanted the job done.' His speech had a curious humming drawl, not altogether following the pattern of the local dialect; brisker, more positive ...

This is a mix of what could be a stereotype, together with a man setting about a job of work, but there is a curious pointing out of the man who comes to do a working class job. Lehmann is asking the reader to share in a new curiosity – notice the odd man who works with his hands. Listen to the expression of his nature.

If one returns to my opening dichotomy between the Bloomsbury mindset and the urge to present a new realism for this world of great social change and war, then there are clear differences. The alleged limitations of the Woolf method, as in *Mrs Dalloway*, were written clearly in a review of that book by Sylvia Lynd (1888–1952), writing in the magazine *Time and Tide*. She wrote:

> For by this method of writing, this snatching at life in handfuls and heaping it chaotically together, by rejecting a central presence and personality to give it order and coherence and inevitably selection and limitation, Mrs Woolf compels us to make impossible demands on her and cry for every life in London in a single book.

One might argue, in Virginia Woolf's defence, that only by showing the internal confusions and distress of one individual can a writer suggest types, classes and/or the human condition itself as a universal. That is, we all have inner lives of confusion and we snatch at life in handfuls.' In fact, Sylvia Lynd's critique could easily be applied to documentary fiction, in that it tends to present 'a cry for every life ... in a single book.' We may see this in an advert for James Hanley's book, *Grey Children*, in 1935: 'Portrait of South Wales: *Grey Children* – a study in humbug and misery ...' The advert has this: 'This is the STARK TRUTH about the DISTRESSED MINING VILLAGES of SOUTH WALES. James Hanley knows all about the HUMBUG and MISERY and he does not mince his words ...'

As well as *New Writing*, there was *Left Review*, and this publication kept MI5 busy, as it was actively communist, and went so far as criticising the cash spent on the 1935 Silver Jubilee. The names most associated with *Left Review* were, once again, mostly male, such as Edgell Rickword (1898–1982) and Tom Wintringham (1898–1949), but there was among them Amabel Williams-Ellis (1894–1984), involved in editorial work. She was linked to the Bloomsbury Group, being the cousin of Lytton Strachey. She married the architect Sir Clough Williams-Ellis (1883–1978) in 1915, and was the literary editor of *The Spectator* from 1922 to 1923. She wrote over forty books, and wrote widely for the magazines of the time, and her books cover several genres. She died in 1984.

THE LONDON MERCURY 669

D. L. MURRAY'S

REGENCY

Gerald Gould in the Observer "recommends it with enthusiasm." 8/6 net

THE SALLY CARSON'S

PRISONER

"This is certainly the finest novel on modern Germany I have read."
LILIAN ARNOLD in John o' London's Weekly
7/6 net

ALISON FLEMING'S

CHRISTINA STRANG

"This beautifully produced book . . . done with a straightforward sincerity and understanding that give it not only a freshness but a sort of sculptural quality." Times Literary Supplement
7/6 net

and ERIC SHIPTON'S

NANDA DEVI

"Mr. Shipton is to be congratulated on achieving one of the greatest mountaineering feats of recent times . . . An outstanding travel book." The Times
With wonderful illustrations 15/- net

HODDER AND STOUGHTON

2X

Above left: Alyse Gregory, author of *The Day is Gone*. (*Madeleine Curry*)

Above right: Book advert, as appeared in the newspaper. Three women writers hyped – now forgotten? (*London Mercury*, April 1936)

Right: 'Clever Women' newspaper story. Report on a talk by Storm Jameson. (*Hull Daily Mail*)

CLEVER WOMEN AND IMMORAL WOMEN.

(By STORM JAMESON, the famous English Novelist, in an Interview.)

MISS STORM JAMESON, one of the most successful of that band of young women novelists whose originality and activity constitute a striking feature of literary life in London—who, by the way, is only 31—when invited to express herself on the subject of careers for married women replied in a positive manner:

"I don't say that it is impossible for a married woman with children successfully to run a separate career as well, but I do say that it is practically so. None but a super-woman can run both,

DALES FOLK by ELLA PONTEFRACT

"*He were nobbut a peeat high,*" *a dalesman said of a small boy.*

"*If there's another Noah's flood, there won't be manny folk left alive i' England when t'watter comes blashin' down oor chimney pots,*" *said another of his high farm.*

"'*Tha's nivver gaen to lig under yon' lump o' clout,*" *a daleswoman said to a camper.*

THIS vividness of expression, owing much to dialect, is an attractive dale characteristic. That there was a hill fair here, that this small town had a market, and this village kept up wedding customs are dead facts until the dalesfolk, by such phrases in their recollections, give them life, making one see the sheep and cattle on the hill, hear the bargaining in the market, and feel the hot pennies thrown at weddings.

We had watched men cutting and setting peat on the fells, but an old lady of eighty made us realise the activity when everybody burnt peat. We saw her as a child setting the blocks, and being taken as a reward to Askrigg Hill Fair. A farmer's wife completed the picture by telling of making stacks on the moor herself because her husband was "neaa peeat man."

As our first friend talked on, the room faded, and became a village shop with scholars sitting in one corner watching the door for a customer to bring a break in lessons.

Two men in different dales showed us the wide importance of Middleham Moor Fair by telling, one how he joined with a neighbour to buy a cow there to salt for the winter's meat, and the other of his early morning journey to the fair over two fell passes and another valley. They spoke naturally of what had been a phase in their lives, their interest in it as a thing of the past intensified by their interest in the life of the dale to-day.

Above: Marie Corelli's house in Stratford-upon-Avon. (*Author's collection*)

Left: 'Dales Folk'. Feature from the first issue of *The Dalesman*. (*The Dalesman*)

Sixteen Companionable Volumes
By
E. V. Lucas

Fcap. 8vo, gilt top, Cloth, 5s. each

The Open Road
The Friendly Town
The Gentlest Art
The Second Post
Her Infinite Variety
Good Company
A Wanderer in Paris
London Lavender
Listener's Lure
Over Bemerton's
Mr. Ingleside
Loiterer's Harvest
Fireside and Sunshine
Character and Comedy
One Day and Another
Old Lamps for New

Methuen & Co. Ltd.
36 Essex Street, Strand, London, W.C.

Above left: Drawing of E.M. Hull, author of the best-selling *The Sheik*. (*Wikicommons*)

Above right: Advert for E.V. Lucas's book. He was a prolific author who collaborated with his wife, Elizabeth. (*Author's collection*)

Right: 'E. Nesbit Story'. A typical illustrated tale from *Strand*, 1898. (*Author's collection*)

The Young Antiquaries.

By E. NESBIT.

Author of "The Would-be-Goods," etc.

THIS really happened before Christmas, but I must tell you about it, because it leads on to the story of what became of the parrot we got from the Chinaman, and you would not understand that unless you understood this first.

It was one Sunday—the somethingth Sunday in Advent, I think, and Denny and Daisy and their father and Albert's uncle came to dinner, which is in the middle of the day on that Day of Rest, and the same things to eat for grown-ups and us. It is nearly always roast beef and Yorkshire—but the puddings and vegetables are brightly variegated and never the same two Sundays running. At dinner someone said something about the coat-of-arms that is on the silver tankards which once, when we were poor and honest, used to stay at the shop having the dents slowly taken out of them for months and months. But now they are always at home and are put at the four corners of the table every day and anyone who likes can drink beer out of them.

After some talk of the sort you don't listen to, in which bends and lioncels and gules and things played a promising part, Albert's uncle said that Mr. Turnbull had told him something about that coat-of-arms being carved on a bridge somewhere in Cambridgeshire, and again the conversation wandered into things like Albert's uncle had talked about to the Maidstone Antiquarian Society the day they came over to see his old house in the country and we arranged the time-honoured Roman Remains for them to dig up. So, hearing the words King-post and mullion and moulding and underpin, Oswald said might we go—and we went and took our dessert with us and had it in our own common room, where you can roast chestnuts with a free heart and never mind what your fingers get like.

Oswald listened as carefully as he could, but Denny always buzzes so when he whispers.

When first we knew Daisy we used to call her the White Mouse, and her brother had all the appearance of being one, too, but you know how untruthful appearances are, or else it was that we taught him happier things, for he certainly turned out quite different in the end: and she was not a bad sort of kid, though we never could quite cure her of wanting to be "lady-like." That is the beastliest word there is, I think, and Albert's uncle says so, too. He says if a girl can't be a lady it's not worth while

Copyright in Great Britain and the United States of America.

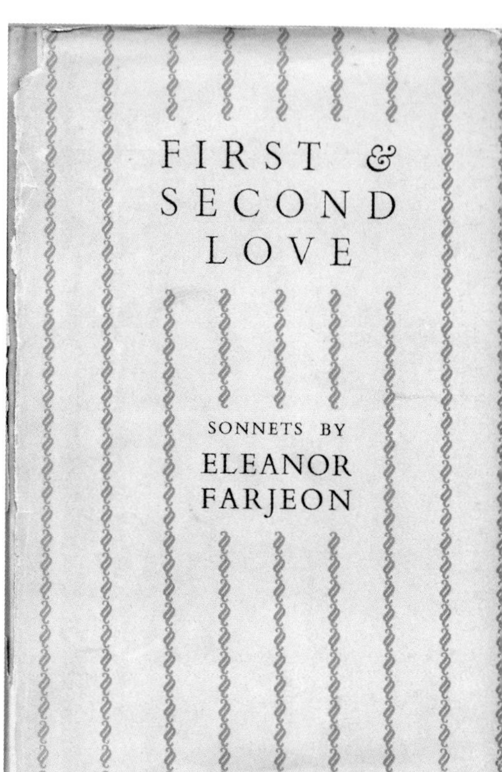

Above left: Cover of *Fact* from the July 1935 edition. (*Author's collection*)

Above right: Cover of Eleanor Farjeon collection, *First and Second Love* published in 1947. (*Author's collection*)

Left: Nellie Ganthony, writer and performer, modelled on George Grossmith. (*Author's collection*)

Above left: Cover of Katherine Mansfield's first book, *In a German Pension*, published in 1911. (*Author's collection*)

Above right: Madeleine Curry, friend and correspondent of Alyse Gregory. (*Author's collection*)

Right: Cover of October 1951 edition of *Magpie*, with Daphne du Maurier included. (*Author's collection*)

MILLS & BOON'S BOOKS for EVERYONE

Ready during January.

HAROLD BEGBIE'S
NEW LONG NOVEL
THE PICTURE BOOK
6/-

A joyous and enchanting story about a great London Duchess and her world. Please write for a Prospectus.

By the Author of 'The RAJAH'S PEOPLE.'
THE SHINING HEIGHTS
By I. A. R. WYLIE.
6/-

A long, powerful, and absorbing novel by one of Britain's most popular novelists.

JACK LONDON'S NEW BOOK.
THE STRENGTH OF THE STRONG
6/-

A remarkable volume of stories in the author's finest style.
The Popular Shilling Edition of "The Little Lady of the Big House" is ready.

By the Author of
"WHEN THE RED GODS CALL."
KRIS GIRL
6/-
By BEATRICE GRIMSHAW.
An Exciting Story of the South Seas.

General Literature

MY SIBERIAN YEAR.
By M. A. CZAPLICKA. With 37 Illustrations from Photographs. Demy 8vo, 10s. 6d. net.

THE EXPERIENCES OF A WOMAN DOCTOR IN SERBIA.
By DR. CAROLINE MATTHEWS. Demy 8vo, 5s. net. Illustrated.

CAPT. HARRY GRAHAM'S
NEW VOLUME.
RHYMES FOR RIPER YEARS
(3/6 net: postage 4d.) is now ready. It is profusely illustrated by NORAH BRASSEY.

BOOKS BY CAPT. HARRY GRAHAM.
Deportmental Ditties 3/6 net
Canned Classics .. 3/6 net
***The Bolster Book 3/6 net**
*Also issued at 1/- net.

THE DOLLS' DAY.
By CARINE CADBY. Illustrated with 29 Photographs by Will Cadby. Second Edition. Crown 8vo, 2/- net. (Postage 3d.)
"One of the most unusual

2/- Edition Nearly Ready.

TRUTH.—"It is a great book, told with the finest detail of artistic finish. A living page of fiction which will stand the test of time."
The *SCOTSMAN.*—"A most vivid picture of the life and amusements of the young American millionaire, his school and University life, his trips to London, his dinners, his dissipations . . . deserves to be widely read."

2/- net. **LOVE** 2/- net.
Postage 5d. **By W. B. TRITES,** Postage 5d.
Author of "Life." 1/- net. (Postage 3d.)
The novel which has sold over one hundred thousand copies.

SELLING in HUNDREDS of THOUSANDS
1/- net each; postage, 3d.

The most Popular Shilling Series in the World.

JACK LONDON
THE LITTLE LADY OF THE BIG HOUSE—THE VALLEY OF THE MOON—THE MUTINY OF THE ELSINORE—JOHN BARLEYCORN—CHILDREN OF THE FROST—THE GOD OF HIS FATHERS—THE CRUISE OF THE SNARK—THE CRUISE OF THE DAZZLER—AN ODYSSEY OF THE NORTH—THE

BEATRICE GRIMSHAW
GUINEA GOLD
COSMO HAMILTON
THE BLINDNESS OF VIRTUE
A. A. LILLEY
TWENTY-FOUR YEARS OF CRICKET
ROY NORTON
THE BOOMERS
THE PLUNDERER

Advert spread for Mills & Boon, 1914. (*Author's collection*)

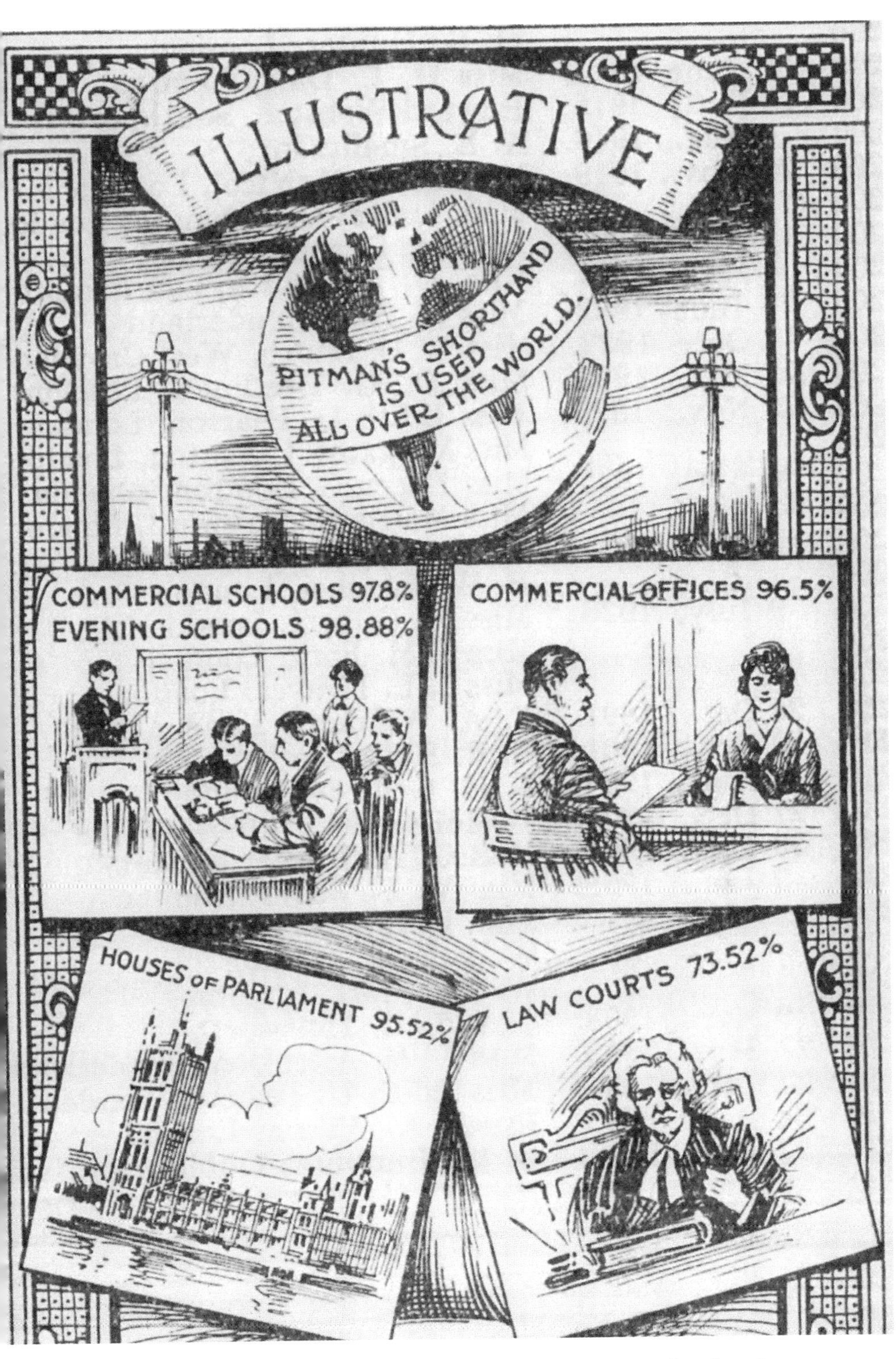

Images showing the offerings of the successful Pitman's shorthand course. (*Author's collection*)

ADAM et ÈVE

Oh ! que fragile est la femme !
L'affreux doute emplit mon âme !
Jure-moi sous ce pommier
Que je suis bien le premier !

14

15

ADAM et ÈVE

RENÉ KIEFFER, ÉDITEUR, RELIEUR D'ART, 18, RUE SÉGUIER, PARIS-VIe

Above: Paris Small Press. Adam and Eve, produced by bookbinder René Kieffer (1876 –1963). Taken from the world of writer Gertrude Stein. (*Author's collection*)

Left: Victorian cover showing *Tinsley's* magazine. Reviews had to cover 896 new novels in 1896. (*Author's collection*)

Above left: Cover of the famous *The Sheik* by E.M. Hull published in 1919. (*Author's collection*)

Above right: Cover of *Yvette* by Guy de Maupassant published in 1884. One of the Flammarion series of modern classics – only one female writer included in fifty-two names. (*Author's collection*)

Right: A typical feature by Eden Philpotts (1862–1960) in 1896, mentor to Agatha Christie. (*The Idler*)

In the Hands of Jefferson.

By Eden Phillpotts.

Illustrations by Ronald Gray.

It is not difficult to appreciate the recent catastrophe in Oceania, where the island of Great Sangir was partially smothered by terrific volcanic and seismic convulsions, when one has visited the Western Indies.

Many of these tropic isles probably owe their present isolation, if not their actual existence, to mighty earthquake throes in remote ages of terrestrial history beyond the memory of man. But

"WHERE LORD NELSON ENJOYED HIS HONEYMOON."

man's memory is not a very extensive affair, and at best probes the past to the extent of a mere rind of a few thousand years. For the rest he has to read the word of God, written in fossil and stone and those wondrous arcana of Nature, which, each in turn, yields a fragment of the secret of truth to human intellect.

Regions that have been produced or largely modified by earthquake and volcanic upheaval may, probably enough, vanish at any moment under like conditions; and the island of Nevis, hard by St.

Left: Dorothy Una Ratcliffe, author of *Dale Folk*, with her then husband, Charles (they married in 1909), and Lord Brotherton (1856–1930). (*Courtesy of Jacey Bedford*)

Below left: Sloppy Joe's. The famous bar in Havana, attracting drinkers as Paris did in the 1920s. (*Author's collection*)

Below right: Cover of *Strangers and a Sojourner* by Nora K. Smith, published by Hodder & Stoughton in 1937. The book was a winning entry from a nationwide writing competition in 1936. (*Author's collection*)

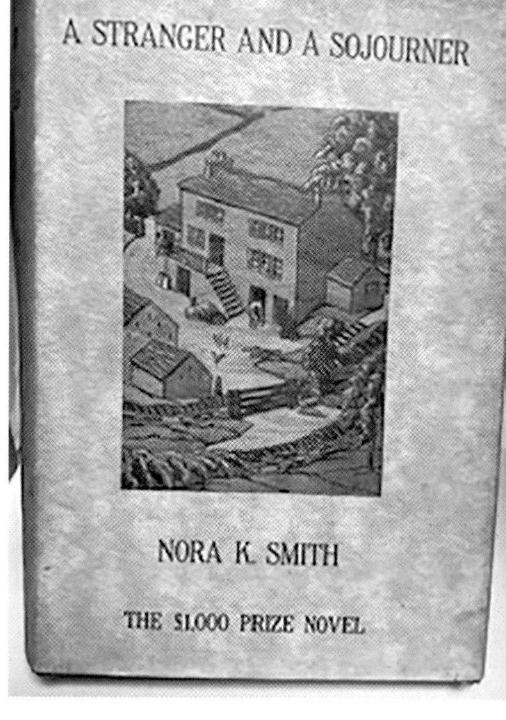

The W.H. Smith Subscription Library. Smith's and Boots' libraries were major sources of sales and income for many women writers up to the 1960s. (*Author's collection*)

Cover of *Out of the Kitchen* by Alice Duer Miller, published in 1916, which was a bestseller. (*Author's collection*)

Dibdene,
Shamley Green,
Guildford, Surrey.

March 30. 53

Dear Miss Holder

I enclosed a letter with your typescript sent by registered post but omitted to refer to your postscript about indicating passages to cut. I think it would be much better if you performed this operation, omitting those paragraphs or pages which you don't consider essential. I think perhaps the story of your childhood is a little too long. To my mind the interest of the narrative increases when you become a nurse.

Yours very sincerely Philip Gibbs.

A letter written by agent Sir Philip Gibbs to an aspiring female novelist. (*Author's collection*)

MADELEINE Walker

From Llewelyn Powys

to help her to remember

the occasion of their

first meeting at (March 26th 1939)

Clavadel and as an offering

to a young and beautiful poet.

"I wander thro' each charter'd street
Near where the charter'd Thames does flow,
And mark in every face I meet
Marks of weakness, marks of woe.
In every cry of every man,
In every infant's cry of fear,
In every voice, in every ban,
The mind-forg'd manacles I hear."

(MANACLES)

For our time is a very shadow that passeth away, and after our ende there is no returning, for it is fast sealed, so that no man cometh again. [illegible] Come on therefore, let us leave some token of our pleasure in every place, for that is our portion, else gett we nothinge.

The Boke of Wysdome.

From Wolf's Bane

The eternal law the deep life stream,
I worship there!
[illegible] shall [illegible] the briefest human dream
[illegible] the fading trees!
[illegible] the frailest human touch
[illegible] the harebells cover the hill,
[illegible] the broken memory of such
[illegible] the heart has had its will.

Death comes, soon, and youth has wings;
Snatch the chance, the time lovers;
Spring alone the crocus brings;
GOD HAVE MERCY
ON ALL LOVERS!

A dedication from Llewelyn Powys written in Davos. (*Author's collection*)

How Many Stories Are There

bought and published every year? And how many articles? If you remember that there are about *four thousand* newspapers, weekly journals, and monthly magazines published in the U.K., nearly all of which require to buy articles and stories from outside sources, you will quickly realize that *thousands* of stories are required and *tens of thousands* of articles.

Almost every daily and evening paper now includes a short story in each issue, and, as regards articles, a leading London evening newspaper lately printed in one issue no fewer than *ten* which were contributed by "free-lance" writers.

There is, in fact, something akin to a "boom" in short stories; many new journals and magazines are now appearing, thus increasing the demand for contributions. "Free-lance" journalism and story-writing are, in short, sharing in this general revival of prosperity, and those who have taken a course of correspondence instruction from The London School of Journalism are reaping their reward.

One woman student recently reported that she had sold over 250 contributions. Another informed the School that, in his first year after completing the course, he had made, by *spare-time* writing, nearly £400. And these are examples typical of many.

The field is immense, the demand is steadily increasing, and the rates of payment are uniformly good. A short story may bring its author anything from six to twenty guineas. Articles can earn from one to five or six guineas, according to length. A single story or a single article once a week means a very acceptable addition to your income. *Why not investigate your possibilities?* It may be that you possess latent ability which an L.S.J. Course will develop and make profitable to you, as so often has been the case. Many of the School's most successful students had never written a line for print before taking a course; others had tried, but with little or no success. The practical and *individual* instruction and guidance which they received enabled them to develop talent which otherwise would not have been discovered.

Here is a suggestion. Write a short article on any subject which interests you, or, if you can think of a plot, write a short story. Send your article or your story to the Secretary (Mr. G. L. Butler). He will submit it to Sir Max Pemberton (Director of Studies), who will then form an opinion as to your literary possibilities and will advise you accordingly. No fee is charged for this, but it may prove the means of opening to you a new and fascinating means of increasing your income by spare-time writing.

One of many adverts for writing courses produced by the London School of Journalism. Note the case study of a female writer. (*Author's collection*)

"The Spell of the Black Woman."

A REMARKABLE NOVEL.

For the very first time in literary history, a woman novelist has utilised the Cameroons as a background for a remarkable story. The authoress is Mrs Charlotte Cameron, F.R.G.S., the woman writer and traveller, whose 26,000 mile trip across Africa a couple of years ago, attracted a deal of attention, and earned for her the title of "The Modern Mary Kingsley." Mrs Cameron was one of the first Englishwomen to traverse the one-time German South-West African Colonies from end to end. It was here that the idea of her forthcoming book, "Zenia, Spy in Togoland." was conceived. "Quite apart from the romantic element in 'Zenia,' explains Mrs Cameron, 'I have limned the life in Togoland as it really is, with the idea of appealing to the colonising instincts of the Englishwoman. I want to illustrate to her how successful the German women have been in adapting themselves to a trying climate, and to conditions that are unusual. But, above all," Mrs Cameron added, "I want her to realise how vitally necessary it is that the spell of the black woman over the European Colonist in Africa shall be broken. There are African Colonies where the black woman reigns supreme; where dusky beauties, with thick lips and hair that is frizzed most comically, usurp the place of the white woman who will not come. Such a state of affairs should no longer mar our colonial record in the days ahead."

'A Remarkable Novel'. Newspaper report from 1915 regarding *Zenia, Spy in Togoland* by Charlotte Cameron, published in the same year. (*Hull Daily Mail*)

THE MEDIATION OF A PIANO.

A TUNING ROMANCE.

By Mary Romney.

Illustrated by Fred Pegram.

I.

MISS STANFIELD was in a hurry, and the brisk tattoo which she delivered on the counter with the handle of her neat umbrella brought the mild youth poring over a ledger off his stool with more than his usual alacrity.

"I want you to send a man to tune my piano," she began, in clear, decisive tones.

"I should prefer the man I always have—Turner, isn't that his name?"

"Mr. Turner is away, madam, on a few days' holiday," returned the mild youth, apologetically. "However, if you will allow us to send our other——"

He hesitated on seeing the gathering frown in her blue eyes.

"When will Mr. Turner be back?"

"'I WANT YOU TO SEND A MAN TO TUNE MY PIANO,' SAID MISS STANFIELD."

A typical fiction contribution by a female writer in 1899 as appeared in *Harmsworth's*. (*Harmsworth's*)

Is the artistic temperament a blessing or a curse? We should first decide what the artistic temperament means. Artistic is a large word. It includes painting, acting, poetry, music, literature, preaching. Whether the temperament is a blessing or a curse largely depends upon the health of the artist. If De Quincey was an artist, the artistic temperament was a curse. So also with Thomas Carlyle. So also with Charles Lamb. The artistic temperament is creative, sympathetic, responsive; it sees everything, feels everything, realises everything, on a scale of exaggeration. It is in quest of ideals, and all ideals are more or less in the clouds, and not seldom at the tip-top of the rainbow. Those who undertake such long journeys are subject to disappointment and fatigue by the way; if ever they do come to the end of their journey it is probably in a temper of fretfulness and exasperation. A sudden knock at the door may drive an artist into hysterics. He is always working at the end of his tether. There is nothing more tantalising than an eternal quest after the ideal; like the horizon, it recedes from the traveller; like the mirage, it vanishes before the claims of hunger and thirst. On the other hand, it has enjoyments all its own. The idealist is always face to face with a great expectation. Perhaps to-night he may realise it; certainly

Dr. Parker says it depends upon the health of the artist.

H H

Is the artistic temperament a blessing or a curse? The subject for discussion in *The Idler*. (*The Idler*)

Left Review played its part in the realism of the documentary trend; but it had a marked difference from the other periodicals such as *Fact*, in that its political aims were forthright, set firmly against fascism and totalitarianism. The content of a typical issue was therefore far more than literary reflections and criticism: there was always a number of political pieces. The contributors included Storm Jameson, together with W.H. Auden, Ralph Fox (1900–1936) and Pearl Binder (1904–1990).

Amabel Williams-Ellis is an interesting writer in many respects. In an article on her life and work written by Jayne Sherratt, the argument makes it clear that Williams-Ellis had many and diverse talents. Her novel *The Big Firm* (1938) seems to merit some special pleading for its exceptional quality. A *New York Times* review called it 'distinguished as a work of literary art' and Sherratt took up her research, reported on the website 'neglected books' She recalls: 'I found that in a career spanning seven decades of the twentieth century Amabel [Williams-Ellis] had published over seventy books. Six of these were novels, mainly written between 1925 and 1939.' One might argue that she had plenty of family and contacts behind her, as she 'grew up where celebrity was normal' as Sherratt notes. But the evidence of her rare talent is in that fourth novel, *The Big Firm*. Sherratt argues the case, 'It was written in an atmosphere of increasing international tensions and crisis' and the central character is a scientist working in microbiology research. Political opinions on current crises play a large part in the story, and it is clear that Williams-Ellis's political views were deeply held. Sherratt points out that she even went to New York to speak at the American Enquiry Commission, which was interested in what was happening in Nazi Germany. As I write this, I'm hoping that Sherratt will perhaps write a biography of Williams-Ellis; this is sorely needed.

Another woman writer linked to the *Left Review* was Nancy Cunard (1896–1965), whose involvement in writing about the Spanish Civil War led to some pamphlets being printed, and she engaged in some *vox pop* research; finally a book on all this was published by the *Left Review*: *Left Review Authors Take Sides on the Spanish War*. Cunard was deeply involved with many of the key features of writing and publishing through the interwar years, from running a magazine, editing and political activism, through to massive social issues, and she was a charismatic person, prominent in fashion trends also. In a literary world where small presses and exclusive literary groups abounded, she tended to meet a large proportion of the movers and shakers in that world. Her influence always seems to be there in these projects, perhaps typified by her joining the Sitwells to create their anthology called *Wheels* (1916). But arguably her most lasting production was the editing of the *Negro Anthology* (1934), in which she gathered together all kinds of writing and testimony to the pain of black lives in the United States. Included were luminaries such as Langston Hughes (1901–1967) and Zora Neale Hurston (1891–1960). The book went into print in 1934 and certainly caused a stir. Cunard herself attracted some acrimony, and even some threats to her life.

Chapter 6

The Poets

'Alas, that ever life's sweet counterfeit,
Convention, should usurp life's very throne.'
Eleanor Farjeon

In the 1820s, Northamptonshire poet John Clare wrote a poem headed, *An Effusion to Poetry*, adding beneath that title these words: 'On receiving a damp from a genteel opinionist in poetry, of some sway, as I am told, in the literary world.' One of Clare's key statements was:

I still must love thee, Poesy,
A poor rude clown, and what of that?

Clare was responding to a negative response to his 'untutored' lines in his working-class poetry, coming from the farms and fields, like Robert Burns (1759–1796) and others known as 'peasant poets'. Whoever the 'opinionist' was, it is clear that he was educated in the classics, and poetry from a man who had no more than an elementary education seemed to him to be unacceptable – below required standards of ability.

This split across British cultural life and the arts ran deeply, and in many ways, still does, in spite of post-modernism and the supposed equality of opportunity given to our citizens by the education system. This poem was written around fifty years before the momentous Elementary Education Act 1870, which gave elementary education to all children; but still, after that date, there was a massive difference between the workers who left school at fourteen to graft in mills, mines and factories across the land; those workers, along with the growing number of clerical workers towards the end of the nineteenth century, naturally formed part of the general readership for the publishing trade, and within that trade there was poetry.

In the latter half of the Victorian age, following Alfred Tennyson's first works in the 1830s, there was a succession of popular poets, such as Elizabeth Barrett Browning (1806–1861) and Christina Rossetti (1830–1894) to the 'Nineties vogues led by Oscar Wilde and the Decadents.' But what is easily missed is the mass of verse produced for the readership who lacked a classical education and a background in English literature. A division was growing in this respect, and there were plenty of John Clares around whose concept of poetry was very different from that of the Oxbridge graduates who knew the subtleties of translations, echoes and derivatives of the great Latin and Greek poets.

Into this situation came the huge commercial success of *A Shropshire Lad* by A.E. Housman, published in 1896, which was vaguely expressed but with a clear appeal to the male generation who fought first in the Boer War of 1899 to 1902 and then in the First World War. It was about romantic attachment to friends and places, country idylls and the beauty of England. It was also about sacrifice and acts of nobility, right and wrong, and tough male behaviour. In short, it appealed to the readers who had no Virgil or Horace, as well as to the middle class readers who had read these poets. It was a collection with a universal appeal, and it showed that poetry could be universal, democratic and passionate.

The First World War brought out the very high poetic abilities of the male poets such as Wilfred Owen, Siegfried Sassoon and Robert Graves (1895–1985), but it also produced women poets. In Jon Silkin's (1930–1997) landmark anthology, *The Penguin Book of First World War Poetry* (1979), there are eight women poets, and these included poets from nations other than Britain. It was a sign of a great change in attitudes. However, the war opened up opportunities for women poets, and also, to a wider spectrum of male poets. In other words, suffering and dying in the trenches was egalitarian, and poetry, being on the sharp edge of extreme emotion, was a prominent expression of a shared experience, way above and beyond any normal peacetime social hierarchy.

One result of this was that much poetry written in the ten years between the 1919 return to normality and the late 1920s depression was that the familiar split in the readership of poetry became more evident. The productions of Bloomsbury and of the more elitist writers who saw poetry as a high art because it was somehow coded against immediate meaning, won a place in the epicentre of debate and discussions of the literary establishment. The poems of that time which appealed to a mass readership, such as volumes published by Mills & Boon, were somehow inferior to the work of T.S. Eliot, Marianne Moore (1887–1972) and David Jones (1895–1974). Why were these works superior? Because they highlighted what caused this division in what poetry was considered to be.

Two Verse Readers

About 1920 then, there were buyers and readers of poetry who expected a book of verse to be difficult; that is to say, it should need a process of hard thinking in order to be understood. Poetry for them was about a deep meaning, something akin to philosophy. If it expressed an immediate meaning, then it must be popular, and if it was popular, it must lack ambiguity, multiple interpretations, rich literary allusion and complex syntax.

The other reader wanted poetry to be clear about its meaning and communication. When Edna St Vincent Millay (1892–1950) wrote 'Conscientious Objector' she put the essential communication of her poem in the line, 'I shall die, but that is all I shall do for Death.'

The full implications to be inferred are there, revealing their meaning quickly. The whole poem progresses in a similar way. No line gives any ambiguity, any possible dispute on multiple meanings. In contrast, Wilfred Owen entitles a poem *Apologia Pro Poemate Meo* (1920) and shows he is a grammar school boy. The working class sapper along the line would read that title and move on to read something like Rupert Brooke's famous *The Soldier* (1915) with its instantaneous statement of universal ideology,

> If I should die, think only this of me:
> That there's some corner of a foreign field
> That is forever England. …

The women poets of the interwar years followed the two routes into being professional poets. To read Marianne Moore's poems of her *Selected Poems* (1935) one needs to check out her copious notes at the back to have a full knowledge of the vocabulary of the poems. One poem, *Camellia Sabina* (1935), refers to six publications, from natural history to literature, including a long explanation of an aspect of viniculture from *The Epicure's Guide to France* (1935).

The importance of this division, particularly in the 1930s with the growing interest in proletarian writing and making the arts accessible to all, is very significant. The resulting thinking from a poem such as Moore's is something like this sequence in the reader's mind: I have read the surface of these words, some of it is puzzling, but I have some footnotes, this leads me to think about off-shoot subjects, what is this all about then? There is no avoiding the conclusion that either the poets of modernism never thought about their readers or that they only had in mind those readers who were highly educated and understood the new discourses in a range of literary genres.

The answer to this question about the apparent schism between storytellers and story experimenters is in a great deal of academic discussion and commentary, and perhaps Maroula Joannou (*b.*1947) has stated the most perceptive and meaningful explanation. She wrote:

> While the modernist separation from what had gone before might cut the woman writer off from oppressive patriarchal structures, controls and responsibilities, it also cut her off from a public community of women and from an important nexus of shared feelings, hopes, experience, and desires. As Suzanna Clark puts it in *Sentimental Modernism* (1991) 'Modernism practised politics of style, but it denied that style had a politics.'

This makes it perfectly clear that in creating Virginia Woolf's 'room of one's own' something special had been establishing, but that had the nature of a monk's cell, a reserved away from the busy activity of life and relationships. Joannou's thinking here suggests that the cutting off from most human contacts with that quotidian life of business affairs, economic necessity, maintaining family and friendships, and so on. It makes creative writing a kind of cell. The statement makes sense, and it implies that following modernist writing practice carries a heavy penalty. In fact, one could argue, there was a middle ground, and my social history of women writers so far has been describing this. In Storm Jameson's life – a totally committed woman of her age, busy with causes – we see a writer quite able to write with intellectual quality, but who is also capable of producing family stories, emotional conflict and realistic scenarios in terms of those male novelists that Woolf saw as severely limited in their portrayal of life.

The women poets of these decades, entering the world of publishing on a level with men, had to take the blows as well as the triumphs, and the accounts of literary life from Ethel Mannin, Phyllis E. Bentley and Agatha Christie all make it clear that they coped extremely well. One of the most telling scraps of biography with this in mind comes from Eleanor Farjeon, who loved the poet Edward Thomas perhaps like a sister more than a passionate lover, but whatever the truth was, she was dedicated to him. In 1913 she had two books in print, but showed Thomas a privately printed novel. Author Matthew Hollis (*b.*1971) explains what happened: 'Thomas made clear that he found the work inauthentic, believing that [Eleanor] Farjeon had suffocated her material by imposing too many authorial aspirations, while failing to draw out any artistic expression … "Is this Brutal?" he asked her.' It does appear so.

Rather than try to produce a comprehensive account of the poetry written by women in these years, it is helpful to look at some important themes and influences. These include bohemian escapism, aesthetic experiment, social commitment and anarchic humour. If there is a swell of real power driving the current of this flood of vigour and adventure in words, it is the desire to be different, to be heard and also to be passionate about ideals as well as ideas.

The Poetry Scene Post-1918

In the years immediately after the First World War, what changed poetry across the board was the accessibility of the image, perhaps even more than the freedom of forms; both were crucially important, but metaphorical discourse in the poetics of language was open to all. Another way of saying this is that for centuries there had been subjects suitable for poets, so that restricted the work, but there were subjects denied to women also. To make this clearer, it could be said that the basis of an image, for a women writer, had a moral substance. Christina Rossetti could write 'How do I love thee? Let me count the ways' and find images suitable for romantic love. Anything too physical, suggestive or rough would not enter the writer's mind. The form would be a constraint also. What we now call 'free verse' was a rare bird and outside the ken of most writers, who produced poetry for particular periodicals or for anthologies. Then there came various 'movements', which were mostly concerned with the power and versatility of the image. Mina Loy (1882–1966) could write, in a poem about a blind youth, in the war:

> The dam Bellona
> littered
> her eyeless offspring
> *Kriegsopfer*
> upon the pavements of Vienna.

In these lines, typical of the poetry freed from set form, restrictions on suitable diction and other constraints, Loy uses all the linguistic resources of the new discourse to say something startling. The German *Kriegsopfer* has a condensed expression that English cannot match – expressing 'war work' – so the 'work' of war is to blind young men? The poor youth is the 'offspring' of a deity of war.

This new freedom, coming along with a number of movements or shifts of consciousness such as cubism, futurism, expressionism and more, was generated by a fusion of many influences, from the malaise of the 'Naughty Nineties' to the spread of Sigmund Freud's ideas on the subconscious, to the communist revolution in Russia. Art and literature was, in its 'higher cultural' quarters, a city made of mixed dwellers, most of them eager for radical change.

The women poets of this time undoubtedly demonstrate the tendency of writers to be strong individualists, and in many ways these poets show something quite the opposite of one of the main tendencies of the high cultural discourse of modernism. There are two tendencies at work here: some poets were clearly influenced by the kind of thinking behind William Wordsworth's (1770–1850) seminal preface to his *Lyrical Ballads* (1800); he stresses here that his work is entirely opposite to the dominant poetry of his time, and is for all:

> The principal object then which I proposed to myself in these poems was to make the incidents of common life interesting by tracing in

> them, truly though not ostentatiously, the primary laws of our nature: chiefly as far as regards the manner in which we associate ideas in a state of excitement. Low and rustic life was generally chosen because in that situation the essential passions of the heart find a better soil in which they can attain their maturity, are less under restraint and speak a plainer and more emphatic language ...

This is completely the adverse of the main thrust of the argument expressed in John Carey's (*b.*1934) *The Intellectuals and the Masses: Pride and Prejudice Among the Literary Intelligentsia, 1880–1939*, in which he traces the development of negative ideas about mass culture, the nature of the crowd, and the growing proletarian population between the last decades of the nineteenth century and the 1930s. Carey gathers evidence from a number of famous writers, from Thomas Hardy to Graham Greene and from George Orwell to E.M. Forster that the nature of the Bloomsbury mindset was directly opposed to, and afraid of, mass culture. That mass culture includes the popular novel, middlebrow interests and partly also a suburban view of society (suburban life was also a target of the literary elite who saw mediocrity there).

In many of the women poets of this time there is an intense interest in the individual within the community, and although the scrutiny of the self was very much a concern of the higher cultural imagination, the middlebrow stance was different. Carey's interest is in showing how many writers, perhaps most brutally in the work of D.H. Lawrence, there was a negative opinion of the working class and their urban culture, embedded in poor living conditions, low aspirations and questionable eating and hygiene habits. In fact, it takes a poet like Stevie Smith (1902–1971) to mount a defence of the worker. In four lines, in her poem *Alfred the Great* she rubs out any preoccupation with such marginal matters as living conditions. For her, love and affection, human warmth and morality come first:

> Honour and magnify this man of men
> Who keeps a wife and children on £2 10
> Paid weekly in an envelope
> And yet he never has abandoned hope.

Documentary in the hands of the writers of socialist leanings, had seen this, but had been more interested in group behaviour and attitudes. Yet mixed with this desire to gather depressing facts about the working life, there was a fresh vision in many of the women poets, who put the focus on self-identity in the quotidian life, a life close to pain and deprivation in many cases, but immersed in the material nature of life.

A survey of these decades also has to account for the tendency of writers to have a political interest and sometimes an axe to grind; it was a time of projects, social awareness, self-help; but it was also a time of shining a light on what had been eclipsed by a biased and selective social history. John Carey's book makes it clear that most writers in the elitist camp aimed at a kind of preservation of the talented few, those who saw themselves as more worthy of praise and validatioin than others down the hierarchy. He notes that the mass market newspaper, the habit of photography and suburban recreation all had a deleterious effect on the quality of art and letters. On F.R. Leavis's (1895–1978) periodical, *Scrutiny*, for instance, he writes: '*Scrutiny* itself made no bid for the popular market, never printing more than 750 copies in the 1930s.' Carey goes further: 'Largely through [T.S.] Eliot's influence, the assumption that most people are dead became, by the 1930s, a standard item in the repertoire of any self-respecting intellectual.' That last word is the thorn in the flesh in this debate: *intellectual.* The boom in literary and political periodicals and anthologies through these decades made it clear that one was supposed to think, to engage with debate about how society was to work and change at a time when first the liberal attitudes to morality were challenging the religious basis of society, and second, when fascism began to work prominently for power. When the Spanish Civil War of 1936 to 1939 created a widespread appeal for volunteers to fight fascism, women went to participate, along with the men. Some, like Stella Jackson (1908–1993) – who used the penname Stella Fitzthomas Hagan – are little known, despite her living with Ewart Milne (1903–1987), who went to Spain and worked with medical aid; others joined any organisation that might play a part in the cause for important change.

The 'mass' so feared by the high culturalists needed close examination. Such was the fear of a threat coming from the new liberalist attitudes that E.M. Forster had to kill off his aspirant literary lower-middle class clerk by having a bookcase fall on him, in *Howard's End*. Forster was having fun, perhaps even writing a message to those who feared the popular culture created by an over population in the cities. But the hatred of the crowd and the mass culture by the Bloomsbury mindset was not always intellectually or morally acceptable. Carey quotes Lawrence: 'The great mass of humanity should never learn to read and write.' Carey adds, 'Without education the masses will, Lawrence hopes, relapse into purely physical life.'

The poets, men and women, often expressed thoughts and ideas to their readers about politics, but just as often they faced up to the dilemmas of their time. The old question: 'what is poetry *for*?' appears to be a very fruitful line of thought when we read the various notably individual women poets of the time, women who understood that there had been so much repression in the women poets of the late Victorian generation. It was an exciting time, packed with self-reflection, surreal language, bold metaphor and freedom of poetic form. The poetry of the age presents us with a heady mix of the bizarre and humorous individuals with person concerns, and the traditional nature of the poet as a commentator on the age, an *agent provocateur* for the writing that would have to defend and explain cultural values.

The women poets may not have been predominantly entrenched in the higher echelons of the literary establishment, but they worked hard in various literary locations to be part of the scene, and to be professional. Jane Dowson (*b*.1955) explains this in *Women's Poetry of the 1930s: A Critical Anthology* (1996):

> As women, it was difficult to penetrate literary circles; they lacked the publicity and promotion which are achieved through making the right social connections; they could not easily integrate into their respective socio-literary milieus as they were often pressed by social duties, cultural constraints and family responsibilities. Unlike her son John, for example, Frances Cornford [1886–1960] could not exchange views and compositions with the young men at the Arts Café in Parton Street ...

Jane Dowson's *Women's Poetry of the 1930s: A Critical Anthology* was long overdue in 1996 when it appeared. Here at last was a representative selection of many of the women poets whose work had appeared in periodicals in the 1930s and later, but who had mostly been overlooked by critical fashions and whose work was often hard to find.

Experiment and Individual Freedom

Stevie Smith, born in Hull in 1902, made her debut as a poet in 1937 with *A Good Time was had by All* (1937), but had first been in print before that with *Novel on Yellow Paper* (1936). Obviously her talent was recognised, as a major publisher wanted both books. The reasons for this are not hard to find. In dealing with the human predicament and the absurdity of existence, linked to questions of faith and belief, she expressed the prominent issues of her time and of all times, in deceptively simple verse forms and diction. In fact, there is a profundity in her work, often hiding behind apparently facile and quirkily entertaining poems. She was a popular performer, and her touch of eccentricity attracted readers to poetry in a turbulent world in which civilised values were under threat. She had published three collections by the end of the Second World War.

Smith represents the kind of writer of her time who distracts from the 'message' by her manner. That is to say, her voices and styles approach subjects obliquely, and although she is perhaps defined today as the author of the hugely successful poem *Not Waving but Drowning* (1957) she deserves much more recognition and appraisal.

She represents the experimental and original thread in the fabric of the poetry of her time. It is possible to align her with Edith Sitwell and Anna Wickham (1883–1947) in this respect. In a world of rapid change and threats to any version of stability, these poets replied with humour and waywardness with words, and they were whimsical in their address to the reader. In many ways, their influence may be seen as something more substantial than their actual writings, but that is only because they have been sparsely represented in anthologies. Today, more of their work may easily be read.

It is interesting to make comparisons sometimes; in 1929, when several of the women writers who were to figure in the politicised writings of the documentary period were beginning, in Germany, *Berlin Alexanderplatz* (1929) by Alfred Döblin (1878–1957) was published. This novel, concerned with so many major themes in writing from Mitteleuropa, includes a philosophical strand that is hard to compare with anything regarding the First World War and its aftermath in England. Its scope is epic, with a working class hero, and its themes reach into historical debate, popular song, criminology and the sexual revolution in the anti-cultural and radical new angles assumed on the nature of society and power across many European states.

This reminds the modern reader of the nature and history of the novel; in Europe and Russia it had always been part of the status and regard of the creative artist; he was expected to take the novel seriously and his views and opinions were sought and respected. Whereas in Britain, the novel between Daniel Defoe in the first decades of the eighteenth century and the novels of Charles Dickens in his mature period (1850s onwards) the novel, existing in twin guises as first a romance and second a fiction pertaining to society through realism or satire, was mostly small scale and many of its creators were women. These women were held down by law and social mores, restricted by genre and publishing, and except for a few individuals such as Mary Wollstonecraft (1759–1797), their work was kept tightly in line with the influential publishers' needs and aims.

In fact, writing all the time by *c.*1920s was at last being influenced more by Europe; the 'Yellow Book' writing and art, together with the decadent trend, shows the influence of French writers. By the 1920s the French presence is strong, as many writers spent time in Paris and learned new approaches to art.

But in poetry, the tendency for British women writers to be dashing and bold in their individual voices makes for interesting and stimulating reading. In Jane Dowson's *Women's Poetry of the 1930s: A Critical Anthology*, it is noticeable that Edith Sitwell, who published on a very large scale through these years, is given only a few pages, whereas other remarkably individual presences are given far more extensive representation. A comparison with the male poets of the time is worthwhile. The word *Macspaunday* was coined to show that Louis MacNeice (1907–1963), Stephen Spender, W.H. Auden and Cecil Day-Lewis (1904–1972) dominated the 1930s decade; of course, there were many women poets working away, dedicated to their craft, whose work was always to be overshadowed by the more forthright and well-known poets. Eleanor Farjeon's poems, as in *First and Second Love* (1947), show her control of form and metrics; but what startled, and was noticed, was the poetry that showed an understanding of the pressing issues of the time.

Valentine Ackland – real name Mary McCrory – (1906–1969) is a case in point. Her poems often depict a lost land, somewhere cut off, its denizens once fulfilled and purposeful, but now aimless. A sense of futility percolates through her lines. In *Communist Poem* (1935) she wrote:

> Here is our life, say: where the dismembered country
> Lies, a dead foeman rises a living comrade.
> Here where our day begins and your day dims
> We part ...

Then, in *Winter* the reader is reminded that there is a sense of weak despair in her experience:

> Clotted together in misery, hungry and time-besotted,
> The drag of time on our hands and on nerves the nag,
> Then we whisper together and the word we say is red ...

Ackland had no shortage of material behind her; not only was she tormented by drinking problems and by the love of two women, she also was very much involved with communist activities and with the Spanish Civil War; her interests were entirely in keeping with her time – pacifism and socialist theory mainly. She lived with Sylvia Townsend Warner (1893–1978), and before that, as Jane Dowson summarises, 'She did not ... become reconciled to physical love for a man, even though by 1932 she is alleged to have had 27 affairs, five of which were with men and one of which resulted in a miscarriage in 1927.'

Themes for Today

Rarely was there a time more acutely aware of the urgency of the age for human survival. By the 1930s, it almost seemed to be a writer's duty to present a commentary on atrocities, totalitarian fears and the ascendency of specific power in a number of world states. Selecting a representative figure in the poetry of the time is a challenge, but it is hard to ignore the claims of Sylvia Townsend Warner in this context. She was born in 1893, and did munitions work in the First World War, also being involved in pacifism and socialism; she became a successful public speaker as well as, by the 1930s, being active in the republican cause in Spain. She visited Spain, and it seems as though she saw that her best contribution to a world under threat from fascism was to communicate; like Storm Jameson, she out in the hours as a delegate, speaker and mouthpiece for good causes. She was at one time working with the Red Cross volunteers in the Spanish Civil War, and then, in contrast, took part in the work of the International Association in Defence of Culture. It was a time when the right thing to do was to be a 'joiner' – and that could be anything from the Left Book Club to a local socialist group.

Some of her poems could stand alongside the most memorable work from both world wars. In *El Heroe* for instance, she produced one of the most resonant and meaningful 'unknown soldier' tributes we have, with the repeated line,

> Nobody knew his name
> pen nor paper will tell it.

At other time she could produce the kind of repugnance and brutal vocabulary readers expect from war poetry, as in these lines from *Port Bou*:

> I am the smell
> On all the winds of Spain.
> I am the stink in the nostrils
> Of the men of Spain.
> I have taken the place
> Of the incense at the burial ...

She was also capable of writing the kind of rhetoric sometimes found in the more overt social commentary poems of W.H. Auden, with that sense of foreboding and moral questioning so common in the 1930s, with lines like these, in which the rhetorical questions accomplish the kind of torment one finds in writing coming out of dire emergency and suffering:

... War is near.
Against that enemy pang of the quickened sense
Is the swiftest weapon, is the surest defence.
There we cling ...

The context of this writing is often one of insisting that the England in the people's mind is as important as the England, which was about to be under threat of annihilation. Some poems were written under a spirit of the kind of love and nostalgia summed up by Robert Browning's (1812–1889) famous lines,

Oh to be in England
Now that April's there

but more common was the kind of perspective found in an odd poem by Marianne Moore with the title of *England* but which begins as if the title will be in focus, in this way: 'with its baby rivers and little towns, each with its abbey or its cathedral with voices – one voice perhaps, echoing through the transept ...' But then the poem moves on to give a series of sharp images of a number of countries, as if reinforcing the view that England was indeed, very small. This writing about the charm of rural England was found across all the genres, and was arguably as prominent in crime fiction as it was in the poetry of warning and doom. In Gladys Mitchell's novel, *The Mystery of a Butcher's Shop* (1930), for example, we have this: 'The road outside the station was deserted except for a decrepit hansom ...' Preceded by, 'There would be a luxurious limousine to meet him outside the station, he reflected happily. There would be tea under the trees or in the summer-house at the Manor. There might possibly be an invitation to stay to dinner ...'

In this search for Englishness, George Orwell wrote one of the most important pieces on the theme, in his essay 'Inside the Whale' and there he found in the work of A.E. Housman and Rupert Brooke as being foundational for much of the 1930s lines of thought.

The women writers mostly escaped the censure that Orwell gave in his essay, when he built up his argument to condemn most of the 1920s male writers. He pointed out what came before the crises of the 1930s:

> But what is noticeable about all these writers is that what 'purpose' they have is very much up in the air. There is no attention to the urgent problems of the moment, above all no politics in the narrower sense. Our eyes are directed to Rome, to Byzantium, to Montparnasse, to Mexico, to the Etruscans, the Subconscious, to the solar plexus – to everywhere except the places where things are happening ...

Quite the opposite is what we find in Jane Dowson's anthology: of the twenty poets represented there, only two could be said to be intensively concerned with an inner landscape of the imagination, eclipsing social commentary, and this is in the works of Edith Sitwell and Kathleen Jessie Raine (1908–2003). Generally, the women writers were a strong part of one of the age's ongoing debates: the poetry dealing with philosophical questions and the poetry 'of today'. This issue is often open to writers of extreme views either way, and we see this in the reviews of poetry anthologies, such as one by Edwin Muir (1887–1959) in *The London Mercury* in which he quotes the anthology editor Michael Roberts as writing, 'The first important thing about contemporary literature is that it is contemporary: it is speaking to us, here, now.' Muir takes issue, responding with, 'If that is really so, then literature is far too specialised an activity to be of permanent interest, for it is not concerned with lasting things but only with the values of here and now ...' Muir completely misread Roberts's remark, and he gave away the fact that his own definition of literature had to be that it must be 'deep'. He even adds, still reacting to Roberts, 'which means that it is shallower than it should be.'

The women writers, as a reading of most writers involved will show, had far too many causes to fight and far too many issues to explore through verse to worry about whether a piece of writing was 'shallow' or not. This narrow attitude also implies that reviewers and critics like Muir were not aware of such works as Eleanor Farjeon's *First and Second Love*, which were written between 1911 and 1917 but were not collected until 1947. Here, Eleanor Farjeon produced forty-four sonnets, in which Muir could find a richness in every poem, and some rhyming couplets to show that the writer had supremely mastered the form, as in these lines from sonnet *XIII*:

Not that I loved too much requires my tears,
I loved too little, and love stopped his ears.

One of her loves was the poet Edward Thomas, and the last poem in the book, *Easter Monday*, in memory of him (he died in France in the First World War). Here, she produced a poem with what must have been explanatory of the situation of thousands of wives and partners during that conflict:

That Easter Monday was a day for praise,
It was such a lovely morning. In our garden
We sowed our earliest seeds, and in the orchard
The apple-bud was ripe. It was the eve,
There are three letters you will not get.

On the whole, the women's poetry of these years was rich, packed with extraordinary individual talents and showing more than average ability with both formal demands and with the pressing desire of the time for writers to 'speak for us, here, now.' The work of Stevie Smith proves that Muir's deep poetry need not be encased in serious formal arrangements of words and themes. It can, in fact, entertain as it provokes thought, and in the 1930s most people sensed that thinking was as urgent as keeping an eye on Germany and Japan. It was an age of reconstruction, and most of that was in the heart and in the mind. After all, who ever said that 'deep' thinking had to be expressed in complex ways? J.B. Priestley had shown this to be false reasoning, as described earlier. Smith's work proves beyond doubt that profound thinking and feeling may be lucidly expressed in plain language.

A Time for the Surreal

One aspect of poetry was always on the publishing scene in these years: the surreal and strange. The poet most easily aligned with the strange and radical is arguably Edith Sitwell, who figures prominently in several memoirs about this time, including the modern classic by Gertrude Stein, *The Autobiography of Alice B. Toklas* (1933).

The phenomenal success of Edith Sitwell illustrates how poets may adopt a range of voices and stances that tend to obfuscate, confuse and dazzle in their sheer eccentricity of approach. Sitwell wrote a book on English eccentrics, and appeared to her contemporaries as one of the notable examples of English oddness in their age. Her poems need decoding. A first reading of a Sitwell poem is to experience a rush of language, most of which provides a smokescreen to meaning rather than a clear exposition. In *Mariner Man* for instance, the opening is this:

'What are you staring at, mariner man
Wrinkled as sea-sand and old as the sea?'
'Those trains will run over their tails,
if they can,
Snorting and sporting like porpoises. Flee
The burly, the whirligig wheels of the train.
...'

Repeatedly in her work, the reader is left floundering in the wake of an enfilade of words, all looking for some kind of attachment to sense. It is often impossible to make sense of images, which go unrestrained, such as in a poem called *Minstrels*, which has these lines,

Beside the sea, metallic bright
And sequined with the noisy light,
Duennas slowly promenade
Each like a patch of sudden shade,
...

It is difficult to assess such surreal approaches. But where this tendency does payoff is in *Gold Coast Customs* (1929), which is explained in a note: 'In Ashantee, a hundred and fifty years ago, the death of any rich or important person was followed by several days of national ceremonies, during which the utmost licence prevailed ...' Once the reader knows such a context, the flights of seemingly dream like language and imagery gather into sense.

Sitwell's preference for sound over sense is still there, but still there are musings springing out like wayward off-shoots of part nonsense:

Chasing a rat,
Their soul's ghost fat
Through the negro swamp,
Slum hovel's cramp
Of Lady Bamburgher's parties above
With the latest grin, and the latest love ...

In the end, most of the techniques and daring images are rootless, not applying any patterns of meaning for their time. For a contrast, in which strange poems are actually hooked into universal, one has to read the remarkably intelligent and coherent though odd poems of Stevie Smith and Anna Wickham.

Edith Sitwell, who will linger in the cultural histories, is surely the one that the reader meets in Gertrude Stein, who knew her in the late 1920s. At one point Sitwell persuaded Stein to come and give a talk in Cambridge; Stein managed to do it, rather bullied into it by Sitwell, but it was a notable success: 'Edith Sitwell, Osbert [Sitwell (1892–1969)] and Sacheveral [Sitwell (1897–1988)] were all present and were all delighted. They were delighted with the lecture and they were delighted with the good humoured way in which Gertrude Stein had gotten the best of the hecklers ...'

Stein's first impression of Sitwell confirms the general image: 'Very tall, bending slightly, withdrawing and hesitatingly advancing, and beautiful with the most distinguished nose I have ever seen on any human being ... I delighted in the delicacy and completeness of her understanding of poetry.'

Stevie Smith, as mentioned above, combined poems with line drawings, and created notably 1930s preoccupations with great, deep perceptive statements made by a lone voice in the dark, wondering about certainties and about faith and death. One might see apparent similarities to many of Sitwell's poems, in a poem such as 'My Soul' for instance, in which a cartoon shows a woman in an armchair, by a window, with her cat standing near. She begins with:

In the flame of the flickering fire
The sins of my soul are few

and then asserts that even in such peace, she is 'on the brink of eternal night.' Smith at this point does what she often does: show a dilemma shared by all in such a way that fear is held in a startling image. How will she resolve this, we ask. She does so with a stunning image that lingers in the mind and leaves after-effects of thought:

Oh feed to the golden fish his egg
Where he floats in his captive bowl,
To the cat his kind from the womb born blind,
And to the Lord my soul.

There is no comfort in the resolution; even the thought of the lord is linked to that eternal night, and the woman's very being is aligned with the fish and the cat.

Stevie Smith is at her astounding best in that kind of poem, in which the diurnal familiar is placed in the kind of unfamiliar we turn away from whenever we can. By reducing any kind of context and placing a weak little figure as a mouthpiece for fear and anxiety, she creates a uniquely modern voice from no specific place; nothing is hooked into a setting.

She stretches this kind of approach in her 1930s poems, sometimes with a very clear contemporary hook into what her readers saw around them or read about. In *Unser Vater* 'Our Father' (*c.*1930s) she draws a woman wearing a little waitress's hat and short skirt, as if perhaps she is from Berlin, and she uses the *Lord's Prayer* at the opening:

Unser Vater,
Du Der im Himmel wohnst,
Behold they child,
His prayers and his complaint ...

She builds on this with an appeal she often states:

Oh Father, heed
thy child, let not the grave
seal him in sin ...

The context of this reminds one of the drawings of George Grosz (1893–1959) where he satirises the abuses and exploitations of street and café life in Germany; but also, Smith may easily veer towards the simplicity and power of William Blake (1757–1827), as she shows in her four-line poem, *Human Affection*:

Mother, I love you so
Said the child, I love you more than I know,
She laid her head on her mother's arm,
And the love between them kept them warm.

Smith proves time and again that strong individuality does not mean that the reader has to work overtime to extract a string of coherent meaning from a poem.

Interestingly, there are similarities between Smith's poetry and some of the verses Dorothy Parker (1893–1967) wrote in these decades. Sometimes Parker provides a short stanza, end-rhymed, carrying lots of thought and reflection around the minimal words, as in *Anecdote*:

So silent I when Love was by
He yawned, and turned away;
But sorrow clings to my apron-strings
I have so much to say.

But equally, Parker can reach more into the basic questions of being, as Smith does, in poems of more substance, as in *Testament*:

Oh, let it be a night of lyric rain
And singing breezes, when my bell is tolled.
I have so loved the rain that I would hold
Last in my ears its friendly, dim refrain.
...

In the poetry of Anna Wickham there is another variety of individual power and impact. In a feature written by Lionel Birch (1910–1982) for *Picture*

Post magazine in 1946, Birch shows, in words and pictures, the lovable 'poet and landlady' who ran a Hampstead rooming house in the 1940s. The photographs show her on the streets, chatting, playing with children and sitting smoking in her kitchen. Brad Bigelow, on his 'Neglected Books' site, notes that 'her poetry might have been more highly regarded now had she put more energy into her writing and less into her fights with the world ...' Bigelow quotes Wickham to great effect in his article:

> I feel that women of my kind are a profound mistake. There have been few women poets of distinction, and if we count only the suicides of Sappho, Laurence Hope [real name Violet Nicolson (1865–1904)] and Charlotte Mew [1869–1928], their suicides have been very high.

There was a terrible irony in that statement. Around one year after the 1946 interview, Wickham hanged herself; it is hard to imagine the horror felt by her son, who found her body. She had ended her life in the kitchen, which was photographed in the *Picture Post* feature. The images used in that interview show her busy with people, and in the life around her, the place that had remained home, even in the Blitz. The feature, 'Anna Wickham: Poetess and Landlady' quotes a notice in the 'mistress of words' that says: 'Tour Bourgeoise. Anna Wickham's stabling for poets, artists and their executives. Creative mood respected. Meals at all hours.' Wickham was born in Wimbledon in 1884, went to Australia, began to train as a singer, but then diverted into poetry, publishing three collections between 1915 and 1921. Lionel Birch depicts her as doing battle with domesticity, and notes that there is space in her life for 'dreams and domesticity'. He presents a lovable eccentric, writing that 'People stare? Of course people stare' and he describes her: 'huge face, corrugated by the astringency of wisdom, the goblin eyes, and the laugh of a naughty little girl ...' Her poetry is strikingly original at times. The following is taken from *The Silent Singer*:

> I have no words that could prevail
> Against the furies of my male.
> When we go out I come behind,
> While he expounds his angry min ...

Everything in her spirit as it worked behind and beneath the surface of her poetry, suggests combat, opposition, and a delight in being contrary. She delighted in imagining voices from deep inside the wars of the sexes, as in *King Alfred and the Peasant Women* where we have this:

> I'd rather he fought me than missed his combats,
> Though I'm not built for blows upon the heart.
> Give me a breast-plate, and I'll at 'em,
> Though that's fool-woman's part!

There is no doubt that her poetic voice was distinctive. It was as wonderful as her personality. Jane Dowson sums up the skill very succinctly: 'Anna Wickham is at her best in telling the story of women whose masks of ordinariness and survival conceal frustration and a losing battle with pain.'

The Norm

What must not be overlooked is the poetry that has not appeared since the years in focus: the everyday verse, the collections of popular rhymes; the various easily absorbed poems that entertain. In other words, what is normally termed 'light verse'. But even this is only a part of the picture; every age in literary history has its anthologies, collections from small presses and minor poets with their single collection in print. This was an age of the small, independent press. In Gertrude Stein's *The Autobiography of Alice B. Toklas*, which is discussed in the next chapter, there are several projects explained involving small press writing.

But there is yet more. A case study helps to explain this situation, and as reference has already been made of Eleanor Farjeon, her work provides that instance. She has always been defined as being on the fringe of the very male Dymock Poets, as she lived among them and was very close to Edward Thomas and his wife, Helen (1877–1967). But she later became a very successful children's author, was on the editorial board of the magazine *Time and Tide*, and published several poetry collections. Marion Shoard (*b*.1949) has made the case for Eleanor Farjeon as being far more than a shadowy figure on the edge of the Dymock Poets. They settled around that village in Gloucestershire, in the years just before 1914, and through to some years after 1918. Shoard points out that Eleanor Farjeon's work was

> taken seriously by other poets. For instance, D.H. Lawrence commented in May, 1915 'There is a dignity and beauty and worth in these sonnets.' [Eleanor] Farjeon took writing seriously and worked as a professional in a number of roles across the publishing world. One of her most telling statements is in relation to her way of working: 'I've been writing hard, which has been a great joy to me – writing in the way I like best too ... with a kind of "possessed concentration" so that I spend perhaps three hours on fourteen lines ...'

Eleanor Farjeon received awards for her work; she published several books for children, but also several works for adults such as *Pan-Worship and Other Poems* (1908) and *The Soul of Kol Nikon* (1923). Some of her works were illustrated by the great artist Edward Ardizzone (1900–1979). Marion Shoard makes Farjeon's part in the Dymock Poets' writing and theorising very clear: 'We owe [Eleanor] Farjeon a huge debt for recording the everyday life of the poets during her stay in Dymock in August 1914, including the cider supper, often first in letters to Maitland Radford, which were incorporated into her book about Thomas, *The Last Four Years*.' The 'cider supper' was a particularly gregarious and productive occasion when all these writers were together, and without Eleanor Farjeon, we would know very little about what passed on that occasion.

The minor writers were, as always, a part of the scene in literature, and they played an important part. In Jane Dowson's anthology, quoted above, she includes poems from important periodicals in the book, pointing out that notably *Time and Tide* and *The Listener*, along with others, played a significant role in the poetry scene. Dowson wrote: 'It modelled itself on *The New Statesman* but had a clear commitment to women's issues. It printed contributions by both sexes, but the editors evidently encouraged women at all stages of its production.'

A summing up of poetry by women writers at this time has to admit that the same kind of situation existed *c.*1920 or *c.*1930 as existed for some decades after 1945: women poets were mostly marginalised in publishing.

As mentioned previously, they were marginal in most anthologies used on school *curricula* for some time. In my own career as a teacher of English, I can say that I used five poetry anthologies over the years between 1974 and 1990, and women poets were rarely included. It took until the emergence of writers such as Gillian Clarke (*b.*1937), Liz Lochead (*b.*1947), Carol Ann Duffy (*b.*1955) and similar for things to change.

It could be said that in the interwar years there had been new uses of poetry, and much of this was related to the previously set definition of 'woman's province' both socially and legally; these new uses were to elucidate woman's situation but also to show that in terms of linguistics, women used language in very different ways from men, and the effects of such developments as Freudian thought on the subconscious and the modernist understanding of narrative had percolated through to the poetry by women, who were writing from a dynamic position of being between old modes in poetry and new, freer form and diction. The work of Mina Loy shows this in her surrealist element. In the 1920s she published in *avant-garde* small magazines, and had made helpful contacts in the literary world. Her work is in focus in the next chapter, as Paris figures in the story.

Chapter 7

Influential Americans: Wharton to Parker

'A dream lies dead here. May you softly go
Before this place, and turn away your eyes ...'
Dorothy Parker

The Age of Innocence

When Edith Wharton's (1862–1937) novel, *The Age of Innocence*, was published in 1920, the theme had so many in-built commentaries and links relating to the new writing of the time that it seems today like an overarching foreshadowing of thoughts that would occupy the Americans travelling to Europe to seek inspiration for their work. There were exceptions, writers who made friendships and found the value of absolutely fresh thinking, such as Robert Frost working with Edward Thomas, in which friendship both gained a great deal of energy and direction for their new work.

Wharton, already established as a writer when this novel appeared, worked into her story of Newland Archer and the Countess Olenska, along with the New York coteries and wealthy culture seekers, a critique of something that suggested an atrophy, a state of frozen mental attitude, and a desire to preserve a conservative life which was preventing change. What is thought of as culture is, in fact, a sort of paralysis, and theme is developed at times with some similarity to James Joyce's *Dubliners* (1914). One comment given early in the novel prepares the reader for this: '"Oh well," said Archer with happy indifference. Nothing about his betrothed pleased him more than her resolute determination to carry to its utmost limit that ritual of ignoring the "unpleasant" in which they had both been brought up.' The New York of the novel – which is set in the 1870s – has a remarkable similarity with the restraints and tastes of the comfortable middle class, something in Germany known as *Biedermeier* and in Britain as high Edwardian stuffiness and indulgence. The city is summed up in this respect very satirically:

> But then New York, as far back as the mind of man could travel, had been divided into the two great fundamental groups of the Mingotts and Mansons and all their clan, who cared about eating and clothes and money, and the Archer-Newland-van-der-Luydentribe, who were devoted to travel, horticulture and the best fiction, and looked down on the grosser forms of pleasure.

This is familiar to readers of Forster's *Howard's End*, in which the epigraph of 'only connect' is more and more impossibly conceived as the novel progresses, as if some fundamental difference has life in a firm grip. But the restlessness inside this tight structure is Edith Wharton's interest, and as a marriage is imminent, that institution is subject to some commentary: 'with a shiver of foreboding he saw his marriage becoming what most of the other marriages were: a dull association of material and social interests held together by ignorance on the one side and hypocrisy on the other.' The crucial word here is *material.* The huge number of Americans and British seeking a kind of freedom in cities such as Paris and Berlin in the interwar years wanted a view of the human world in the modern age as being free from such shackles.

Olenska dwells in that alternative world in which disorder and individual escape from the material bonds of the acquisitive class are depicted:

> It was certainly a strange quarter to have settled in. Small dressmakers, bird-stuffers, and 'people who wrote' were her nearest neighbours; and farther down the dishevelled street Archer recognised a dilapidated wooden house ... in which a writer and journalist called Winsett ... lived. Winsett did not invite people to his house ...

Sometimes a writer senses a widespread trend, a significant moment of cultural change, and Wharton does this. Katherine Mansfield's criticism of the novel, was that the characters were 'arranged for exhibition purposes' but then, that could be applied to Thomas Hardy or Arnold Bennett for instance. Judgement depends on how the purpose and theme are thickened and substantiated by character, and in *The Age of Innocence*, arguably the theme is one which extends across many decades, and settles, in the 1920s, in a place where its relevance is profound.

Paris

Where did Wharton's 'people who wrote' go to? What attracted them to continue their bohemian life elsewhere, beyond the New York in which they were, for some great families and clans, beyond the pale? They went to Europe, and many went to Paris.

If the focus is switched to the French angle on the literary history of the first half of the twentieth century, first of all one notices the dominance of male authors, and second, that there were movements in France that lie as a creative background to the kind of writing the literary visitors found. For instance, in a comprehensive guide to French literature and influential literary groups and fashions through the centuries, Genevieve Winter includes 'Lunanisme at le groupe de l'Abbaye. Winter notes that this "anonymism" developed by Jules Romains (1885–1972) was on the fringe of surrealism, naturalism and symbolism.' That is to say that the aesthetic climate the writers and artists found was open to a multitude of ideas, statements of artistic interest, and plain influence. What is for sure is that the writers arriving in Paris would encounter the truly original ideas and performances related to writing and performing that have stayed, and been an influence. A perfect example of this is Dada, developed by Tristan Tzara (1896–1963). Through the poet Guillaume Apollinaire (1880–1918), Stein encountered these ideas, and most visiting writers would have met with discussion of Dada in the 1920s.

One central idea in Dada was the nature of writer, performer and audience. The receiver of the art should be either involved or engaged, in the theme expressed, or ideally made to wake up, to be alive, and never to be a basic watcher or listener, a passive mind being entertained. One may see how this thinking relates to the fashionable notions of stream of consciousness and dramatic monologue in modernist writing, in which the sharing of subjective experience, of awareness of the nature of being, was always a major artifice towards the new 'truth' of writing about existence.

Of all the persistent images of the post-First World War years in society and culture, surely we think of café and dancing, parties and balls, and over all this, the 'Jazz Age' and the attitudes of *laissez-faire* and 'live for today'. The firm representations of the 1920s in literature and biography are surely those of long evenings and early mornings spent in bars. The novels of Evelyn Waugh capture much of this, along with the works of Nöel Coward (1899–1973) and Aldous Huxley (1894–1963). In Joseph Moncur March's (1899–1977) graphic novel, *The Wild Party* (1928), there these lines about the flappers and boozers, living the life of sensual excess:

> Books?
> Books?
> My God! You don't understand.
> They were far too busy living first-hand
> For books.
> Books!

There were many infamous and celebrated places for such hedonism and escape. One thinks of Sloppy Joe's Bar for instance, in Havana. In a cocktail manual for 1933 there is an illustration of the kind of place Americans made for in the age of prohibition. It shows well-dressed and drunken people chatting, lounging and raising their glasses. The bar was owned by Joe Otero, and his place attracted the wealthy. The story is that some customers, looking at the run-down condition of the place, teased Otero and someone said, 'Why Joe, this place is certainly sloppy. Look at the filthy water running from under the counter.' But conditions didn't matter. Life was too short to think of hygiene.

The places of escape were many, across Europe, but for the writers and artists, the magnet was Paris. After 1918 it could hardly have seemed, looked at objectively, as a paradise: Alistair Horne (1925–2017) has summarised the economic situation:

> While Britain and America were already emerging from the world slump, France remained in depression. Between 1928 and 1934, her industrial production fell by 17 per cent; between 1929 and 1936, average income slipped 30 per cent; and by the end of 1935 more than 800,000 were unemployed. So the financial crisis ran on into the 1930s ...

The poorer young Parisians had a tough life; there was widespread deprivation, and Horne points out that most Parisian buildings had no running water until 1940. Building had slowed down considerably also:

> [by the end of the] thirties construction from over six thousand storeys per year in 1914 to around 400. This was hardly the kind of place where one might have expected a boom in the artistic colonies of foreigners, pursuing art and culture, but so it was. We could even add the fact that there was bubonic plague in the Porte de Clignancourt. But the foreigners came, particularly the young Americans.

Horne once again has the relevant statistics:

> In 1921 foreign residents of Paris comprised 5.3 per cent of the population; ten years later the figure had almost doubled to 9.2 per cent. One factor in the American arrivals was the advent of prohibition in the States. The Volstead Act 1919 had driven them out towards places where booze was freely available. The notable writers who were in Paris at this time includes some first class celebrities such as John Dos Passos [1896–1970], Robert Benchley [1889–1945], e.e.cummings [*sic*] [1894–1962] and Dorothy Parker. By 1927 there were probably around 40,000 Americans in the city.

It was Gertrude Stein who called these creative types 'the lost generation' and they have been fully represented in words and on film. One of the fullest, most informative accounts of the life in the city at the time comes from Jean Rhys's (1890–1979) novel, *Quartet* (1928). In this, the central character, Marya Zelli, is a drifter, spending hours in lonely cafes in between mixing with various trendy crowds. She meets chancers, wealthy players, small-time crooks and struggling artists, but finds a kind of temporary stability in a ménage a trios in which she is the live-in mistress of a man called Heidler. At the same time, she has a man who is more of a partner to her, but he is sentenced to a stretch in jail, and so Zelli becomes dependent on charity from the Heidler couple.

The residents are tragic and pathetic; one character says, 'Mrs Heidler paints too. It's pretty awful to think of the hundreds of women round her, painting away, and all that, isn't it?' But the arty inhabitants are not fully functional, nor living fully in the present, in spite of the round of hedonistic activities, drifting from bar to bar: 'Here yes were beautiful, clearly brown, the long lashes curling upwards, but there was a suspicious, almost a deadened look in them.' Zelli moves into a kind of secondary life, never really engaged with reality: 'She began to live her hard and monotonous life very mechanically and listlessly …' and 'she remained apart, lonely, frightened of her loneliness, resenting it passionately.' Everyone becomes depressed and lost. Even Heidler, who has money and a business of sorts, says, 'Well, I'm sick of myself ... And yet it goes on. One knows that the whole damn thing's idiotic, futile, not even pleasant, but one goes on. One's caught in a sort of trap, I suppose.' It is a novel that alternates relentless gloom with frantic insistence on pleasure.

When Zelli loses both men – Heidler and her convict Stephan, there is rock bottom, and she sees it: she has a letter from Heidler. He has sent her farewell cash before he moves on and her response is: 'Nothing mattered just then. It was extraordinary that anything had ever mattered at all. Extraordinary and unbelievable that anything had ever mattered.' On the other hand there is another Paris, and now we see this principally through the eyes of Gertrude Stein (among the women writers); in her puzzling, enigmatic work *The Autobiography of Alice B. Toklas*, we have the imagined viewpoint of her friend and helper, Alice B. Toklas (1877–1967), as the two live at the heart of bohemian Paris in the Rude de Fleurou and so began one of the most remarkable literary lives from that period and time; what a time it was for the arts: James Joyce's *Ulysses* was being read and considered by the Shakespeare Head, the bookshop and publisher in the city run by Sylvia Beach (1887–1962); Ernest Hemingway (1899–1961) as was Edward FitzGerald were there, and so were many of the great artists such as Pablo Picasso (1881–1973) and Henri Matisse (1869–1954). In this set, Gertrude Stein is one of the most puzzling of the successful and still highly-rated modernists. But there is something bizarre about her rise to success. Her now classic work, *Three Lives* (1909), reminds us that some great writers began by buying themselves into print. That book cost her, in

2024 values, almost £20,000 to be printed by New York vanity publishers, Grafton Press.

Strangely, in the pretend and playful Alice B. Toklas book, there are odd assertions of genius and praise, along with half-cooked accounts of the roots of Stein's genius. Here were two women living in Paris, with Picasso dropping in, along with a host of other artists and writer on the rise, such as French poets and drifting talents on the make. One comment in the autobiography gives us an insight: 'In those days most of the guests were living more or less precariously, no-one starved, someone always helped, but still most of them did not live in abundance.' Their fame grew, and the women were clearly a magnet for hopeful artistic types: 'the word had spread ... any village where there was a young man who had ambitions heard of 27 rue de fleurus ... he lived but to get there and a great many did get there.' Certainly, Gertrude Stein worked in her own way, and didn't follow any standard rules about writing. One account is: 'she had then the habit of beginning her work at eleven o'clock at night and working until the dawn. She said she always tried to stop before the dawn was too clear and before the birds were too lively ...' On several occasions, the reader is told that Stein 'meditated and made sentences' and increasingly, the work becomes a spoof of the kind of work usually written to make a literary artist into some kind of guru or genius. It becomes a humorous work in fact. Not only does Alice B. Toklas devote her life to the genius-guru, but then along comes Etta Cone (1870–1949), who works at typing the manuscript of *Three Lives*.

There had to be fabulous wealth here. Not only was the cash found for vanity publishing, but the summer brought a holiday in Fiesole near Florence, Italy. Time and place were devoted to a great work, of course, and in this case it was *The Making of Americans: Being a History of A Family's Progress* (1925). This was to be a family history, but in the autobiography we have: 'It was getting to be a history of all human beings, all who ever were or are living ...' The humour now approaches the method of Monty Python.

Stein's world was a familiar one to anyone who studies the microcosm of the literary clique. The literary network tends to nurture those who are thought to be special. Then the aficionado of press and promotion steps in. In this case it was at first George Hugnet (1906–1974). He was a multi-talented artist who was a figure in major artistic movements such as surrealism and Dada. In Paris in Stein's time he started to edit and produce the *Editions de Montagne*. One of his productions was the first sixty pages of Stein's *The Making of Americans: Being a History of A Family's Progress*, and this is entirely in keeping with what tends to happen in the networks and cliques. A work is generally considered to be high art of such quality that it is promoted, often in a small press or other format; efforts are made to have it known across the members of the clique and their contacts. In that way a literary reputation grows. So it happened with Stein.

A similar thing happened with Elliot Paul (1891–1958). He had been asked to edit a new magazine. He chose one of Stein's short works for the first issue, and this prompted her to make a remark which opens up some of the salient facts of this microcosmic literary situation: 'After all ... we do want to be printed. One writes for oneself and strangers but with no adventurous publishers how can one come into contact with those same strangers.'

Time and time again in literary history, one sees the values of self-belief; this may tip over into arrogance, but one has to ask what tends to happen when there is an absence of self-belief? Why, obscurity and failure of course. There are two words that never seemed destined to be in the vocabulary of Gertrude Stein. Of course, vanity plays a part, and George Orwell admitted, when he asked the question, 'why I write' that vanity is an important spur. In Stein's case, promotion happened, and the comment in the autobiography is, 'It was easy to get the book put in the window of all the book stores in Paris that sold English books. This event gave Gertrude Stein a childish delight amounting almost to ecstasy ...'

Then there was Mina Loy. Here was a writer who defied categorisation. She was poet and painter, and in her Paris phase she produced remarkably original work. She knew Stein of course – everyone did. But she also appeared before the public in the small magazines of the time and her reputation grew among the *cognoscenti*. So many of the women writers of this time could be said to be in that situation. Many of them appear to have lived on salad leaves and hope.

Now that time has passed and writers from decades ago are featured in the standard works, a glance at how Loy is remembered is helpful. One summing-up is: 'The collection of poems *Lunar Baedecker* (1923) looks at specifically female experiences ... *Last Lunar Baedecker* (1982) forms her collected verse.' This simply leads the reader to the books, and maybe that is enough, but thankfully, criticism and assessment are now in rich supply. Much of the interest in her work today in concerned with the surrealist image: that fresh conception of the uses of imagery that formed originally a part of the Imagist platform for Ezra Pound (1885–1972) and others early in the twentieth century. One part of this is the 'refutation of logic' as in an individual's perceptions and actions are always at the mercy of chance and bizarre mixes of responding to the world through an irrational channel.

The proof of quality is in the writing, and in *Three Moments in Paris* (1915) Loy sets out to express the nature of this thinking. In these three poems she provides sharp instances of this imagery, jutting into the logic of each poem like some alien threat in the first, 'One o'clock at Night' for example, we have:

> And the only less male voice of your brother pugilist of the intellect
> Booms as it seems to me so sleepy
> Across an interval of a thousand miles
> An interim of a thousand years
> But you who make more noise than any man in the world when you clear your throat
> Deafening wake me
> And I catch the thread of the argument
> Immediately assuming my personal mental attitude
> And cease to be a woman ...

Loy allows the reader to slowly enter the dramatised scene as an outsider but also as someone allowed to be close to the woman's inner life of the senses.

The three poems repeatedly present images that demand to be re-read and pondered, such as '"Little tapers" ... "Leaning to the breath of baited bodies/like young poplars fringing the Loire."' Later, we have,

> The woman
> as usual
> is smiling as bravely
> as it is given to her to be brave
> in winking glasses ...

If we admit that at the very least these techniques push one towards paying more attention to both the form of the poem and the words, then the poem has been properly engaged with and will have a chance for its power to work.

Loy was a true original, along with Stevie Smith and Anna Wickham, and her work, as is also the case with them, is surely ready to find new readers in the twenty-first century.

Dorothy Parker

In an interview with *The Paris Review* in 1956, Dorothy Parker referred to her first writing, at *Vogue* magazine, given the chance to do so by a certain Frank Crowninshield (1872–1947). The meteoric career of Crowninshield began when Condé Nast bought the society magazine, *Vogue*, and also *Vanity Fair*. In 1914, Nast said 'We as a nation have come to realize the need for more cheerfulness, for hiding a solemn face, for a fair measure of pluck, and for great good humour.' When he discovered Dorothy Parker, he had found a genius of those subjects. She was incapable of writing or uttering a false sounding, artificial word, and humour marked her view of the world at all times. Her beginnings as a writer, as she told the interviewer for the review, were meagre: 'After my father died there wasn't any money. I had to work you see, and Mr. Crowninshield paid $12 for a small verse of mine and gave me a job at $10 a week.'

Dorothy Parker emerged steadily from basic editorial work to become a major writer, producing work for the stage, for humorous magazine writing, popular verse and short stories. Like Sitwell, she became known as a unique character, but she had a rare talent with words, and was incapable of producing a dull sentence. Much of her fame came from her cultural life as a member of the Algonquin Round Table, which was a meeting place of a bunch of writers associated with literary journalism in New York. They met to eat, drink and talk at the Algonquin hotel. The other writers in the circle included Robert Benchley (1889–1945), Alexander Woollcott (1887–1943), Edna Ferber (1885–1968) and George S. Kaufman (1889–1961). One writer recalled, 'We were all of the theatre or allied trades.' But for Parker, that was only one arrow in her quiver.

Parker was capable of writing excellent stories, sometimes equalling Anton Chekhov or Katherine Mansfield in the power of the themes mixed with the use of highly expressive scenes within the developed storyline. She is arguably at her best in a story such as *Big Blonde* (1929) in which the main character, Hazel Morse, experiences life through poorly selected men and booze. Parker is adept at a strong vignette such as, 'She prided herself upon her small feet and suffered for her vanity ... The curious things about her were her hands, strange terminations to the flabby white arms splattered with pale tan spots – long, quivering hands with deep and convex nails ...'

Hazel Morse enjoys life; she laps up the sensual experience open to her, and loves to spend time with men who have a limited range of sensitivity and sensibility. Hard life, drink and circumstances wear her down to the point of an attempted suicide, for which she travels to New Jersey where she can buy the write drug to send her into a deep sleep and eternity. But this fails. There is an intense formative moment, evoking a European or Russian element:

> As she slowly crossed Sixth Avenue, consciously dragging one foot past the other, a big, scarred horse pulling an express-wagon crashed to his knees before her. The driver swore and screamed and lashed the beast insanely, bringing the whip back over his shoulder for every blow, while the horse struggled to get a footing on the slippery asphalt. A group gathered and watched with interest ...

Parker shows in this story, as in another beautifully paced fiction, *The Lovely Leave* (1944), that she has the ability to create a story in which an element reaches out into universal feelings and qualities, while at the same time using a specific detail or scene to drive home a strong theme. The horse is an extension of the woman: it provides a metaphor for her struggles as well as for the futility of life really, in its fundamental qualities of sacrifice and labour. The theme is strengthened for the reader and the story has a potent after-effect of emotional *éclat*.

Parker was also a very perceptive and ironical commentator on the business and the craft of writing; in *The Paris Review* interview, she is asked, what work did she do at *Vogue*, and in the rely she says, 'Now the editors are what they should all be: all divorcees, and chic, a collection of Ilka Chases ... [a forthright radio host and actress of the time].' She pointed out that the Americans in Paris, though fond of drink, 'worked damned hard all the time.'

When it comes to writing itself and her development, as part of her general abilities and genius for humour, she said that she 'fell into it'. But she is candid about where she belongs in the geography of the American women writers of her age: she referred to some as 'providers of oil-wells'. The meaning was that they were constantly productive; but for Parker, the cases was that she did not want to be labelled as a humourist: 'It makes me feel guilty. I've never read a good quotable female humorist [*sic*] and I never was one myself ... "A smart cracker" they called me and that makes me sick and unhappy.' She was also a careful and fussy writer: 'I can't write five words but that I change seven.'

Parker perhaps would not have liked to be compared to some of the masters of short fiction, but there is a strong argument possible that such forms are her at her best. She said that 'I'm not going to do those he-said-she-said things anymore, they're over, honey. I want to do a story that can only be told in narrative form ...'

She had perceived that her variety of storytelling needed the presence of a directly attuned voice and a sharing of a character's story through intimate and contemporary language. My feeling is that she saw in her best fiction a narrative voice that was very close to her fine-tuned angle on the world and on her contemporaries. The individual and the universal come together.

Yet still there is the other Parker: the entertainer in verse and the never solemn book reviewer. In her volumes of poems, from *Enough Rope* to *Death and Taxes*, she made simplicity and with go tightly together, so that short forms surprised and entertained. In *Portrait of the Artist* she manages a slight parody of very early ballad form, placed together with what could have been rhetoric, all made to fit a neat formal bed:

Oh, wrap my eyes with linen fair,
With hempen cord go bind me,
And, of your mercy, leave me there,
Nor tell them where to find me.

In her book and theatre reviews she produced short essays of delight, appealing to anyone who knew the territory of the cultural life of the metropolitan. The openings say it all:

> There is always this to be said for the epidemic of Spanish influenza – it gave the managers something to blame things on ...
>
> Review of *Redemption* (1899)
> by Leo Tolstoy (1828 –1910), 1918

> In my present state of almost impenetrable gloom brought on by night after night of April, Nancy Lee and Once Upon a Time you don't know what it means to me to be able to say a few kind words about something ...
>
> Review of *Hedda Gabler* (1891)
> by Henrik Ibsen (1828–1906), 1918

> Misfortune, and recited misfortune in especial, may be prolonged to that point where it ceases to excite pity and arouses only irritation.
>
> Review of *No More Fun*, 1931

Dorothy Parker, had she lived to understand just what a huge influence she has been on women writers, but also on all writers, would probably have scoffed and asked for another drink. But the fact is that humour and satire of the interwar years is one of the outstanding features of women's writing of that time, and Parkers stands supreme as a true original – and in several genres.

Alyse Gregory and Llewelyn Powys

In a 1978 feature written for the *Antiquarian Book Monthly Review*, Glen Cavaliero (1927–2019) usefully explains the literary phenomenon of the years *c.*1929–1975 that emerged around the Powys family from Montacute. In doing so, he had to mention and explain a number of women writers who were part of that circle, and foremost of these is Alyse Gregory (1884–1967), an American who married Llewelyn Powys (1884–1939). The family of writers includes John Cowper Powys (1872–1963), Littleton Charles Powys

(1874–1955), Theodore Francis Powys (1875–1953) and Philippa Powys (1886–1963) as well as Llewelyn Powys. As Cavaliero explains, they were a significant part of the literary scene, but divided the ratings. Of John Cowper Powys he wrote, 'In retirement in upstate New York and after 1934 in North Wales, he wrote the six great novels, and the autobiography by which he is most likely to be remembered.'

Philippa Powys had a novel and a poetry collection in print before the Sundial Press published two of her novellas in 2011; her earlier novel, *The Blackthorn Winter* (1930), was reissued in 2007.

Alyse Gregory came to know Llewelyn Powys late in his life, when he was going to Davos Platz in Switzerland for treatment; he had tuberculosis, and while there, he met a number of other writers, and another circle of creative types gathered, and with this came correspondence. Gregory was not a minority figure, however, she had edited the prestigious literary journal *The Dial* and had published several books by the time her husband died in 1939; she was to follow these with her autobiography, *The Day is Gone* (1948).

Gregory had a difficult time, of course, as Powys was seriously ill; but she did make friends in Davos, including a young woman who was in the sanatorium with Powys. This was Madeleine Curry, who had aspirations to write – mainly in poetry – and whose work had been in the journal, *Horizon*. Gregory and Curry had a lengthy correspondence, with Gregory living down in Powys country while Curry (married to a doctor in the Royal Army Medical Corps serving in India) worked to help young women industrial workers in the Midlands, at one time during the Second World War setting up a special centre for these young women in Newark. She also came to know the wife of Ignazio Silone (1900–1978) and they corresponded.

Gregory when young had been potentially a professional singer, and had then been involved in political reform and women's rights. But her literary importance, apart from her marriage to Powys, was her time as editor of *The Dial*. In her autobiography, *The Day is Gone*, she writes vividly about her difficult years, living in unsavoury digs and slumming it in bohemian areas of New York. At one time she had a room positively swarming with rats. She started by writing literary essays and criticism – hardly a money-spinning genre – but she was noticed. Gregory writes with feeling about this tough stage in her development:

> To make one's living by writing has usually, however, little enough to do with art. As soon as we mingle with the crowd, our most original insights are jostled from us. I was far from aspiring to be an artist. If I could find a place any where [*sic*] in the long procession of honest, anxious scribblers who earned a bare living in the literary market, I thought I should be delighted ...

Yet she was fortunate in that she had friends in the world of writing and editing, and two of these – Scofield Thayer (1889–1982) and Dr James Watson (*b*.1928); they were planning to have a new manager for their periodical, *The Dial*, and they wanted Alyse Gregory.

The magazine had a long history, first appearing in 1840, when it was related to the very influential literary thinking behind Transcendentalism, in which Ralph Waldo Emerson (1803–1882), Frederic Henry Hedge (1805–1890) and Theodore Parker (1810–1860) were dominant. Emerson wanted the magazine to be 'so broad and great in its survey that it should lead opinion of this generation on every great interest ... A great journal people must read ...'

But by 1916 when the owners sold the publication, there was an opportunity for a new life and purpose. When Scofield Thayer put some backing in place, the re-launch was imminent, and he had his editor in focus: Gregory. It was then a literary magazine, and during its existence, it published many of the established celebrity writers of the time, including Djuna Barnes (1892–1982), Marianne Moore, Hart Crane (1899–1932), Sherwood Anderson (1876–1941), Anatole France (1844–1924), Amy Lowell (1874–1925), Ezra Pound and W.B. Yeats between early 1920 and the end of 1921.

Gregory edited the magazine only for two years between from 1923 until 1925 but she made an impact. The magazine was far more than a large office dedicated to printing and editing. Gregory explains the social side: 'The top floor of the magazine was given up to a dining room where the contributors could meet for a meal when they pleased, and where eminent authors and artists visiting New York were entertained for dinner ...' But she adored the work, and it gave her a unique place in the literary world; more important for her, there was much more to report regarding its effect and influence:

> Into what delightful paths had my days at last carried me! Surrounded by sympathetic people, subjected to the dilemmas incident only upon nice aesthetic judgements, with young men and old paying me artful compliments, in touch with minds original and imaginative – the pick of all Europe and America what higher fortune could I desire?

The American writers after the First World War undoubtedly had a notable influence on British writing; the freer, more open approaches and the loose attitudes to form were part of it, but then generalisations are dangerous. There was plenty of artistic discipline around too. What can be said, so well explained by D.H. Lawrence in his essays on American writers, is that the geography and topography, together with the new sense of unity and nationhood after a very long struggle, made Americans look again at their own land and its history, and this ran parallel to the factual and documentary impetus behind much British writing still to come. Of course, the verbal adventures of modernism were still there, arguably going into a second phase during the Second World War, with writers such as James Hanley, Denton Welsh (1915–1948) and Henry Green (1905–1973); the women writers were prominent as well, and it is time to conclude this survey with a look at some of them: Radclyffe Hall perhaps most prominently.

Chapter 8

Some Special Cases

'What am I, in God's name – some kind of abomination?'

Radcliffe Hall,
The Well of Loneliness

There are some topics that expand to fill the space available when it comes to the interwar years in Britain. One was sex and love, and other is best summarised by 'abroad' – a place that Philip Larkin would not visit because it was 'bloody'. The former theme is always there in art and literature of course, but between the two world wars there are many aspects of social history that open up a very mixed, confused and hard-faced morality. It was the era of Marie Stopes's (1880–1958) *Married Love* (1918), which had offered a controversial guide to legal sex; but it was also at this time that in Britain prostitutes and sex workers in general faced repression and prejudice at every turn; it was also a time when the words *dirt* and *smut* were applied to both pornography and to affairs of the heart.

Nowhere is this strange morality more visible than in the criminal courts. In the case of Bywaters-Thompson, in which Percy Thompson was murdered by his wife's lover, Frederick Edward Francis Bywaters (1902–1923), it was clear that there was no room for the French 'crime of passion' in the British order of things; through her passionate and romantic letters to her lover, Edith Jessie Thompson (1893–1923), was revealed as an accessory to the killing. This was in 1922. Four years later, a woman in the Leeds sex trade was hanged for the murder of a client; she did not speak at her trial, advised not to speak, although, since 1898, she had the right to do so. The verdict was inextricably mixed with moral judgement.

Then, at this very time, there was also D.H. Lawrence, *Lady Chatterley's Lover* (1928), and notions of pornography as opposed to approved romantic feelings. Marriage was indeed an institution, and through these years freedom from its bonds had to be done through the ritual business of acquiring a 'witness' to an affair, proving a partner to be faithless. Hotels ran a very profitable trade in backing this, and photographers had a nice little income in providing evidence.

Pornography and obscenity were the difficult words. It was not until 1960, long after Lawrence's death in 1930, that the famous trial of his novel for obscenity took place, but at the heart of this subject there was the notion of sexual passion. What was its place? When was it proper, other than in procreating the species, in the marriage bed? The results of illicit unions were there for all to see: the orphans, the broken families, the rejected women, and the horrendous habit of removing 'disgraced' women from the social scene and placing them in institutions. In other words, sex was difficult to cope with from education to marital morality. In Agatha Christie's *The Murder at the Vicarage*, the vicar accidentally sees a couple *in flagrante delicto* in the man's art studio. A conversation takes place between the 'sinner' and the vicar:

> As soon as we were alone his manner changed. His face became grave and serious. He looked almost haggard.
> 'You've surprised our secret Sir,' he said, 'What are you going to do about it?'
> I could speak far more plainly to Redding than I could to Mrs Protheroe, and I did so. He took it very well.
> 'Of course' he said when I had finished,
> 'You're bound to say all this. You're a parson I don't mean that in any way offensively ... But this isn't the usual sort of thing between Anne and me.'

There is the central issue in a nutshell. It is a sordid affair in the eyes of society, but to the lovers, their affection is special, different, genuine. There is real love and there is lustful desire. How society and morality cope with that was, in these years, a matter of applying a morality unchanged from the Victorian years.

The Spanish Civil War

When Franco's version of fascism rose into a confrontation with the republicans in Spain in 1936, politics came out of the seminar and into the streets. When Nazi and Italian intervention, siding with the Nationalists in July of that year, there was an appeal for help and a call to arms. The confrontation of democracy and fascism – which was threatening to break out elsewhere – foreshadowed much worse to come. But one of the sources of help for the republican cause was the International Brigade. Paul Preston summarises this well in his book on the war, *A Concise History of the Spanish Civil War* (1996): 'Volunteers from over the world flocked to fight for the Republic. Some were out-of-work, others were adventurers, but the majority had a clear idea of why they had come: to fight fascism.'

Naturally, writers and artists came along in those ranks too. One of these, Jason Gurney (1910–1973), explained the thinking very concisely:

> The Spanish Civil War seemed to provide a chance for a single individual to take positive and effective stand on an issue which appeared to be absolutely clear. Either you were opposed to the growth of fascism and went out to fight against it, or you acquiesced in its crimes and were guilty of permitting its growth.

As far as the women writers were concerned, not all arrivals to participate were pro-the Republic. Lara Hartmann's research on women writers and this war includes an account of Florence Farmborough (1887–1978) for instance: she was for the Nationalists. Hartmann writes,

> Farmborough presents Franco as the only 'decent' or 'civilised' side in the war ... the Republican side ... is addressed as 'Red Hordes'. More typical is the contribution of Helen Nicholson, as explained in her 1937 book, *Death in the Morning*. She also wrote a novel, *The Painted Bed* [1938]. She married a Spanish academic, and so, living in the midst of such a horrendous war meant that she had much to contribute to the general understanding of the situation. She remarks at one point, 'In those days it was quite a simple matter to murder

> anyone you wished to, provided you were of the left wing, and your victim a member of the right.'

Hartman points out that Nicholson 'puts all the violent acts in other people's mouths. She herself rarely gives her own opinion on the Republicans or their actions, aside from being stressed that the Alhambra is being bombed, and therefore so is her own house ...'

Like the First World War though, the war in Spain was in many ways a poets' war. Mention has already been made of Sylvia Townsend Warner, and she figures again here with the element in her work of reportage as well as her poetry. She and Ackland joined the Red Cross volunteers. Mercedes Aguirre has explained Warner's activism: '[she] became involved in the activism ... Her interest in the war was connected to her involvement with the Dorset branch of the British Communist Party, which Warner and her partner Valentine Ackland had joined in 1935.'

In September 1936, they went to Barcelona to work with the Spanish Medical Aid Committee. They did what they could, and Aguirre makes it clear that Warner had a lot to say on the conflict. Warner wrote extensively about Spain throughout the duration of the conflict, and in a variety of genres. She wrote articles stressing the need for foreign intervention in the conflict' as well as short stories and poems.

There is also a personal perspective in her poems: 'The poems suggest that, while their 1936 trip to Barcelona was initially driven by their ethical and political commitment, it also represented a liberation for their relationship, and they provide a new perspective on Warner's relation to the Spanish conflict.'

The Well of Loneliness

In Ethel Mannin's book *Confessions and Impressions*, she includes an interview with Radclyffe Hall, and she makes it clear that Hall's novel *Adam's Breed* (1926), was a work she admired above the notorious *The Well of Loneliness*, but she adds, the latter work she found 'profoundly beautiful and moving.' Mannin had a special interest in this writer; it is clear from the memoir that she has strong opinions on the British and sex. She had read D.H. Lawrence and had seen the sense in his views on men, women and sex. She wrote,

'We have made sex a smutty story; but for them [the English people] it is life and in their acceptance of it as such they have laid hold of the art of living. At the back of all our shame about sex is the puritanical hatred of life, and its fear of happiness.'

The interwar years certainly experienced a steady evolution of the place of sexuality in culture; not only was sex for sale in the cities, but it was studied and discussed by thinkers and theorists; Lawrence saw what he thought was a basic fear of life, as Mannin states. When Christopher Isherwood went to Berlin in the late 1920s, he came across the Magnus Hirschfeld Sexology Institute. This had been founded in 1919. Jonathan Fryer (1950–2021) notes that

> Hirschfeld had succeeded in winning a precarious status of respectability for his brainchild, so that it was accepted as an asylum for sex offenders ... until their cases were heard in court ... Hirschfeld was a supporter of Russian Soviet legislation which had decreed that an individual's sex life was private and therefore outside the law ...

Yet of course, matters in this respect run deep. *The Well of Loneliness* ends with a vision, and the impassioned poetic closure, coming from 'her own voice, into which millions had entered' builds up to 'Acknowledge us, O God, before the whole world. Give us the right to our existence.' This unique novel deals with some profound aspects of sexual identity, and makes it clear that, a century on from its appearance in print, our modern world has made room for far more understanding and tolerance of difference than perhaps Radclyffe Hall had ever imagined. In her story of Stephen, the 'invert' as she wished to be known, she sets the action in rural England initially (around Malvern) but moves things around to London, Paris and elsewhere. The theme is a bunching of multiple strands, covering varieties of loving relationships, but what binds these into a strong central preoccupation is the inability of the wealthy, mostly rural and traditional morality of Stephen's family and their peers.

Stephen loves horses, books and writing, and she eventually becomes a successful and admired novelist, like her creator; but one feature of the novel is that as it progresses, new characters are introduced; at times this seems like an effort to provide a full spectrum of varieties of the 'type' or 'condition' – as in a suicide pact in Paris towards the end. However, the reach and depth are far more subtle and refined than that, because several masculine personalities are included, from bullies to bores; the book also includes scenes from the First World War, and even rural idylls of real significance, but it is always a search for selfhood.

For much of the book, there is a rhythmic pulse to the prose, similar to some of D.H. Lawrence, and these novels make an interesting comparison. *Lady Chatterley's Lover* and *The Well of Loneliness* appeared in the same year, 1928. Although both encountered the worst of repressive law, Lawrence provides a high level of rhetoric and an insistent sense of instructive prose, as if, notably in the explicit sex scenes, Lawrence felt that his readers needed to be both entertained and instructed regarding the morally free pleasure of sex. Puritanism was there in his own people, he said, and Ethel Mannin agreed. Both wrote extensively about the sexual repression evident in British society and morals.

Yet, in spite of the impact of the book, Radclyffe Hall's momentous account of lesbian love has not a trace of physical sexuality: it has ample sensuality and a great deal of romantic affection, but percolating through the prose is an appeal for understanding and a strong theme of urgent change: in the handling of the story and in the treatment of the characters' affections and desires, there is a repeated clamour for attention and enlightenment. The reader follows Stephen's climb to success as a writer, running concurrently with the losses and sadness in her emotional life, from the death of her favourite horse to her failures in love in a number of ways.

There is rejection following rejection as we follow the course of Stephen's life, and even late in the novel, after meeting Lady Massey (1938–2024) and feeling again that here might be a true friend, we have the kind of rejection she is inured to, as in a letter from Massey to her:

> certain things that I don't want to enter into – have simply forced me to break off our friendship and to say that I must ask you not to come here for Christmas. Of course a woman of my position with all eyes upon her has to be extra careful. It's too terribly upsetting and sad for me; if I hadn't been so fond of you both [Stephen and Mary] – but you know how attached I had become to Mary...

And so it went on: 'a kind of wail full of self-importance combined with self-pity.' Although there is not a really substantial part of the novel allotted to Stephen's writing and how it plays a part in her inner liberation, nevertheless that theme is there. In her early teens she began writing, encouraged by her father; then later she learns the demands of the art and it moves from therapy to profession.

At the very centre of the writing there is far more than the professional writer and her life, however. It is existential. At one point in one of her many meditations, Stephen speaks to her father's memory:

> You knew! All the timer you knew this thing, but because of your pity You wouldn't tell me. Oh father – and there are so many of us – thousands of miserable, unwanted people, who have no right to love, no right to compassion because they're maimed, hideously maimed and ugly – God's cruel; he let us get flawed in the making ...

But the thickening of the existential concerns offer a strong insight into what Stephen has gained: her faithful friend and servant, Puddle, says:

> You've got work to do. Come and do it! Why, just because you are what you are, you may actually find that you've got an advantage. You may write with a curious double insight – write both men and women from a personal knowledge. Nothing's completely misplaced or wasted, I'm sure of that.

In 2024, this insight has settled and been absorbed within the whole gamut of women's writing, through the vicissitudes of feminist writing and theory, through to popular women's writing. Naturally, the trajectory from banned book up to respected modern women's classic has happened, and in fact, we can safely omit the word 'women's' from that statement, as the novel is now a universal classic.

An interesting comparison may be made, when it comes to the notion of obscenity, if we refer to the idea of 'moral corruption' as it was placed in the dialogue around the trial of D.H. Lawrence, his publishers and *Lady Chatterley's Lover* in 1960. Then, over twenty years after Radclyffe Hall's confrontation with obscenity, the concept of corruption was little different from the idea applied to prisons in which 'contamination' was applied to avoid first-time offenders mixing with old lags. But in literature, as the obscenity linked to James Hanley's *Boy* in 1931 shows, there is a deep basis of repulsion behind the laws, and this is linked to sexual offences which had made problems for the criminal justice system through the centuries. In *Boy*, it centres of sodomy, the offence that had sent Oscar Wilde to prison; but Hanley based his novel on habits and behaviour he had seen himself as a boy sailor in the merchant marine. The issue becomes not *what is obscene*? But *why are we afraid of this behaviour*?

After all, Radclyffe Hall knew as much about lesbian love as James Hanley did about the subject of the old cliché, *rum, sodomy and the lash*. What must be validated now is that Hall was a trailblazer in this respect, as Lawrence and Hanley were. If we return to the topic of Britons travelling to Paris and Berlin to learn about sex, and to experience a society that had open-minded views on this, then surely it was a very negatively set and rather restricted moral compass here *c.*1930, and it hardly changed at all during the years between 1939 and 1960. In my own secondary modern boys' school in Leeds, when I was a student there in 1960, every boy in the school seemed to know where the Penguin paperback copy of *Lady Chatterley's Lover* was in the school library. I recall finding the book on the shelf, with its band of dirt down the closed pages, showing all curious children where the offending pages could be found.

This is the kind of cultural shock that occurs when there is fear and closed-mind attitudes present. Anecdotal evidence often conforms that the kind of sex education we have now – open, explicit and informed – did not exist until very recent times. *The Well of Loneliness* played an important part in the struggle by creative artists to highlight serious flaws in British cultural life.

One thing that Hall knew and expressed really powerfully was the place of writing in her character's life (and her own of course): 'Writing, it was like heavenly balm, it was like the flowing out of deep waters, it was like the lifting of a load from the spirit; it brought with it a sense of relief, of assuagement. One could say things in writing without feeling self-conscious, without feeling shy and ashamed and foolish ...'

Under all the plotting, relationships and images, though, one figure remains of Hall's Stephen: one persisting insight, that reaches out from literature to life: 'there was a kind of enlarged splendour about her – absurd though she was, she was splendid at that moment – grotesque and splendid, like some primitive thing conceived in a turbulent age of transition.' The last four words relate again to Lawrence:

> [the] essentially 'tragic age' of Lawrence and Hall's uneasy reality from which Stephen falls and rises again – these are a world in slippage. As politics snatched all the front pages in the decade following Hall's classic, so the footnotes – the sexual unrest and the gender identities – were waiting their turn to make the headlines and make yet another 'turbulent age of transition'.

The feature of this period we must hang on to is that so many established and unquestioned beliefs were being questioned. The kinds of aims and goals expressed in so many of the generation of writers who went to be educated in ways beyond the textbooks are found in so many memoirs, but one of the most explicit comes from Christopher Isherwood, in his book, *Christopher and His Kind* (1976), where he wrote:

> At the Cosy Corner Christopher met a youth whom I shall call Bubi ... appealing blue eyes, golden blond hair and a body which was smooth-skinned and almost hairless, although hard and muscular ... Christopher experienced instant infatuation. This wasn't surprising; to be infatuated was what he had come to Berlin for ...

That 'infatuation' could be applied as much to the café culture of Paris as to the more sleazy part of London that so many women writers knew at the first stage of their careers. Most had known the 'underworld' behind the smart, modern cityscapes. Most filled their notebooks and stocked imagery in their minds. The great adventure of daring to become a professional writer went arm-in-arm with the metropolitan identity, and in the key locations of these places there was a fresh kind of freedom. Shaking off that baggage of morality was a tough ask – especially when one recalls that the First World War, in its popular propaganda and literature – used a set, intractable morality to make the foundations of the conflict. After all, as all the young men were told, didn't the Germans commit all those atrocities in Belgium? In the world of England in 1914, everything had to conform. In the *Windsor Magazine* of early 1915 one advert, showing a woman donning a corset, proclaims 'Let there be no more undeveloped women ...'

The task facing the writers and artists coming to their zenith in the 1920s was as much concerned with challenging conformity as with 'finding themselves' through art. Even the Bloomsbury mindset had to exist in a world in which the sergeant majors of morals were as evident in society as the Lord Chamberlain's office.

In the Shadow of the Second World War

For many years, the women's writing produced at the time of the Second World War or immediately after appears to have been dominated by memoirs, and the massive influence of the Mass Observation movement. This vigilance for all things mundane under the shadow of the bombers of Hitler's *Luftwaffe*, from Blitz to Doodlebugs, entered so much of the diaries, journals and letters of that war, and large-scale paperbacks such as *Nella's Last War: The Second World War Diaries of Housewife 49* (2006) by Nella Last (1889–1968) did a lot to create the experience of the Home Front for modern readers.

Last's book *Nella's Last War: The Second World War Diaries of Housewife 49* and the kind of material it covered relates clearly to the fiction and poetry of the time. Yet the women creative writers of the time have been most prominent in anthologies. One of the most recent of these is *A Different Sound: Stories by Mid-Century Women Writers* (2023), edited by Lucy Scholes. This partly answers the question on what these women tended to write about. Editor Lindsay Duguid, in a review of the book, summarises helpfully: 'What is under threat is the ideal of an old-fashioned life, delicately described in terms of lace mats and napkins, a vase of pink roses, photographs in silver frames, warm beds and firesides.' As so often, the male writers on that war have been promoted for some considerable time. For instance, the fiction of Henry Green, William Sansom (1912–1976), James Hanley, Frank Sargeson (1903–1982) and others, along with J.B. Priestley, have been more noticeable in the general press than a number of female writers. But the discoveries and retrievals have been, and are still being, done. What strikes us now is the determined realism of these women writers: their need to highlight a domestic perspective for many, but for others, there is the obvious impetus of using their foreign war experience as part of their central store of 'material'. Storm Jameson wasted nothing in this respect; others made the obvious move of putting their own patch of experience centre-stage and using the fear and threat around the scenes of peace and former stability.

Women were still a major part of the small magazine industry in the post-Second World War years. John Lehmann has this to say in an editorial of 1946: 'We salute the founders of the new magazines whose flattery took the sincerest form ... and last but far from least, Miss Frost and Miss Cooper, without whose patient labours behind the scenes we would hardly be taking this butterfly flight today.' The small magazines, together with the fiction magazines in anthology format, were booming at this time. They were not only a platform for new writers, but established and highly-rated writers were part of that scene. In the October 1951 issue of *Magpie*, for instance, Daphne du Maurier's story, *The Escort*, appeared with Eve Ballantyne and L.A.G. Strong (1896–1958). Ballantyne appears not to have published a book, but the magazine encouraged beginners.

It is hard to find a typical women's novel of this period, but certainly in *The Rich House* by Stella Gibbons, as in so much of the crime fiction by women, the profound interest taken in a small community is a basic foundation for exploring and creating characters. In *The Rich House*, the reader puts together a map of the town of Seagate. Gibbons's founding line of thought in her writing sometimes runs along with Tolstoy's notion of 'the practical life of each individual.'

This 'practical life', since the outbreak of the Second World War in 1939, had meant hard times, making do and sacrificing much of what constituted the pleasures and comforts of everyday living. In wartime issue of *The Countryman*, for example, through the 1940s, there was a constant supply of instruction and information about food, domestic work and basic husbandry and agronomy. At one time the journal imagined a 'rural school' and asked writers what could be learned in it, but the scope was wider than that, including not only how to keep bees but how a single housewife could 'quell that fire single handed' with a North British Auto-Spray.

The creative writing by women at the time shows that the successful and popular categories were crime, historical romance, contemporary romance, social problem fiction, and autobiographical or saga regional fiction. One statistic is also useful. At the London Library between 1954 and 1959 the number of volumes added averaged 6,000 per year, and even in just 1 year, 1954, there was an increase of 843 volumes in circulation.

For the more serious writers, there were hugely significant themes and explorations to be done in fiction. Storm Jameson, for instance, in *The Hidden River* (1955), gave this reply to a question about the book, 'hung about in my mind for several years before it got itself written.' What had been conceived as a plain story of treachery turned itself into a story about what happens to the man who takes justice into his own hands. I do not know the final answer, but what, after all, is a book worth if it does not raise questions which cannot be completely answered?

Similarly, in *Cloudless May* (1943), she uses her knowledge of France, and she explained the genesis of the novel in this way: 'The idea for *Cloudless May* was born of that devotion [to France] emerged in the Spring of 1939 in Paris, when she realised with a shock how little, morally and spiritually, France was ready for the war that loomed.'

Naturally, in the years immediately after a world war, there would be a plethora of experience and experience in writers' minds that related to a re-examination of past experience.

Part of that revisionist stance taken by so many writers may be seen in the fiction embedded in the topography of the post-Second World War Blitz landscape, and in the impoverishment of everyday life. But it was also a landscape rich in potential threat and fear: this world was one in which petty crime had thrived, but also serious crimes against the person; there had been a 'Blackout Ripper' and there had been bodies found in the ruins on bomb craters which turned out to be suspicious deaths and often to be murders. The fiction of the 1940s used this, for sure, but also it used the intimacy and togetherness of small, circumscribed communities. In *The Rich House* this cosy domesticity and the everyday effectively suggests the closeness of the emotional ties: 'They had not got out of their beds until twelve o'clock, and later still Louise had carried up to them kippers and coffee and two new packets of cigarettes and some chopped liver for Vinnie, Myra's little dog.'

George Orwell, writing in 1948, commented, 'This is a political age. War, Fascism, concentration camps, rubber truncheons, atomic bombs etc., are what we daily think about and therefore to a great extent what we write about ...' He was right, but the word 'political' also embraces the daily politics, covering forced action, individual pressures and the need for conformity. The women writer has consistently through the years covered in these pages, revealed the other politics: that of the household and the human relationship. Her teaching is still there in the writing from the interwar years, and there are still important discoveries to be made in this body of work. One is tempted to think that many of the women knew exactly what aspects of women's lives were in need of this desperate, incisive revision through the lens of fiction.

Conclusions

'Think of what our nation stands for,
Books from Boots and country lanes,
Free speech, free passes, class distinction
Democracy and proper drains ...'
John Betjeman (1906–1984)

From the outset, I have tried to survey the women's writing of these two decades from the viewpoint of creative writing itself, regardless of the marketplace, and also from the position taken in search of understanding how the highbrow and middlebrow fiction developed together. Included in this has been the knowledge I have gleaned from my many years as a tutor teaching the skills involved in creative writing. From that experience, I am fully aware of the huge differences between writing for oneself and writing for an identified reader.

This difference brings into focus all kinds of factors influencing the basics of narrative: style, voice, point of view, setting and so on. There is no doubt that one of the 'tests' of the literary or 'serious' work of fiction is whether or not the work stands multiple readings and has what is commonly called 'depth'. But this is such a shifting concept that one perhaps has to settle for the more simplistic contrast that rests on the question of whether or not there is some strand in a novel or short story that demands of the reader some tough thinking or feeling. It seems to me that it is never enough to claim that a literary work simply needs more 'brainwork' or something similar. No, in many cases the challenge of such a read is one of layers of themes or poetic and imaginative devices.

In the case of the last point it surely follows that for a novel which uses such devices (*A Passage to India* by E.M. Forster (1924) for instance, or many of Mansfield's stories) asks of the reader something different. Arguably this demand is to do with the bedrock of knowledge: the knowledge that is extraneous to the actual interplay of events in the novel. We need to reflect on the questions asked about the 'weight' a novel carries in every sense. This was used by Italo Calvino to distinguish between categories of books, and it is helpful. He suggests light and heavy novels in terms of everything they carry during the demands made of the reader. This includes such items as long, tortuous sentences, references to knowledge of the factual elements in the story (from history to biology perhaps) and with the addition of the level of abstraction in the narrative language. In other words, we might expect popular novels to be a 'light read' as used in common vocabulary, but there is probably also the 'lightness' of all these other senses in which a work of fiction presses into our faculties and demands thought.

Still matters are not so simple: what about the degree and quality of feeling, one might ask? Surely, a novel appeals to our sense of empathy as well as to our packed brains of acquired information? That is to say, arguably a novel's depiction of a human relationship is as demanding on the reader as the intellectual content. We tend to judge the material in a story that is placed somewhere on the spectrum between realism and sentimentality, and we perhaps judge the latter always with a negative judgement.

The most persistent line of thought regarding what is learned from this body of writing is that middlebrow Britain still finds itself in a moveable position regarding high and low cultural media and products. On the one hand, sociologists might argue that the social hierarchy has been eroded or at least made irrelevant. But still the evidence is there with regard to literature when one looks at the state of English literature taught in schools. The 'classics' appear to have lost the place of honour and admiration, and perhaps it is no very negative tendency to observe that writing dealing with the immediacy of living in such a secular, material world is thrust into main focus. But the attitude of almost worshipping literature perhaps began to see decline – inevitably – when writers without public school and university backgrounds began to reach the heights of being 'establishment' and had set readerships, or as they would be called in today, 'followers'.

That middlebrow Britain certainly had women writers in its ranks, and also a growing readership for all the media outlets relating to arts and culture. In an exhibition presented in 2021 there was a section headed 'Reading

Women' and in that was featured *Time and Tide* magazine. This began in 1920, with Helen Archdale (1876–1949) as editor. Then Lady Rhondda took over for decades. The publication was enthusiastically behind campaigns of a feminist hue and of left-wing issues. Some of the women contributors in the interwar years were: Vera Brittain, Emma Goldman (1869–1940), Charlotte Haldane (1894–1969), Naomi Mitchison (1897–1999), Rebecca West (1892–1983) and Winifred Holtby. The headings of an issue in 1925 shows the range: review of the week's events, book reviews, the theatre, music of the week, fiction and verse and a literary competition. *Time and Tide* was produced 'by and for' the women of Britain.

Several contrasts and comparisons have emerged in the course of writing the book. One fundamental subject is the contradistinction between the emotional, imagination-led writer who creates in an almost trance-like state, and the writer of craft and structure. One of the best reflections on this issue came from Storm Jameson in her autobiography, *Journey from the North*, in which she considers a writer called Romer Wilson (1891–1930). Like Jameson, Wilson was a Yorkshire woman, and they were similar in some ways but Jameson sees something different in one respect: 'her form of insanity – which was partly a total indifference to appearances and partly the dangerous lucidity with which, when she was writing, she heard and saw.'

But Jameson saw and wondered about this fundamental comparison in ways of working:

> She told me once that she did not write with the conscious or deliberate intention of writing what, when she came to read it through, was there on the page. For weeks, months, she felt no impulse to write at all; then the wish seized her, she shut herself away from everyone, husband, infant son, friends, and wrote until she was physically and mentally exhausted.

Jameson was far too deeply concerned with writing as a craft in need of dedication: something to be learned and mastered by application to hard work. Her reflection on the Wilson approach was, 'If Mr X or Miss Y had told me that their admirably mechanically-articulated novels were in this way given, I should not have believed a word of it. I believed Romer Wilson – if only because no fragments she left, however trivial, is less than alive.' This is one reflection to be drawn from the social and professional history that forms the bedrock of writing is that both approaches are possible, but no golden rules exist that might guarantee success, and all the writing manuals in the world will not provide a magic wand and a publishing deal.

Some conclusions are provoking and not a little complex in that they emanate from two decades that saw perhaps a series of cataclysmic changes; much of this was domestic, in that there was a heap of problems awaiting the various governments between the first Labour one and the eve of war under Neville Chamberlain (1869–1940). But what stands out in terms of the women writers is that in their adult years there were a series of events and trends, which energised women's lives across the social hierarchy. These topics included a revisionary attitude to sex and sexual manners, together with the understanding of sex and emotion rather than simply sex and reproduction. It is hard to deny the influence of D.H. Lawrence in this respect, and also Radclyffe Hall. But as Christopher Isherwood's work shows, the after-effects of the First World War reached into every avenue of life. It is also easy to overlook the revolution in Germany, with the chaotic devaluation of the mark and the social deprivation. As the writers across Britain wrote their new realism and documentary stories, there was Bertolt Brecht (1898–1956) in Germany, with the production of a theatre aimed at shaking people into an epiphany of realisation about issues of humanity and survival. This came along with the bold and subversive drawings of George Grosz, and the urban chaos was soon to come after *c.*1930 when the Nazi Party expanded in power and influence.

Most significant of all, in the context of this book, however, is surely the nature of women and creativity. Some theorists have spoken of the 'feminine sentence' and the sustained introspection of the fiction in Virginia Woolf and Katherine Mansfield can be shown to illustrate the specific inward-turning preoccupation of writing about a selfhood in need of being revealed and understood. One of the most useful insights into this line of thought has come from Professor Judy Simons, in her study of women writers and their journals or diaries. One of the key questions in this is a particular wording about writing method:

> Should we assume from this that she saw life only as material for her art as a novelist? Is it true that by keeping herself deliberately apart from the social experience, she gave the impression of waiting to transform it into something else, to sift it and modify its character?

This is entirely contrary to the realistic imperative of many women's writing of this period. After all, most of these women writers had a great deal of life experience to reveal, to express as a previously unheeded part of human life. In doing so, there was no point in 'waiting to transform it' but rather to try hard to tell it as it actually is. Hence the 1930s was a decade in which a general realisation emerged that Britain was not as previously understood because it had only been *partially* so. For centuries there had been, moving amongst the men who led industry, farming and transport, politics, the sea and the skies, another version of humanity, whose role in life had been defined as child bearing and kitchen cleaning.

Something of the prevailing attitudes to women and creativity is in an anecdote about Edith Evans, when she was told that Nancy Mitford (1904–1973) was at someone's house, finishing a book. Evans replied, 'Oh, really? What exactly is she reading?'

When this time of women being able to write on an equal footing with men, there was so much time to make up. There were points to prove and triumphs to define. Gillian Clarke expresses this in her poem, *October* when she writes:

> I must write like the wind, year after year
> Passing my death day, winning ground.

Looking at the social history of the first decades of the twentieth century, the evidence for fiction by women being found in all areas of publication is not hard to find, from the new popular magazines and their short stories, through to literary and political outlets. Among all this, there were opportunities to use fiction in an Agitprop manner, as in the hugely best-selling medical publications written to inform women about their feminine 'health and hygiene' concerns. Apart from Lydia E. Pinkham's (1819–1883) best-seller, *Private Textbook upon Ailments Peculiar to Women* (the origin of The Scaffold song *Lily the Pink*) there was the phenomenon of Dr Hall's Hygiene Co. and its book, *Woman: Her Generative Functions and Diseases*, which contained a short story *Woman's Martyrdom – Founded on Fact*, which contains this:

> The hurrying rap-raps of clog-shod feet reached the ear from all sides, as Raw youths, set-faced men, and shawl-shrouded girls and women passed along briskly. Close by a corner near the mills, two female figures almost collided whilst hurrying from opposite ways.
> 'Hullo [*sic*] Miriam!' exclaimed one, 'didn't see you coming.'
> 'Didn't see you, either' said the other, 'Oh this wind! Doesn't it cut one's face this morning? How's your mother doing this morning?'
> 'Oh, dreadful!' exclaimed Mary Hard, 'She gets no sleep, no rest, and that terrible pain always gnawing at her inside.'

Fiction by women, it strikes a modern reader, was not only a significant expansion of narrative across all parts of the nation's cultural life: it was very handy for getting the message across in an age in which mass communication was advancing fast. It is not so far from this writing of Dr Hall's text to outright propaganda, and, of course, as the documentary writing shows, this was close also to political writing and the work of the committed individual. These decades were, after all, the age of 'the common man and woman' – the new clerks, the new voters and the new politics.

There is no doubt that of all the various forms and genres of writing, crime fiction flowered in this period. It was the 'Golden Age' of the genre, in which rules were agreed on the matters of plot in a murder story, very much with the reader in mind. By the late 1930s, Agatha Christie, Dorothy L. Sayers, Gladys Mitchell and a host of others were established, and in 1936 a review essay on new crime novels, including Christie's *Cards on the Table* (1936), made her the notable star turn: 'Poirot, with his vanities, his little grey cells and his moustache, is endearing. Evan Pinkerton is even more so ... It is enough to say that Mr Pinkerton has indeed got the clue and also the wits to use it, and that he comes triumphantly out of an episode which has put him in many painful situations.'

The feature included remarks on an increasingly familiar title: *How to Write Crime Stories* by Nigel Morland (1905–1986), and this was to become a common aspect of publishing through the war and beyond. His instruction was 'all on the technical points' and he advised on avoiding even the smallest error. The reviewer notes that 'readers are apt to be touchy when they find the novelist moving clumsily on ground that is well known to them.' This touches on another growing readership and related genre: true crime.

Although true crime writing in these decades was dominated by men, it is clear that the readership was expanding, encouraged no doubt by the crime story on film. The early crime dramas and police tales, leading to such classics as *Dixon of Dock Green* and dramas of the Flying Squad, were the province partly of the crime reporters of the newspapers, such as Percy Hoskins (1904–1989) of *The Express*, but the time was not far off when women would write in true crime areas.

If one had to distinguish a truly major feature of the two decades, covering a large proportion of all fiction and popular non-fiction, one would have to point to England and Englishness as the central preoccupation. The changes in social hierarchy and documentary, discussed in an earlier chapter, had a strong element of the worker in their narratives, and the topography of the country was changing rapidly, owing partly to the First World War and the demands made on the land and coast for defences, but more prominently to the results of the decline of the landed aristocracy in these years. Viewers of *Downton Abbey* will be familiar with the tales of the home's decline in the 1920s owing to taxes and to the loss of male family members. The domestic servants were reduced in number; estates were sold, in part at least, and investment in them was limited.

The old standard description of England with its three-tier classification no longer held in everyone's mind, and the British Empire was now questioned, examined in literature and the arts, and the purpose of the landed aristocrats reassessed. Extremes of wealth and poverty were now everyday apparent and somewhat shaming regarding the sequence of governments who failed to deal with this. Together with such developments there was the rise of interest in communism. Reading about visits to Russia was not difficult; major public figures such as H.G. Wells and George Bernard Shaw had done so.

Part of this questioning of traditional superiority and the men of power who had run the place, going back to the Plantagenets and the constant wars with France and Ireland, which had entailed the duties of the feudal system, taking away working men on the land to become soldiers abroad, was deeply embedded in the situation of power. In Kate O'Brien's award-winning novel, *Without My Cloak* (1931), we have different time references sections, and in an early establishment scene there is a profile of the typical Victorian paterfamilias, man of power and standing:

> he became a silent, self-reliant man, whose wife feared and venerated him and whom even his mother approached with caution. Uncouth and simple he remained in life, but growing rich, loaded his womenfolk with silks and gauds ... His wife bore him thirteen children, of whom eight, four sons and four daughters, reached maturity.

There was a 'Man Problem' in this relentless revolution in writing: as the traditional social hierarchy was eroded, so the reasons for questioning this central male power increased and intensified. The spectrum of this fictional depiction is wide: it reaches from the writer in Angela Thirkell's *High Rising* (comic but convincing) to Daphne du Maurier's Max de Wynter. Now, throughout the late 1920s and into the next decade, women had been shown by the media to be entirely capable of independent control of dangerous and daring situations, from the fiction (*The Sheik*) to the works of travel, as in the books of Beryl Markham (1902–1986). The women's clubs were places where the career women could gather and learn, ask questions and share experience. Ethel Mannin's memoir, *Confessions and Impressions*, in which she meets and interviews prominent people from these times, includes Ellen Wilkinson MP (1891–1947), actor Elsa Lanchester (1902–1986) Gwen Otter, and writers Radclyffe Hall and Sheila Kaye-Smith.

The 'England in the mind' – the myth of the traditional land of Arthur, King Henry V (1386–1422) and then the British Empire and its heroes, played a part in the mediation of the English virtues and national qualities, at a time when fascism was the outside threat. As is known from so many instances in history, something from outside a society – some kind of fear – tightens the sense of togetherness of those under threat. With this came a fresh depiction of robust authority, ranging from horrendous abuse of power, as in James Hanley's novel, *Boy* in which a boy sailor is exploited and abused to an enraging extreme, to the cruelty against women in the work of Jean Rhys.

The Spanish Civil War of the mid-1930s shone a light on many of the new humane, socialist and radical attitudes of the same writers and artists who had worked to show the results of inequality at home in Britain. The general public view and evaluation of the writer became less sure and understood. In the years between the end of Queen Victoria's reign and the end of the First World War, the writer's province had been circumscribed: it covered reportage from the verge of empire; entertainment and escapism; travel narratives and home commentary. That is to say, where dissent was found, it crept in stealthily. Then with first the Anglo-Boer War (1899–1902) and then the Battles of Loos (1915), Ypres (1914 and 1915) and the Somme (1916) came the shaking of the strong base of all this: writers might be, in fact, rather more of the European variety, who had (many of them) lived with an empire, but had known a very different literary culture, one in which multiple voices, from multiple societies, could go to work and create sub-cultures, such as the Parisian bohemian scene as depicted by Henri Murger (1822–1861) in *Scènes de la vie bohème* (1851), – 'Scenes of Bohemian Life' – or the Middle-European café culture which engendered so many subversive writers from Joseph Roth (1894–1939) to Franz Kafka (1883–1924).

The fear of something so free and powerful being unable to appear in Britain is seen in George Orwell's essay of 1945, 'The Prevention of Literature', in which he wrote: 'Everything in our age conspires to turn the writer, and every other kind of artist as well, into a minor official, working on themes handed to him from above and never telling what seems to him the whole truth. But in struggling against this fate he gets no help from his own side ...' Interestingly, in the world of the adherents of the higher culture and the Bloomsbury mindset there is arguably 'help from his own side' even if that is no more than a leg up towards being published or simply being welcomed into a coterie of people with similar interests.

In the world of writers' clubs, described in an earlier chapter, it is evident that women found welcoming and helpful sisterhoods and support groups, but these women were a minority. Most aspiring writers in the shires, many holding down a job or keeping a house and home together, saw a view from a distance, from a periphery in which the lonely writer toils away, with a dream of being one of the women like Storm Jameson, Phyllis E. Bentley or Agatha Christie, whose vision and talent led them to metropolitan acknowledgement and success.

The middlebrow revolution was a tough process, but it was happening, and only part of it was actually happening at a marked distance from the movers and shakers of the establishment. There was a reaction to the signposting of urgent issues about women's lives; this was a feature that insisted on describing and explaining female selfhood, both in similarity to men, and in the gender differences. In much of the humour and fun, there was an appeal to this understanding to be about aspects of women's lives, which had been blotted out like a grey cloud over the sun.

However, the genuine efforts to validate the women writers, from inside the literary establishment, had to be made by determined participants in this feature of the middlebrow revolution. This activity is seen in the social history of the *Left Review*, the literary magazines like *Fact* and in the local and regional writing groups. Phyllis E. Bentley writes extensively about the gregarious nature of writers and their groups in Calderdale when she was first established: 'Still, the Women's Luncheon Club enlarged the horizon, as did the University Extension Society' and she adds that there was the Bradford Library and Literary Society, and then also she comments on her own active involvement in these matters: 'Deeply involved in all Thespian affairs, president of the Authors' Circle, still joint secretary of the Women's Luncheon Club and the University Extension Society I find myself in my diary increasingly sitting at the typewriter and answering the telephone.' If one takes a more distant evaluation of the supposed freedom in these new careers for women, perhaps some restraint is needed, rather than sweeping generalisations. In Reay Tannahill's (1929–2007) ambitious and thought-provoking *Sex in History* (1980) there is this assessment:

> all the new toys and diversions of the post-war [First World War] era were showered upon them [women]. Cosmetics, lightweight clothes, cheap jewellery, phonograph records, holidays by the sea, dance halls, restaurants, coffee shops, tea rooms and above all, the cinema, conspired to absorb the brief spending power ... Men had possessed women, and women had been possessed by men, for more than 5,000

years, and it was to take more than a vote and a salary to break the marriage habit.

In the past there have been many simplistic evaluations of the women writers who worked in the shadow of the modernist challenge to conventional realism, and it has never been enough to quote the words of the song:

How you gonna keep 'em
Down on the farm
Now that they've seen Paree

Yes, they were women of that generation who experienced the 'Roaring Twenties' and the fascist 1930s, but in terms of creativity, some aligned with the more overtly intellectual writers who kept 'literature' as a concept separate from *writing*, while others put an immersion in life at the level of dealing with work, relationships and politics as their main focus.

Few women writers of this era could have seen and done as much as Cecily Mackworth (1911–2006), who was 'writer, traveller, war correspondent and rebel' in the words of her obituarist, Gordon Bowker (1934–2019). She died in 2006, aged 94, and she saw most of Europe, settled for a while in Paris and knew Henry Miller (1891–1980) there in 1937; after writing *I Came out of France* (1941), T.S. Eliot befriended her, and she lived through the Blitz, then back to France again. Her novels came in the 1950s but had written poetry and essays before 1945. Bowker adds, 'As a child she had been introduced to Thomas Hardy, and later enjoyed friendships with her fellow Welsh poets Vernon Watkins [1906–1967] and Dylan Thomas [1914–1953]. As well as being in the Blitz, she had seen the Reichstag burn.'

Cecily Mackworth, probably more than any other woman writer of these decades, lived a life that illustrates perfectly the trajectory of the professional writer: married but restless, endlessly travelling, and always committed to some cause or project. She was, as Bowker explains, always living a double life: 'Cecily Mackworth to her artistic friends, the Marquise to her aristocratic ones' because she had married a French marquis, and acquired the title of Marquise de Chabannes la Palice.

Sadly, so many of the women writers of this time are listed in the volumes dealing with forgotten writers, as in Christopher Fowler's *The Book of Forgotten Authors* (2017), which lists twenty-five women in his main categories, but one may take comfort from the fact that among these are Georgette Heyer, Gladys Mitchell and Barbara Pym (1913–1980), who have all been in print again after that compilation. One looks for reasons for the oblivion, and Fowler has a category of 'forgotten for writing too little or too much.' The 1930s has two fascinating instances of this: death prevented the talented Dorothy Edwards from writing more than her two books, and as for fecundity, the interwar years has plenty of examples, an outstanding one being Naomi Jacob, who has fifty-three titles listed in reference works. However, her name and works still remain, thanks to Kindle.

In choosing to write about two decades in which writing first of all found delight in experiment, in startling difference, thrived on novelty, and then turned around to the domination of social criticism and documentary, I have switched from fantasy to fact. But if I had to choose a writer whose work opened up the heart of the first decade in terms of women's lives, it would be Raymond Chandler (1888–1959), because in creating Philip Marlowe and a host of women characters, he examined the gentlemanly code of behaviour and attitudes, as well as showing powerfully the absence of that code. If I had to select one writer from the 1930s who showed the way for women and creativity, it has to be Dorothy Parker. She proved that nothing stands in the way of sheer determination when there is ample talent to back it up.

Lastly, if I had to choose two works that show both sides of the coin on women and their lives, then the negative would be in Joseph Moncur March's tour de force, *The Wild Party*, and in opposition, showing women as they were in the new, emerging forms of femininity, perhaps Stevie Smith would be the choice, as she turned away from nothing in life or death.

Appendix I

Other Women Writers of the Period

There is insufficient space to name all of the well-known female authors of the late nineteenth and early twentieth centuries, but some of the most successful ones are referenced below.

Valentine Ackland (20 May 1906 – 9 November 1969)
Mary Kathleen Macrory Ackland was born in London. Known as 'Molly' to her family and friends, Ackland was brought up in Norfolk and attended a convent school there. She married Richard Turpin (1903–1979) in 1924 but their marriage was subsequently annulled. She later changed her name to Valentine Ackland. She met writer Sylvia Townsend Warner in 1930 with whom she would have a lifelong relationship. Ackland was a member of the Communist Party.

Joan Aiken (4 September 1924 – 4 January 2004)
Joan Delano Aiken was born in Rye Sussex. Her father, Conrad Aiken (1889–1973), and her sister, Jane Aiken Hodge, were also writers. Aiken was home educated by her mother until she was 12 and she subsequently attended Wychwood School for Girls. She started writing as a teenager. She married Ronald George Brown (*d.*1955) in 1945 but he sadly died in 1955. Aiken's second marriage was to American painter Julius Goldstein (*d.*2001) in 1976. She is known for her supernatural fiction books.

Djuna Barnes (12 June 1892 – 18 June 1982)
Barnes was born in New York, United States. She spent the majority of her childhood caring for her siblings. She was home educated, and later attended the Pratt Institute and the Art Students League of New York.

Janet Begbie (1897–1953)

Janet Muriel Begbie was born in London. She also used the penname Elizabeth Croly. Her father was writer Harold Begbie (1871–1929) who encouraged her to pursue writing. Begbie married her music teacher in 1926.

Phyllis E. Bentley (19 November 1894 – 27 June 1977)

Phyllis Eleanor Bentley was born in Halifax, West Yorkshire. Her family was wealthy. She knew the Calderdale textile industry very well; her father was a mill owner. Bentley attended Halifax High School for Girls and later Cheltenham Ladies' College. During the Second World War, she worked in the munitions industry. At the end of the war, she returned to Halifax where she taught English and Latin. She concentrated on writing the regional novel, and *Inheritance* (1932) was part of a successful series, eventually televised. She took a serious view of the novel and perhaps would not approve of responses to her work that saw her genre as 'sagas'.

Pearl Binder (28 June 1904 – 25 January 1990)

Binder was born in Salford, Greater Manchester. Known as 'Polly' to her family and friends. She married barrister and Labour politician Frederick Elwyn Elwyn-Jones – commonly known as Elwyn Jones – (1909–1989) in 1937 and they had three children.

Elizabeth Bowen (7 June 1899 – 22 February 1973)

Elizabth Dorothea Cole Bowen was born in Dublin, Ireland. Her family was very wealthy. Her father suffered from mental health issues and in 1907 Bowen and her mother moved to England. Sadly, her mother died in 1912 and she went to live with her aunts. Bowen was educated at Downes House School. She associated with members of the Bloomsbury Group and fellow writer Rose Macaulay helped her find a publisher for her first book. She married Alan Cameron in 1923. During the Second World War, Bowen worked for the Ministry of Information reporting on the issue of Irish neutrality.

Mary Braddon (4 October 1835 – 4 February 1915)

Mary Elizabeth Braddon was born in London. Her parents separated when she was a young child. She was home educated and worked briefly as an actor. She met already married John Maxwell (1824–1895), they began a relationship and moved in together. He was a publisher of periodicals. Maxwell's wife died in 1874 and he and Braddon were able to marry. Braddon became stepmother to his children and they had six children of their own together. One of their sons, William Babington Maxwell (1866–1938), was also a writer.

Vera Brittain (29 December 1893 – 29 March 1970)

Vera Mary Brittain was born in Newcastle-under-Lyme, Staffordshire. She lived a comfortable life and attended Somerville College, University of Oxford where she studied English literature. She delayed her degree at the start of the First World War in 1914 to become a nurse with the Voluntary Aid Detachment. Her brother, Edward (1895–1918), and her fiancé, Roland Leighton (1895–1915), were killed during the war. She found it difficult to return to 'normal' life post-First World War. Brittain married Sir George Caitlin (1896–1979) in 1925. A number of her novels were published throughout her successful writing career.

Frances M. Brookfield/Mrs Charles Brookfield (*c.*1858–1926)

Frances Mary Grogan was an actor and writer; best known for her book *The Cambridge Apostles*. She married writer Charles Brookfield (1857–1913). When acting she adopted the stage name Ruth Francis but used the penname Mrs Charles Frances for her book. She used her own name Frances M. Brookfield for her book *My Lord of Essex*.

Eleanor Alice Burford/Philippa Carr/Victoria Holt/Jean Plaidy etc. (1 September 1906 – 18 January 1993)

Burford was an exceptionally prolific writer. She wrote under a number of pennames, principally Jean Plaidy, Philippa Carr and Victoria Holt. Most of her work was in historical fiction, and she sold around 1 million copies of her books. She started in 1945 and wrote thrillers, mysteries and crime fiction. Burford had written nine unpublished novels in the 1930s while doing well in the expanding short story market. She was always best known for her works featuring the Tudor period, notably her series of novels on King Henry VIII (1491–1547), which began publication in 1949.

Carine Cadby (1864–1957)

Katherine Mary Simpson Stevenson was born in Brighton, East Sussex. She was a successful photographer. She married fellow photographer William Arthur Cadby (1866–1937) in 1894 and adopted the penname Carine Cadby.

Charlotte Cameron (*c.*1872 – 9 December 1946)

Cameron was born in Rhodes Island, United States. Her father was a captain in the Royal Navy and her mother a Suffragette. She was well travelled, visiting Australia as young adult. She was married twice but both marriages ended in divorced – firstly to Major Donald Cameron and secondly to Auguste Ernest George Jacquemard de Landresse.

Dorothy Carrington (6 June 1910 – 26 January 2002)

Frederica Dorothy Violet Carrington was born in Perrotts Brook, Gloucestershire. Her family was wealthy and she had a comfortable upbringing. Sadly, both her parents died before she was 11. She studied at Lady Margaret Hall, University of Oxford, and later married Franz von Waldschultz. She became a noted expert on the history and culture of Corsica.

Barbara Cartland (9 July 1901 – 21 May 2000)

Although Cartland is known as the quintessential romantic novelist of the age when romance meant gentlemanly behaviour, high style and fulfilling marriage, she started out as a writer of thrillers; her first book, *Jigsaw* (1923), was in that genre. She also wrote plays, with a certain success with *Blood Money* (1926), which was deemed to be immoral by the Lord Chamberlain and banned. Arguably, her media image has become bigger than the books, but whatever the establishment thinks of her literary achievement, the statistics of her publication are staggering: 723 novels published and 750 million books sold.

Mrs Ellis H. Chadwick (1882–1928)

Real name Esther Alice Chadwick, she wrote under the penname Mrs Ellis H. Chadwick. She is known for her book, *Mrs Gaskell: Haunts, Homes and Stories.*

Agatha Christie (15 September 1890 – 12 January 1976)

Agatha Mary Clarrissa Miller was born into a wealthy upper-middle class family in Torquay, Devon. Christie also used the penname Mary Westmacott. She married Archibald 'Archie' Christie (1889–1962) on 24 December 1914 and their only child, Rosalind Margaret Clarissa Christie (1919–2004), was born on 5 August 1919. Christie 'disappeared' in August 1926 when her husband asked for a divorce following his affair. She was found ten days later. In February 1930, Christie met her future husband, Sir Max Mallowan (1904–1978); they married in September of that year. Christie is known for writing sixty-six crime novels and short stories – with her famous detective characters, Hercule Poirot and Miss Marple – and she also wrote the play *The Mousetrap* (1952).

Colette (28 January 1873 – 3 August 1954)

Sidonie-Gabrielle Colette was born in Saint-Sauveur-en-Puisaye, France. Her family was wealthy but they made some poor financial decisions and their fortune dwindled. She attended school until the age of 17. She married writer Henry 'Willy' Gauthier-Villars (1859–1931). They separated in 1906 but their divorce was not completed until 1910. Colette did not have access to the earrings from her books as the copyright belonged to Gauthier-Villars. Therefore, she pursued her stage career. Her second marriage was to journalist Henry de Jouvenel (1876–1935) in 1912.

Lettice Cooper (3 September 1897 – 24 July 1994)

Lettice Ulpha Cooper was born in Eccles, Lancashire. She studied at Lady Margaret Hall, University of Oxford. During the Second World War, she worked for the Ministry of Food. After the war, she was a fiction reviewer for the *Yorkshire Post*.

Marie Corelli (1 May 1855 – 21 April 1924)

Mary Mills was born in London. Her mother, Mary Elizabeth Mills, was a servant of Scottish poet Dr Charles Mackay (1814–1889) who was Corelli's father. He was married to another woman at the time of Corelli's birth. His wife died shortly thereafter and he married Corelli's mother; Corelli then took the surname Mackay. She was embarrassed by her illegitimacy and adopted the penname Marie Corelli.

Alba de Céspedes (11 March 1911 – 14 November 1997)
Alba de Céspedes y Bertini was a Cuban-Italian born in Rome, Italy. Her father was the Cuban ambassador to Italy and her mother was Italian. She worked as a journalist during the 1930s and was imprisoned in 1935 for her anti-fascist views. She was imprisoned again in 1943 for her assistance with resistance radio broadcasts. Following the end of the Second World War, de Céspedes resided in Paris, France.

Nancy Cunard (10 March 1896 – 16 March 1965)
Nancy Clara Cunard was born in London into a wealthy upper-class family. Her father was heir to the Cunard Line shipping company. She was brought up on the family estate in Leicestershire. Cunard married army officer and cricketer Sydney Fairbairn (1892–1943) in 1916. They lived in London and separated in 1919 but did not divorce until 1925. She moved to France in the early 1920s. Cunard had a brief relationship with writer Aldous Huxley and later a relationship with Peter Broughton-Adderley (*d.*1918) who was sadly killed during the First World War. She was a political activist who dedicated much of her time to eradicating fascism and racism.

Ethel M. Dell (2 August 1881 – 17 September 1939)
Ethel May Dell was born in London into a middle-class family. She started to write at a young age and her works were published in various magazines. She married Lieutenant Colonel Gerald Tahourdin Savage in 1922. She was a very private person and never gave any media interviews.

Daphne du Maurier (13 May 1907 – 19 April 1989)
Born in London into a family of actors. She married Lieutenant Colonel Frederick Arthur Browning (1896–1965) who was a senior officer in the British Army. Her book *Rebecca* was adapted into a play and film.

Dorothy Edwards (18 August 1903 – 5 January 1934)
Born in Ogmore Vale, Glamorgan. She won a scholarship to attend Howell's School for Girls in Llandaff and later attended the University College of South Wales. She was a socialist. Edwards had a very good singing voice and

she had hoped to become an opera singer. Tragically, she committed suicide by throwing herself under a train.

Annabel Farjeon (19 March 1919 – 8 February 2004)
Eve Annabel Farjeon was born in Bucklebury, Berkshire. Her father, Herbert 'Bertie' Farjeon (1887–1945), was a theatre critic and her mother, Joan Farjeon, was an artist. Her uncle, Joseph Jefferson Farjeon (1883–1955), was also a successful crime writer and her aunt, Eleanor Farjeon, was an established writer. She had comfortable upbring and trained as a ballerina.

Eleanor Farjeon (13 February 1881 – 5 June 1965)
Born in London into a well-establish literary family. She was known as 'Nellie' to her family and friends. She suffered from poor eye sight and ill-health throughout her childhood. After the First World War, Farjeon became a journalist but her work was often published under a pseudonym.

Florence Farmborough (15 April 1887 – 18 August 1978)
Farmborough was born in Aylesbury, Buckinghamshire. She found work as a governess for a family in Kyiv (then part of Russia) and a couple of years later she moved to Moscow where she worked as an English tutor. During the First World War, Farmborough worked as a nurse with the Red Cross. She also worked as a reporter for BBC radio and for *The Times* as well as lecturing at university. Farmborough was in Spain during the Spanish Civil War; returning to England during the Second World War, where she worked for the Women's Voluntary Service.

Edna Ferber (15 August 1885 – 16 April 1968)
Born in Michigan, United States but she moved to Iowa as a young child and then to Wisconsin as a teenager. She was Jewish. She briefly studied at Lawrence University. After graduating from university, Ferber went to work as a reporter for the *Appleton Daily Crescent* and then at the *Milwaukee Journal*. She was known for being out spoken.

Rosita Forbes (16 January 1890 – 30 June 1967)

Joan Rosita Torr was born in Lincoln. Her father, Herbert James Torr (1864–1935), was a landowner and a justice of the peace. Her grandfather, John Torr (1813–1880), was the Conservative member of Parliament for Liverpool from 1873 until his death in 1880. She had a comfortable upbringing. She married Colonel Robert Foster Forbes in 1911 but they divorced in 1917. Her second marriage was to Colonel Arthur Thomas McGrath (*d.*1962) in 1921 but he sadly died in 1962. Forbes was well travelled and often wrote about this.

Pamela Frankau (3 January 1908 – 8 June 1967)

Pamela Sydney Frankau was born in London. Her father abandoned the family when she was a teenager and she was sent to boarding school, Burgess Hill Girls' School. She became a successful writer at a young age when her first book *Marriage of Harlequin* was published in 1927. During the Second World War, she served with the Auxiliary Territorial Service.

Stella Gibbons (5 January 1902 – 19 December 1989)

Stella Dorothea Gibbons was born in London, and had a chaotic childhood. She was home educated by a governess until a teenager when she attended school in London. Gibbons furthered her studies at University College London. Her first job was with British United Press. She subsequently went to work as a secretary for the editor of *The Evening Standard*. Gibbons married Allen Webb in 1933. In fiction, her notable success was *Cold Comfort Farm*, which is an established humorous classic, poking fun at the rural novels of Mary Webb, which had enjoyed great success. But she also wrote poetry, and her first work was a poetry collection: *The Mountain Beast* (1930).

Charlotte Perkins Gilman (3 July 1860 – 17 August 1935)

Charlotte Perkins was born in Connecticut, United States. Her family was not wealthy and she had a difficult childhood. She attended several different schools. Gilman married Charles Walter Stetson (1858–1911) in 1884 but they divorced ten years later. Her second marriage was to Houghton Gilman in 1890. Gilman was heavily involved in social reform movements. She is also known by her first married name Charlotte Perkins Stetson.

Susan Glaspell (1 July 1879 – July 1948)

Susan Keating Glaspell was born in Iowa, United States. She had a comfortable but conservative upbringing, and attended local schools. By the age of 18, she already had a job as a journalist for a local newspaper. Glaspell later studied at Drake University. She married George Cram Cook (1873–1924) in 1913 with whom she founded the Provincetown Players – a group of writers, artists etc. (similar to the Bloomsbury Group).

Emma Goldman (27 June 1869 – 14 May 1940)

Goldman was born in Kovno (now part of Lithuania, formerly part of the Russian Empire). She emigrated to the United States in 1885 where she became heavily involved with women's rights. She married Jacob Kershner (1814–1906) in 1887 but they divorced the following year. Her second marriage was to James Colton (1860–1936) in 1925. Goldman was deported to Russia in 1919 following a prison sentence for inciting rioting. She later lived in Canada, England and France.

Elizabeth Goudge (1900–1984)

Goudge's first book, in 1919, did not sell well, but by 1945 she was a Fellow of the Royal Society of Literature, and in 1960 she was a founding member of the romantic Novelists' Association, and her novel, *The Little White Horse* (1946), has been acknowledged by J.K. Rowling (*b.*1965) as an influence on her Harry Potter books. Goudge won awards, such as the Carnegie Medal, and her writing career made the popular press, notably in a plagiarism scandal in 1993, but most of her life was steadily creative and productive, working in several categories: adult fiction, children's fiction and non-fiction mainly. For much of her life, Goudge nursed her seriously ill mother, and through the Second World War air raids, there was more pressure and demands made on Goudge's time. But she kept working on her book, which was to become *Green Dolphin Country* (1944).

Alyse Gregory (19 July 1884 – 27 August 1967)

Born in Connecticut, United States. She was musically talented from a young age; she went to Paris, France to further her musical studies, continuing her musical studies upon her return to the United States. Gregory visited England briefly during the First World War before settling in New York. She worked as a copywriter for an advertising agency for a few years before earning a living as a freelance writer. She married English writer Llewelyn Powys in 1925 and they resided in Dorset. Gregory was well travelled. Powys died in 1939 and Gregory went to stay with his two sisters in Dorset. She later moved to Devon.

Beatrice Grimshaw (3 February 1870 – 30 June 1953)
Beatrice Ethel Grimshaw was born in Dunmurry, Ireland. She studied at college in Belfast, and then in Caen, France and London. She was well travelled and became a publicist for Cunard Line shipping company.

Stella Fitzthomas Hagan (1908–1993)
Born Stella Jackson, she used the penname Stella Fitzthomas Hagan. Her father, Thomas Alfred Jackson (1879–1955), was a communist activist and her mother, Kate Hawkins, a Suffragette. As a young adult she had a relationship with poet Ewart Milne. She only had one book published, *The Green Cravat: A Memorable Novel of Turbulent 18th Century Ireland* (1959). She did, however, write a number of plays that were unfortunately never performed.

Charlotte Haldane (27 April 1894 – 16 March 1969)
Charlotte Franken was born in London. She moved to Antwerp, Belgium when she was a child but returned to England a few years later. Haldane was a Suffragette and became a journalist for *The Express*. In later life, she joined the Communist Party of Great Britain and became the editor of the magazine *Women Today*.

Radclyffe Hall (12 August 1880 – 7 October 1943)
Marguerite Antonia Radclyffe Hall was born in Bournemouth, Dorset. Her family was wealthy and she received a considerable inheritance. Hall was a member of the PEN International – an association of writers. There is no doubt that *The Well of Loneliness* will always be a classic, a truly innovative work.

Cicely Hamilton (15 June 1872 – 6 December 1952)
Born in London. Hamilton was educated in England and Germany. She was a teacher for a brief period before becoming an actor with a touring company. She adopted the stage name Cicely Hamilton. In 1907, together with Bessie Hatton (1867–1964), Hamilton founded the Women Writers' Suffrage League. During the First World War, she was an auxiliary in the British Army. Hamilton was a regular contributor to *Time and Tides* magazine.

Timothy Hanley (1902–1980)
Born Dorothy Enid Thomas Heathcote in Lincolnshire into a wealthy family. She married author James Hanley in 1947 but they already had a son, Liam Powys Hanley (1933–2019). They lived in North Wales. She was a talent artist and also a writer, publishing her books under the penname Timothy Hanley. She was overshadowed by the success of James, but there is no doubt that they were happy together, and wrote without any urgent need to follow trends in writing.

Marie Hartley (29 September 1905 – 10 May 2006)
She was born in Morley, West Yorkshire into a wealthy family of wool merchants. Hartley attended Leeds College of Art and later the Slade School of Fine Art in London. She returned to Yorkshire and resided in Wetherby.

Georgette Heyer (16 August 1902 – 4 July 1974)
Born in London, she spent her childhood in France, returning to Britain shortly after the start of the First World War. Heyer was encouraged to read by her father. She married George Ronald Rougier in 1925. Heyer also used the penname Stella Martin. Heyer began writing in her teens, and became a very popular romantic novelist, with a deep knowledge of the Regency and, in particular, of the language of that period. The novelist Kate Walker (*b.*1950) has noted, in conversation, that Heyer carried her learning lightly but probably knew more about the social history and mores of the late Georgian society than most. She began by writing thrillers, and told stories to divert and amuse her haemophiliac brother; calling her an instinctive writer and a naturally-gifted storyteller would be an accurate compliment.

Inez Holden (21 November 1903 – 30 May 1974)
Beatrice Inez Lisette Holden was born in Wellesbourne, Warwickshire into a wealthy family. She wrote short stories for various newspapers. She never married but had relationships with painter Humphrey Slater (1906–1958) and briefly with George Orwell.

Winifred Holtby (23 June 1898 – 29 September 1935)
Born in Rudston, East Yorkshire. She was educated by a governess at home and attended Queen Margaret's School in Scarborough, North Yorkshire. During the First World War, Holtby joined the Women's Army Auxiliary Corps and was sent to France. After the war, she attended the University of Cambridge where she met fellow writer Vera Brittain and they became friends. She lectured for the League of Nations Union.

E.M. Hull (16 August 1880 – 11 February 1947)
Edith Maud Henderson was born in London. Her father was American and her mother Canadian. They travel a lot throughout her childhood. She married Percy Winstanley Hull in 1899 and they had one child.

Zora Neale Hurston (7 January 1891 – 28 January 1960)
Born in Alabama, United States, Hurston moved to Florida as a young child. She was employed as a maid for a brief period before studying at Morgan College, Morgan State University. She then won a scholarship to attend Barnard College, Columbia University. Hurston married jazz musician Herbert Sheen in 1927 but they divorced in 1931. Her second marriage was to Albert Price in 1939. They separated after only a few months but did not divorce until 1943. Hurston's third marriage was to James Howell Pitts but this marriage also ended after a matter of months.

Naomi Jacob (1 July 1884 – 27 August 1964)
Naomi Eleanor Clare Ellington Jacob was born in Ripon, North Yorkshire. She was educated locally and later trained to be a teacher although she left the teaching profession shortly thereafter to pursue her acting career. She contracted tuberculosis, which impacted her long-term health. In the

1930s, Jacob moved to Lake Garda, Italy. She sometimes used the penname Ellington Gray.

Storm Jameson (8 January 1891 – 30 September 1936)
Margaret Ethel Storm Jameson was born in Whitby, North Yorkshire. Her family were wealthy shipbuilders. She went to school in Scarborough, North Yorkshire before attending the University of Leeds and then King's College London. She was president of PEN International. During the Second World War, the organisation helped refugee writers and their families to flee occupied Europe. Jameson was a socialist who was involved with politics throughout her lifetime. Her autobiography, *Journey from the North*, was reprinted in 2024 by the Pushkin Press, and arguably her work will now be re-read and re-assessed; she tackled profound and serious themes in her novels, and had a European perspective on politics and the ideologies of the left. Her early ventures in writing and editing included a very left-wing engagement with the urgent issues around the growth of fascism and the road to world war.

Pamela Hansford Johnson (29 May 1912 – 18 June 1981)
Born in London, Johnson's father died when she was 11 years old, leaving the family with debts. She attended Clapham County Girls Grammar School. Johnson married journalist Gordon Neil Stewart (1912–1999) in 1936 but they divorced in 1941. Her second marriage was to writer C.P. Snow (1905–1980) in 1941.

Jane Aiken Hodge (4 December 1917 – 17 June 2009)
Hodge was born in Massachusetts, United States. Her father, Conrad Aiken, and her sister, Joan Aiken (1924–2004), were also writers. She moved to England as a young child old and lived in Sussex; her parents separated. She studied at Somerville College, University of Oxford. She married Alan Hodge (1915–1979) in 1948. He had divorced his first wife, Beryl (1915–2003), who subsequently married poet Robert Graves.

Sheila Kaye-Smith (4 February 1887 – 14 January 1956)
Born in St Leonards-on-Sea, East Sussex, Kaye-Smith grew up there apart from a short spell living in London. She married an Anglican clergyman

Theodore Penrose Fry (1892–1971) in 1924 but they both subsequently converted to Catholicism.

Nella Last (4 October 1889 – 22 June 1968)
Nellie Lord was born in Barrow-in-Furness, Cumbria. She married joiner Will Last in 1911. They had two sons. During the Second World War, Last served with the Women's Voluntary Service and the Red Cross.

Rosamond Lehmann (3 February 1901 – 12 March 1990)
Rosamond Nina Lehmann was born in Bourne End, Buckinghamshire into an affluent family. Her brother, John, also became a writer. Lehmann was home educated by a governess but she won a scholarship in 1919 and attended Girton College, University of Cambridge. She met her first husband Leslie Runciman (1900–1989) here and they married in 1923. Their marriage was an unhappy one and they divorced in 1927. Lehmann's second marriage was to Wogan Phillips (1902–1993) in 1928 and they lived in Oxford. It was here that Lehmann became associated with members of the Bloomsbury Group. Lehmann and Phillips divorced in 1944.

Amy Lowell (9 February 1874 – 12 May 1925)
Amy Lawrence Lowell was born in Massachusetts, United States. She attended a local school but she did not attended college as allegedly her family did not consider this appropriate for a female. She was an avid reader and book collector.

Marie Belloc Lowndes (5 August 1868 – 14 November 1947)
Marie Adelaide Elizabeth Raynor Belloc was born in London but raised in France. Her brother, Hilaire, was also a writer. She married Frederick Sawrey A. Lowndes (1868–1940) in 1896. Her book *The Lodger* was adapted into an Alfred Hitchcock film, and later into an opera.

Mina Loy (27 December 1882 – 25 September 1966)
Mina Gertrude Löwy was born in London. Her father was Hungarian and Jewish; her mother was English and a Christian. Loy studied art at St John's Wood School. She went on to study in France and Germany. She married

painter Stephen Haweis (1878–1969) in 1903 although it is understood that she did so under pressure as she was already pregnant and their marriage was not a happy one. Following the marriage, she changed her surname to Loy. She had a difficult labour and sadly her child died shortly after her first birthday.

Lady Lugard (19 December 1852 – 25 January 1929)
Flora Louise Shaw was born in Woolwich into a large but wealthy family. Lugard wrote a number of children's books before writing a novel; she also wrote a number of articles for various newspapers. Marrying Sir Frederick Lugard (1858–1945) in 1902, she became Lady Luguard. During the First World War, she helped to establish the War Refugees' Committee.

Sylvia Lynd (1888 – 21 February 1952)
Sylvia Dryhurst was born in London. Her parents were both from Dublin, Ireland. Lynd studied at the Slade School of Fine Arts and the Royal Academy of Dramatic Art. She married journalist Robert Wilson Lynd (1879–1949) in 1909 and used the penname Sylvia Lynd thereafter.

Rose Macaulay (1 August 1881 – 30 October 1958)
Emilie Rose Macaulay was born in Rugby, Warwickshire. She was educated at Oxford High School for Girls and subsequently attended Somerville College, University of Oxford. She was an active feminist.

Cecily Mackworth (15 August 1911 – 22 July 2006)
Cecily Joan Mackworth was born in Llantilio Pertholey, Monmouthshire. Her aunt, Margaret Mackworth (1883–1958), was editor of *Time and Tide*. Her father died when she was a young child and she moved to Devon. She married Belgian Leon Donckier de Donceel. They had one daughter but de Donceel sadly died only three years after their marriage. Mackworth spent time in Hungary, Germany and later France. After the Second World War, she travelled to Algeria and Palestine. Her second marriage was to Frenchman Marquis de Chabannes La Palice in 1956.

Ethel Mannin (6 October 1990 – 4 December 1984)
Edith Ethel Mannin was born in Lonon. Her father was a socialist and he passed on his left-wing views. She married John Alexander Porteus in 1919,

but they divorced later that year. Mannin's second marriage was to Reginald Reynolds (1905–1958) in 1938. It is alleged that she had affairs with the poet W.B. Yeats and philosopher Bertrand Russell.

Katherine Mansfield (14 October 1888 – 9 January 1923)
Katherine Mansfield Beauchamp was born in Wellington, New Zealand. She attended a local school before attending Wellingtons Girls' School. Mansfield emigrated to England when she was 19, where she attended Queen's College London. Mansfield became friends with Virginia Woolf and D.H. Lawrence. She married John Middleton Murry in 1918.

Beryl Markham (26 October 1902 – 3 August 1986)
Markham was born in Ashwell, East Midlands but she moved to Kenya (then British East Africa) aged 4. Markham married three times but she used her second husband, Mansfield Markham's (1905–1971), surname. She allegedly had an affair with Prince Henry, Duke of Gloucester (1900–1974) and with King Edward VIII – then Prince of Wales (1894–1972). Markham returned to England where she continued her affair with Prince Henry. She later had an affair with aviator Hubert Broad (1897–1975). Markham was also an aviator herself and, in 1936, she made a solo flight across the Atlantic from British to North America.

Dr Caroline Matthews (25 September 1877 – 1927)
Caroline Twigge was born in Liverpool. She was privately educated and later studied medicine in Edinburgh. She married surgeon Joseph Matthews in 1907. Matthews received the King Victor Emmauel's Medal for volunteering medical assistance following the Messina earthquake in 1908. She was a surgeon in the Montenegrin army during 1912 and 1913, and later a war correspondence for *The Sphere*.

Betty McCabe
McCabe was born in Scotland but came to London where worked as a housemaid. She allegedly came to England as she was 'inspired by a speaker who said that we in England could not produce such good film scenarios as the Americans.'

Charlotte Mew (15 November 1869 – 24 March 1928)

Charlotte Mary Mew was born in London and known to her family and friends as 'Lotti'. Her father, Frederick Mew (1833–1898), was an architect and her mother, Anna Maria Marden, was the daughter of architect Henry Edward Kendall Jr (1805–1885) for whom Frederick Mew had worked. Henry Edward Kendall Sr (1776–1875) was also an architect. Mew attended Gower Street School and then University College London. Tragically, Mew committed suicide in 1928.

Edna St Vincent Millay (22 February 1892 – 19 October 1950)

Born in Maine, United States, her parents divorced in 1904. She attended Vassar College in New York. Millay married Eugen Jan Boissevain in 1923 but they both allegedly had affairs throughout their marriage. During the First World War, Millay was an active pacifist although she did advocate for the United States to join the Second World War; she was involved with creating propaganda throughout the war.

Alice Duer Miller (28 July 1874 – 22 August 1942)

Alice Duer was born in Staten Island, New York, United States. Her family were wealthy although they later lost their fortunate due to a banking crisis. She married Henry Wise Miller (1875–1954) in 1899 and they moved to Costa Rica. Miller's husband's investments failed so they returned to New York, where they had to use her income to support the family until he secured a job as a stockbroker.

Gladys Mitchell (21 April 1901 – 27 July 1983)

Gladys Maude Winifred Mitchell was born in Cowley, Oxford. She attended school and furthered her educated at Goldsmiths College, and then University College London. After graduating, she became a teacher. Mitchell was one of the first members of the Detection Club – a group of mystery writers. She also used the male pennames Stephen Hockaby and Malcolm Torrie. Her work has remained in print and is highly rated by crime fiction *aficionados*.

Naomi Mitchison (1 November 1897 – 11 January 1999)
Naomi Mary Margaret Haldane was born in Edinburgh. Her parents held different political views but were both from wealthy families. She attended school in Oxford as well as being educated at home by a governess. She later studied at the University of Oxford where she was involved in science. During the First World War, she became a nurse with the Voluntary Aid Detachment but her service was cut short when she caught scarlet fever. She was a socialist and was a campaigner for women's rights.

Nancy Mitford (28 November 1904 – 30 June 1973)
Nancy Freeman-Mitford was born in London into a wealthy family; she had a privileged upbringing. She married Peter Rodd (1904–1968) in 1933 but they divorced in 1957 after a lengthy separation. After the Second World War, Mitford moved to France.

L.M. Montgomery (30 November 1874 – 24 April 1942)
Lucy Maud Montgomery was born in New London, Canada. Her mother died when she was only 21 months old, her father struggled with grief and she went to live with her grandparents. Montgomery later trained to become a teacher at the Prince of Wales College. She went on to study at Dalhousie University in Halifax, Nova Scotia.

Marianne Moore (15 November 1887 – 5 February 1972)
Marianne Craig Moore was born in Missouri, United States. Her parents had separated before she was born. She was a devoted Presbyterian who studied at Bryn Mawr College. Moore moved to New Jersey in 1916 and then to New York in 1918.

Mary L. Moreland (23 December 1859 – 17 March 1918)
Mary Leona Moreland was born in Massachusetts, United States. She attended local schools and then studied at university in Chicago, Illinois. She later became a pastor.

Edith Nesbit (15 August 1858 – 4 May 1924)
Born in London, Nesbit also lived in Brighton, East Sussex, Halstead, Kent and France as a child. Nesbit married Hubert Bland on 22 April 1860, already pregnant with his child. Their marriage was not always a happy one as it is alleged that Nesbit's husband had a number of affairs and fathered children with other women. She was never involved with the Suffragette movement. Nesbit is famous for her book, *The Railway Children*.

Helen Nicholson
Born in the United States, Nicholson was caught up in the Spanish Civil War in 1936 while visiting her daughter and son-in-law in Granada, Spain. She and her family were supportive of Francisco Franco and the Nationalists.

Kate O'Brien (3 December 1897 – 13 August 1974)
Kathleen Mary Louise O'Brien was born in Limerick, Ireland. She was known as 'Kate' to her family and friends. Her family was middle class and she had a comfortable upbring but her mother sadly died when O'Brien was 5 years old. She attended Laurel Hill Convent and later University College Dublin. Following her graduation, she moved to London where she worked as a teacher for a short period. She was also briefly a governess in Spain. Once she returned to England, she worked as a journalist for *The Manchester Guardian*. She married Dutch journalist Gustaaf Reiner (1892–1962) in 1922 but they divorced shortly thereafter.

Edith Olivier (31 December 1872 – 10 May 1948)
Olivier was born in Wilton, Wiltshire. She was home educated before attending Hugh's College, Oxford. She was only there a short time as she had to leave because of her asthma. She was a distant relative of actor Laurence Olivier (1907–1989). In 1916, Olivier helped to form the Women's Land Army in Wiltshire.

Carlota O'Neill (27 March 1905 – 20 June 2000)
Carlota Alejandra Regina Micaela O'Neill y de Lamo was born in Madrid, Spain. She later moved to Barcelona where she met her husband soldier Virgilio Leret Ruiz (1902–1936). They had two children. Ruiz was

assassination shortly before the start of the Spanish Civil War and O'Neill was later imprisoned for over three years. She later moved to Venezuela and then Mexico.

Bessie Parkes (16 June 1829 – 23 March 1925)
Elizabeth Rayner Parkes was born in Birmingham, West Midlands. She attended a boarding school and had a cultured childhood. She married Louis Belloc (1830–1872) who was the son of writer Louise Swanton Belloc (1796–1881). Their children were writers Hilaire Belloc and Marie Belloc Lowndes. Parkes was an activist for women's rights.

Dorothy Parker (22 August 1893 – 7 June 1967)
Dorothy Rothschild was born in New Jersey, United States. She was known as 'Dot' or 'Dottie' to her family and friends. Parker had a comfortable upbring but her mother died when she was young and her father remarried. She attended a finishing school in New Jersey. Parker married stockbroker Edwin Pond Parker II (1893–1933) in 1917 but they divorced in 1928. Her second marriage was to writer Alan Campbell (1904–1963) in 1934 but their marriage also resulted in divorce in 1947. She later remarried Campbell in 1950.

Ella Pontefract (1896 – 23 February 1943)
Born in Yorkshire into a wealthy family. She attended a girls' grammar school in Dewsbury, West Yorkshire and then a prep school in Harrogate, North Yorkshire. She went on to study at the Slade School of Fine Art.

Beatrix Potter (28 July 1866 – 22 December 1943)
Helen Beatrix Potter was born into a wealthy upper-middle class family in London. She preferred to use her middle name. As a child she had several pets, and this is perhaps what inspired her children's books. Potter was a shrewd entrepreneur and sold her illustrations as merchandise. In 1905, Potter was engaged to her editor Norman Warne (1868–1905), but their engagement only lasted a month as her family objected to their proposed marriage, and he died suddenly. She married solicitor William Hellis (1872–1945) in 1913. Potter was a talented writer and illustrator and her twenty-three 'Tales of' books have sold millions of copies.

Philippa Powys (8 May 1886 – 11 January 1963)
Catherine Edith Philippa Powys was born in Montacute, Somerset. She had no formal education. She came from a literary family; three of her brothers were also writers. Powys spent her early adult life farming. In later life, she moved to the Dorset coast.

Barbara Pym (2 June 1913 – 11 January 1980)
Barbara Mary Crampton Pym was born in Oswestry, Shropshire. She was educated at Queen's Park School and later attended Huyton College, and then St Hilda's College, University of Oxford. During the Second World War, Pym joined the Women's Royal Naval Service. Her work was championed by the poet Philip Larkin, and her novels have been reprinted and reviewed well as her reputation has grown.

Dollie Radford (3 December 1858 – 7 February 1920)
Caroline Maitland was born in England. She used the penname Dollie Radford. She was an acquaintance of Karl Marx (1818–1883). She married poet Ernest Radford (1857–1919) in 1883. They had three children, one of whom was writer Maitland Radford.

Kathleen Jessie Raine (14 June 1908 – 6 July 2003)
Raine was born in Ilford, Essex. Her father was a school teacher. During the First World War, she stayed with her aunt in Northumberland. Raine was educated locally in Essex at County High School before attending Girton College, Cambridge. She married writer Hugh Sykes Davies (1909–1984) in 1930 but they divorced. Her second marriage was to poet and *Daily Mirror* reporter Charles Henry Madge (1912–1996). They had two children together.

Dorothy Una Ratcliffe (20 April 1887 – 20 November 1967)
She was born in Preston, West Sussex. Her father was a Yorkshire man and a barrister; her mother was a Londoner. Ratcliffe attended the local school before attending finishing schools in France and Germany. She married Charles Frederick Radcliffe, nephew and heir of wealthy business tycoon Edward Allen Brotherton (1856–1930), in 1922. They divorced in 1930.

Radcliffe's second marriage was to Noel McGrigor-Phillips in 1932 until 1943 when he died suddenly. Radcliffe's third marriage was to journalist and photographer Alfred Charles Vowles. Following their marriage, Vowles adopted the surname Phillips. Radcliffe sometimes used the penname D.U.R.

Jean Rhys (24 August 1890 – 14 May 1979)
Ella Gwendoline Rees Williams was born in Roseau, Dominica in the Caribbean. She used the penname Jean Rhys. Her early education was in Dominica but in her late teens she moved to England to live with her aunt. She studied at Perse School for Girls in Cambridge and then the Royal Academy of Dramatic Art in London. She was the mistress of wealthy stockbroker Lancelot Grey Hugh Smith (1870–1941). During the First World War, Rhys was a volunteer in a soldiers' canteen. By 1918, she worked in a pension office. She married Dutch journalist Willem Johan Marie Lenglet, known as Jean Lenglet (1889–1961), in 1919. They had two children but one tragically died. They divorced in 1933. Rhys's second marriage was to editor Leslie Tilden-Smith (1885–1945) in 1936 until his death. Rhys's third marriage was to solicitor Max Hamer (*d*.1966) who was Tilden-Smith's cousin. He was later convicted of fraud and served time in prison.

Vita Sackville-West (9 March 1892 – 2 June 1962)
Victoria Mary Sackville-West, known as 'Vita' to her family and friends, was born in Kent. Her parents were cousins; they were an extremely wealthy family and she was brought up at Knole, a country house. She was home educated by a governess but later attended an exclusive school in Mayfair. Sackville-West spent a lot of time in France and was a fluent French speaker. She married Sir Harold Nicolson in 1913.

Dorothy L. Sayers (13 June 1893 – 17 December 1957)
Dorothy Leigh Sayers was born in Oxford. She attended Godolphin School in Sailsbury, Wiltshire and then Somerville College in Oxford. Sayers was gravely ill with measles in her youth, but she recovered. Together with Charis Ursula Barnett (1892–1985) and Amphilis Middlemore (1891–1931), she established the Mutual Admiration Society – a literary association. Sayers married journalist Oswald Arthur Fleming (1881–1950) in 1926. She

achieved a rare status in literature: being highly regarded in both popular writing and in the scholarship around and about literature; she was both a Dante expert and one of the outstanding fiction authors of the 'Golden Age' of crime writing between the wars.

May Sinclair (24 August 1863 – 14 November 1946)
Mary Ameila St Clair was born in Rock Ferry, Cheshire. Her father died when she was a child and the family moved to Iford. She attended Cheltenham Ladies' College and later was a Suffragette. In later life, she sadly suffered from Parkinson's disease. Today, her writing on the Brontës is perhaps better known than her fiction.

Edith Sitwell (7 September 1887 – 9 December 1964)
Edith Louisa Sitwell was born in Scarborough, North Yorkshire. She had an unhappy childhood and a distant relationship with her parents. She later resided with her governess. In adulthood, she resided in France for a brief period. In 1955, Sitwell converted to Catholicism and asked writer Evelyn Waugh to be her godfather.

Nora K. Smith (5 February 1889 – 1961)
Smith was born in Sheffield, South Yorkshire. Her father, Reverend Frederick Robert Smith, was a vicar in Burnley, Lancashire where Smith grew up but he was also a successful writer himself writing under the penname John Ackworth. She had a comfortable upbringing. Smith trained as a teacher and was the assistant headmistress at the Red Lion School before becoming headmistress at Patricroft Council School in Manchester.

Stevie Smith (20 September 1902 – 7 March 1971)
Florence Maragret Smith, known as 'Peggy' to her family and friends, was born in Kingston-upon-Hull, East Yorkshire. She acquired the name 'Stevie' as a young woman when a friend commented that when riding a horse she looked like jockey Steve Donoghue (1884–1945). Her father was a shipping agent and often away at sea. She moved to London with her mother and sister as a young child and resided there for the rest of her life. Her mother died when she was 5 years old and she and her sister went to live with their

aunt. Smith spent three years of her childhood in hospital after contracting tuberculosis. She attended Palmers Green High School and North London Collegiate School for Girls. As a young adult she worked as a secretary for Sir Neville Pearson (1898–1982) who was a publisher at Newes Publishing Company. In later life, she often gave poetry readings on the BBC.

Gertrude Stein (3 February 1874 – 27 July 1946)
Stein was born in Pennsylvania, United States into an upper-middle class family but they moved to Vienna, Austria and then Paris, France before returning to the United States and settling in California when she was a child. She was Jewish and could speak both English and German. She attended Ratcliffe College and later John Hopkins School of Medicine but she left before qualifying as a doctor. Stein moved to Paris, France in 1903 where she remained for the rest of her life. Her reputation has grown relentlessly, and the volume of critical interest in print continues to expand also.

G.B. Stern (17 June 1890 – 20 September 1973)
Gladys Bertha Stern (also known as Gladys Bronwyn Stern) was born in London. Her family was wealthy but they lost their fortune during the Vaal River diamond crash. She was educated in England until her late teens when her family travelled to Europe and she studied in Germany and Switzerland. She married Geoffrey Lisle Holdsworth (1894–1955) in 1919 but they divorced shortly thereafter. Her family were Jewish but she later converted to Catholicism.

Mabel St Clair Stobart (3 February 1862 – 7 December 1954)
Mabel Annie Boulton was born in Woolwich. Her family was wealthy and she had a comfortable upbringing. She was a keen sportsperson. She married St Clair Kelburn Mulholland (1861–1908) in 1884. He died at sea in 1908 and her second marriage was to John Herbert Greenhalgh (1854–1928) in 1911. St Clair Stobart was involved in the Suffragette movement.

Marie Stopes (15 October 1880 – 2 October 1958)
Marie Charlotte Carmichael Stopes was born in Edinburgh but she moved to London as a young child. She was home schooled but then attended St

George's School for Girls in Edinburgh and later North London Collegiate School. She then studied at University College London and Birkbeck College, University of London.

Angela Thirkell (30 January 1890 – 29 January 1961)
Angela Margaret Mackail was born in London. She was a distant relative of Rudyard Kipling and Prime Minister Stanley Baldwin. Her brother, Denis Mackail (1892–1971), was also a writer and her godfather was J.M. Barrie. She was educated at school in London and then attended a finishing school in Paris, France. She married singer James Campbell McInnes (1874–1945) in 1911. They divorced and her second marriage was to George Lancelot Allnut Thirkell (1890–*c.*1940) in 1918.

Flora Thompson (5 December 1876 – 21 May 1947)
Flora Jane Timms was born in Oxfordshire. As a young child she attended a parish school. In 1903, she married Post Office clerk John William Thompson and they moved to Bournemouth, Dorset. They had three children.

Alice B. Toklas (30 April 1877 – 7 March 1967)
Alice Babette Toklas was born in San Francisco, United States into a middle class family. She moved to Seattle as a teenager. She was educated at a local school and then attended the University of Washington. After graduating from university, she returned to San Francisco; she was in the city during the earthquake of 1906. She subsequently moved to Paris, France. Toklas became the partner of writer Gertrude Stein.

Mrs Alec Tweedie (1 January 1862 – 15 April 1940)
Ethel Brilliana Tweedie was born in London. Her family was wealthy and she had a privileged upbringing. In 1887, she married an insurance broker Alexander Leslie Tweedie. She used the pennames Mrs Alex Tweedie and Ethel B. Harley.

Katherine Tynan (23 January 1859 – 2 April 1931)
Tynan was born in Dublin, Ireland. She was educated at a convent school. She married writer and barrister Henry Albert Hinkson and moved to England. Tynan sometimes used the penname Katherine Tynan Hinkson.

Mrs George de Horne Vaizey (1857 – 23 January 1917)
Jessie Bell was born in Liverpool. She married cotton broker Henry Mansergh in 1883 but they later divorced and her second marriage was to George de Horne Vaizey in 1898. She wrote under her married name, Mrs George de Horne Vaizey. Their son, George, was also a writer.

Hilda Vaughan (12 June 1892 – 4 November 1985)
Hilda Campbell Vaughan was born in Builth Wells, Powys. She had a comfortable upbringing and was home educated. During the First World War she was in the Women's Land Army and worked with the Red Cross. She married fellow writer Charles Landbridge Morgan (1894–1958) in 1923 and they had two children.

Mrs Humphry Ward (11 June 1851 – 24 March 1920)
Mary Augusta Arnold was born in Tasmania, Australia. She had a pleasant upbringing and attended various boarding schools before returning to England as a young child. She married tutor Humphry Ward (1845–1926) in 1872 and adopted the name of Mrs Humphry Ward for her books.

Beatrice Webb (22 January 1858 – 30 April 1943)
Martha Beatrice Potter was born in Standish, Gloucestershire. She preferred to use her middle name. She was self-educated. Sadly, both of her sisters died as young adults – one committed suicide and the other died from an overdose. She married Sidney Webb (1859–1947) in 1892. She was a social reformer and campaigner for women's rights. Webb was also a founder of the London School of Economics.

Mary Webb (25 March 1881 – 8 October 1927)
Mary Gladys Meredith was born in Shropshire. Her father was a private school teacher and this is probably where Webb's love of literature stemmed from. She attended a finishing school in Southport, Merseyside. She suffered from ill health throughout her life. Webb married Bertram Law Webb (1885–1939) in 1912 and they lived briefly in Weston-super-Mare, North Somerset before returning to Shropshire. They later bought a second home in London.

Rebecca West (21 December 1892 – 15 March 1983)
Cicily Isabel Fairfield was born in London. Her father, a journalist, often discussed current affairs and politics with the family. She was an active Suffragette. West had a brief affair with author H.G. Wells and they had a son together. She married Henry Maxwell Andrews in 1938.

Anna Wickham (1883 – 1 May 1947)
Real name Edith Alice Mary Harper; she was born in London but brought up in Brisbane and Sydney, Australia. She returned to London in 1904 where she obtained a scholarship for drama. She went on to pursue a singing career in Paris, France. Wickham married solicitor Patrick Hepburn in 1906 and they had four sons. She sometimes used the penname John Oland.

Amabel Williams-Ellis (10 May 1894 – 27 August 1984)
Amabel Nassau Strachey was born in Newlands Corner, Surrey. Her father was a journalist and owner of a newspaper; her cousin was writer Lytton Strachey. She had a pleasant childhood. During the First World War, she served as a nurse with the Voluntary Aid Detachment. She married architect Sir Clough Williams-Ellis in 1915 and they had three children. Williams-Ellis was literary editor of *The Spectator* during the early 1920s.

Romer Wilson (26 December 1891 – 1930)
Florence Wilson was born in Sheffield, South Yorkshire. She used the penname Romer Wilson. She was educated at West Heath School and then Girton College, University of Cambridge – which was the first female college in Britain. During the First World War, Wilson sold potatoes for the Board of Agriculture and Fisheries. She married writer Edward Joseph Harrington O'Brien (1890–1941) in 1923.

Virginia Woolf (25 January 1882 – 28 March 1941)
Adeline Virginia Stephen was born in London into a wealthy family. She preferred to use her middle name. As a child she was home educated but later attended King's College London. She married Leonard Woolf (1880–1969) in 1912, and the couple went on to establish Hogarth Press.

Gamel Woolsey (28 May 1895 – 18 January 1968)
Elizabeth Gammell Woolsey was born in South Carolina, United States. She attended a local school. Woolsey moved to New York in 1921. She married journalist and writer Rex Hunter (1889–1960) in 1923 but later allegedly had an affair with writer Llewelyn Powys (1884–1939). Her books were published posthumously.

I.A.R. Wylie (16 March 1885 – 4 November 1959)
Ida Alexa Ross Wylie was born in Melbourne, Australia but brought up in England. Her family were not wealthy and moved often. She was involved in the Suffragette movement while in England but eventually moved to Hollywood in the United States where she sold her novels. Many of her books were made into films.

Charlotte Yonge (11 August 1823 – 24 March 1901)
Charlotte Mary Yonge was born in Otterborne, Hampshire. She was home educated by her father and was fluent in French and Latin. Her family was very religious. She lived in Hampshire her whole life and taught at the local Sunday school. Yonge was the founder and editor of the magazine *The Monthly Packet*.

Note: although many female authors who influenced literature throughout the late nineteenth and early twentieth centuries are referenced throughout this book, there were many who weren't mentioned, and many who came before and after who have written some of the most famous books – covering many different genres, which are still in print today. Some of these well-known authors are listed below – unfortunately, it wasn't possible to name them all.

Louisa May Alcott (1832–1888)
Aphra Behn (1640–1689)
Enid Blyton (1897–1968)
Gwendolyn Brooks (1917–2000)
Frances Hodgson Burnett (1849–1924)
Mary Butts (1890–1937)
Rachel Carson (1907–1964)

Kate Chopin (1850–1904)
Catherine Cookson/Catherine Marchant (1906–1998)
Emily Dickinson (1830–1886)
O. Douglas (1877–1948)
Susan Ertz (1894–1985)
Betty Friedan (1921–2006)
Patricia Highsmith (1921–1995)
Margaret Kennedy (1896–1967)
Judith Kerr (1923–2019)
Harper Lee (1926–2016)
Doris Lessing (1919–2013)
Margaret Mitchell (1900–1949)
Hannah More (1745–1833)
Mary Norton (1903–1992)
Emmuska Orczy (1865–1947)
E. Arnot Robertson (1903–1961)
Mary Shelley (1797–1851)
Muriel Spark (1918–2006)
Harriet Beecher Stowe (1811–1896)
Jan Struther (1901–1953)
Edith Wharton (1862–1937)
Dorothy Whipple (1893–1966)
Antonia White (1899–1980)
Dorothy Wordsworth (1771–1855)
E.H. Young (1880–1949)

Appendix II

The Bloomsbury Group

The Bloomsbury Group or Bloomsbury Set as they were sometimes known was a group of intellectuals, mainly wealthy upper-class writers, artists and philosophers. Members of the group included the well-known E.M. Forster, Duncan Grant, John Maynard Keynes and Lytton Strachey. Female members included Virginia Woolf and her sister Vanessa Bell (both née Stephen). Several members of the Stephen family, including brothers Adrian and Thoby, belonged to the group. Virginia Woolf's husband, Leonard, was also a member.

The Bloomsbury Group deeply influenced literature of the time. They were well known for their modern approaches towards and views on feminism, sexuality and pacifism. Most of the members were closely associated with the University of Cambridge and King's College London, and a lot of them lived in the Bloomsbury area of London; hence their name. Members of the group supported and promoted the work of other members.

Perhaps of most significance is that this group of people were friends before their works became famous. This begs the question: how did such a small group of people have just a considerable influence on British literature in the early nineteenth century? It must be recognised, however, that many male and female writers were successful and famous without having been a member of the Bloomsbury Group.

During the 1930s, the Bloomsbury Group's influence on literary affairs started to dwindle and following the deaths of key members of the group, such as Virgina Woolf and Lytton Strachey the group no longer existed.

There is no doubt that all kinds of divisions are easily perceived when one considers the attitudes to literature evident both in their writings *per se* and in the theorising and dissemination of the aesthetics behind their works. Anyone who has had to study T.S. Eliot's poem *The Waste Land* for a literature course will know that notes and clarifications are needed in order to 'decode' and understand this complex work. The poem includes extracts and quotes in French, German, Greek and Sanskrit, and also has extensive reference to a wide European culture, religious narratives and texts from philosophy and theology. The basic question of readership is often used to criticise this attitude to writing: what readership did Eliot have in mind? The fact that the poem was first published in a periodical with a small readership says a great deal about the concept of literature behind Eliot's thinking.

However, critiques of such attitudes to writing have not always been fair. The extreme alternative view of writing is perhaps summed up in a remark by novelist Mickey Spillane (1918–2006) contrasting authors and writers: 'the difference is that writers get paid.'

Appendix III

Women Writers and Changes to the Law

A summary of legislation that had an impact on women's lives is always useful when reading the women's literature of the interwar years. The obvious basic landmarks are the 1918 and 1928 Acts establishing women's suffrage. The latter date is the momentous establishment of the vote without any property qualification. That proviso had been a bugbear for all campaigners and reformers for a very long time, reaching back to the fundamental issue of owned land and voting rights at the basis of the campaigns of the Chartist years of the 1830s.

Of course, the 1919 Act was the real turning point regarding how women were seen as citizens and as independent minds and intellects; they were, after that legislation, as Virginia Nicholson (*b.*1955) put it in her book, *Singled Out* (2007), 'For every disappointed spinster gnawed at by poverty and blighted hopes, there was another who looked into the future full of bright possibilities – for personal satisfaction, for social value, for the betterment of her world.'

This is a checklist of the legislation for quick reference.

England and Wales Acts of Parliament

There was various legislation passed in England and Wales that affected women and women writers throughout the late nineteenth and early twentieth centuries.

Education Act 1944

This legislation established proper secondary school education. It provided access to secondary schools for girls and the working class. The term 'elementary school' was abolished.

Elementary Education Act 1870

This law established the framework for children aged 5 to 12 to gain access to a school education but this was neither compulsory or free so it did little to help girls or the working class.

Married Woman's Property Act 1882

This law established a married woman's right to buy, own and sell her own property.

Prisoners' (Temporary Discharge for Ill-Health) Act 1913

'Cat and Mouse Act'

This legislation was passed following hunger strikes by Suffragette prisoners. It enabled prisoners who had been on hunger strike to be released from prison for a period of time until their health recovered at which point they would be re-arrested and returned to prison to serve their sentence.

Sex Disqualification (Removal) Act 1919

This law stated that a person should not be disqualified from certain exercises because of their sex or marriage.

> A person shall not be disqualified by sex or marriage from the exercise of any public function, or from being appointed to or holding any civil or judicial office or post, or from entering or assuming or carrying on any civil profession or vacation, or for any admission to any incorporated society (whether incorporated by Royal Charter or otherwise), and a person shall not be exempt by sex or marriage from the liability to serve as a juror.
>
> British Government
> (https://www.gov.uk/government/news/the-sex-disqualification-removal-act-1919)

The Representation of the People Act 1918

This legislation transformed the English and Welsh voting system. It enable men aged 21 and over and women aged 30 and over, who met specific minimum property qualifications the right to vote. The act discriminated against women only giving them the right to vote aged 30 not 21 as following the significant loss of males during the First World War there would have been more females eligible to vote than males.

The Representation of the People (Equal Franchise) Act 1928

This legislation followed on from The Representation of the People Act 1918. It gave women the right to vote at the age of 21 regardless of their property qualifications.

United States Acts

There was also new legislation passed in the United States in the early twentieth century.

The National Prohibition Act 1919

'The Volstead Act'

This act established the prohibition of alcoholic drinks in the USA.

Bibliography

Note: date of first publication in given in the first brackets.

Books Cited

Abse, Dannie, *Goodbye, Twentieth Century* (2001) (Parthian, Cardigan, 2011)
Agate, James, *A Shorter Ego* (Harrap, London, 1947)
Belloc Lowndes, Marie, *The Lodger* (Methuen, London, 1913)
Belloc Lowndes, Marie, *The Philosophy of the Marquise* (Publisher unknown, United Kingdom, 1899)
Begbie, Janet, *Morning Mist* (Mills & Boon, London, 1916)
Bennett, Arnold, *Anna of the Five Towns* (Chatto & Windus, London, 1902)
Bentley, Phyllis E., *Carr* (Ernest Benn, London, 1929)
Bentley, Phyllis E., *Inheritance* (Victor Gollancz, London, 1932)
Bentley, Phyllis E., *O Dreams, Oh Destinations* (Victor Gollancz, London, 1962)
Bentley, Phyllis E., *The Spinner of the Years* (Fisher Unwin, London, 1928)
Bentley, Phyllis E., *The World's Bane* (Fisher Unwin, London, 1918)
Betjeman, John, *The Best of Betjeman* (John Murray, United Kingdom, 1978)
Blyth, Ronald, *Akenfield* (Penguin, London, 1969)
Bowen, Elizabeth, *The Death of the Heart* (1938) (Penguin, London, 1981)
Brett, R.L. and Jones, A.R., *Lyrical Ballads* (Routledge, London, 1971)
Brewer, E. Cobham, *Brewer's Dictionary of Phrase and Fable* (Cassell, Petter & Galpin, United Kingdom, 1870)
Brittain, Vera, *Testament of Friendship* (1940) (Virago, London, 1981)
Broad, Leah, *Quartet: How Four Women Challenged the Musical World* (Faber & Faber, London, 2023)
Brontë, Anne (Bell, Acton), *Agnes Grey*, (Thomas Cautley Newby, London, 1847)
Brontë, Charlotte (Bell, Currer), *Jane Eyre* (Smith, Elder & Co., London, 1847)
Brontë, Emily (Bell, Ellis), *Wuthering Heights* (Thomas Cautley Newby, London, 1847)
Brookfield, Mrs Charles, *The Cambridge Apostles* (Charles Scribner & Sons, New York, United States, 1907)

Brookfield, Frances M., *My Lord of Essex* (Sir Isaac Pitman & Sons, London, 1907)
Cadby, Carine, *The Doll's Day* by Carine Cadby (Mills & Boon, London, 1918)
Calvino, Italo, *Six Memos for the Next Millenium* (1988) (Penguin, London, 2016)
Cannadine, David, *Class in Britain* (1998) (Penguin, London, 2000)
Carey, John, *The Intellectuals and the Masses: Pride and Prejudice Among the Literary Intelligentsia, 1880–1939* (Faber & Faber, London, 1992)
Carrington, Dorothy, *Granite Island: A Portrait of Corsica* (Longman, London, 1971)
Cartland, Barbara, *Jigsaw* (Duckworth, United Kingdom, 1923)
Chadwick, Mrs Ellis H., *Mrs Gaskell: Haunts, Homes and Stories* (Sir Isaac Pitman & Sons, London, 1910)
Christie, Agatha, *An Autobiography* (1977) (HarperCollins, United Kingdom, 1993)
Christie, Agatha, *Cards on the Table* (Collins Crime Club, United Kingdom, 1936)
Christie, Agatha, *The Murder at the Vicarage* (Collins Crime Club, United Kingdom, 1930)
Christie, Agatha, *The Mysterious Affair at Styles* (John Lane, United States, 1920)
Christie, Agatha, *The Seven Dials Mystery* (1929) (Agatha Christie Limited, United Kingdom, no date)
Clark, Suzanne, *Sentimental Modernism: Women Writers and the Revolution of the Word* (Indiana University Press, Indiana, United States, 1991)
Clarke, Gillian, *Selected Poems* (Carcanet, Manchester, 1985)
Colette (Sidonie-Gabrielle), *My Mother's House and Sido* (1922) (Penguin, London, 1980)
Cameron, Charlotte, *Zenia, Spy in Togoland* (Thomas Werner Laurie, London, 1915)
Conrad, Joseph, *Lord Jim* (*Blackwood's Magazine*, United Kingdom, 1900)
Cunard, Nancy, *Negro Anthology* (Wishart & Co., London, 1934)
Dean, R. Storry, *Notable Trials: Romances of the Law Courts* (Cassell and Company, London, 1906)
de Céspedes, Alba, *Forbidden Notebook* (1952) (Pushkin Press, London, 2023)
Defoe, Daniel, *Robinson Crusoe* (William Taylor, United Kingdom, 1719)
Dell, Ethel M., *The Way of an Eagle* (Fisher Unwin, London, 1920)
Dickens, Charles, *The Pickwick Papers* (Chapman & Hall, United Kingdom, 1836)
Dowson, Jane (editor), *Women's Poetry of the 1930s: A Critical Anthology* (Routledge, London, 1996)
du Maurier, Daphne, *Rebecca* (Victor Gollancz, London, 1938)
du Maurier, Daphne, *The Loving Spirit* (1931) (Arrow, London, 1994)

du Maurier, Daphne, *The Escort* (1945) – see *Magpie: The Complete Short Story Magazine* (pp.3–18)

du Maurier, George, *Trilby* (*Harper's*, New York, United States, 1894)

Edwards, Dorothy, *The Conquered* (Publisher unknown, United Kingdom, 1926)

Edwards, Dorothy, *Rhapsody* (1927) (Parthian, Cardigan, 2007)

Edwards, Dorothy, *Winter Sonata* (1928) (Honno, United Kingdom, 2007)

Farjeon, Eleanor, *First & Second Love* (Michael Joseph, London,1947)

Farjeon, Eleanor, *Pan-Worship and Other Poems* (Elkin Matthews, London, 1908)

Farjeon, Eleanor, *The Soul of Kol Nikon* (Collins, London, 1923)

Forster, E.M., *A Passage to India* (Edward Arnold, London, 1924)

Forster, E.M., *A Room with a View* (1908) (Penguin, London, 1974)

Forster, E.M., *Howard's End* (Edward Arnold, London, 1910)

Forster, E.M., *Maurice* (Hodder Arnold, London, written in Edwardian times but not in print until 1971)

Forster, Margaret, *Daphne du Maurier: The Secret Live of the Renowned Storyteller* (Chatto & Windus, London, 1993)

Fowler, Christopher, *The Book of Forgotten Authors* (Riverrun, London, 2017)

Frankau, Pamela, *Marriage of Harlequin* (Harper & Brothers, New York, United States, 1927)

Freud, Sigmund, *Civilization and its Discontents* (1930) (Penguin Classics, London, 2014)

Fryer, Jonathan, *Isherwood: A Biography of Christopher Isherwood* (New English Library, United Kingdom, 1977)

Gibbons, Stella, *Cold Comfort Farm* (1932) (Penguin, London, 2006)

Gibbons, Stella, *The Mountain Beast* (Longmans, Green & Co., London, 1930)

Gibbons, Stella, *The Rich House* (1941) (Penguin, London, 2012)

Gilman, Charlotte Perkins, *The Yellow Wallpaper and Selected Writings* (2009) (Virago, London, 2018)

Gissing, George, *New Grub Street* (Smith, Elder & Co., London, 1891)

Glaspell, Susan, *The Glory of the Conquered* (Stokes, New York, United States, 1909)

Goudge, Elizabeth, *Green Dolphin Country* (Hodder & Stoughton, London, 1944)

Goudge, Elizabeth, *The Little White Horse* (University of London Press, London, 1946)

Graves, Richard Perceval, *The Brothers Powys* (Oxford University Press, Oxford, 1983)

Gregory, Alyse, *The Day is Gone* (E.P. Dutton and Company Inc., New York, United States, 1948)

Grimshaw, Beatrice, *Kris-Girl* (Mills & Boons, London, 1917)
Grossmith, George and Weedon, *The Diary of a Nobody* (*Punch*, United Kingdom, 1888)
Hagan, Stella Fitzthomas, *The Green Cravat: A Memorable Novel of Turbulent 18th Century Ireland* (Hodder & Stoughton, London, 1959)
Haggard, H. Rider, *King Solomon's Mines* (Cassell and Company, London, 1885)
Hall, Dr A. Wilford, *Woman: Her Generative Functions and Diseases* (Dr Hall's Hygiene Co., Manchester, 1910)
Hall, Dr A. Wilford, *Woman's Martyrdom – Founded on Fact* (short story included in *Her Generative Functions and Diseases*) (Dr Hall's Hygiene Co., Manchester, 1910)
Hall, Radclyffe, *Adam's Breed* (Cassell and Company, London, 1926)
Hall, Radclyffe, *The Well of Loneliness* (Jonathan Cape, London, 1928)
Hanley, James, *Boy* (Boriswood, London, 1931)
Hanley, James, *Grey Children: A Study in Humbug and Misery in South Wales* (Methuen, London, 1937)
Heyer, Georgette, *The Black Moth* (Heinemann, London, 1921)
Hoggart, Richard, *The Uses of Literacy* (Routledge, London, 1957)
Holtby, Winifred, *South Riding* (1936) (Virago, London, 1988)
Hope, Anthony, *The Prisoner of Zenda* (Arrowsmith, Bristol, 1894)
Horne, Alistair, *Seven Ages of Paris* (Pan Books, London, 2002)
Housman, A.E, *A Shropshire Lad* (Privately Published, London, 1896)
Hull, E.M., *The Sheik* (E. Nast & Grayson, United Kingdom, 1919)
Irvine, A.M., *The Frantic Misfortunes of a Nurse, or, The Probationer* (S.W. Partridge & Co., London,1910)
Isherwood, Christopher, *Christopher and His Kind* (1976) (Eyre Methuen, London, 1977)
Isherwood, Christopher, *Exhumations* (Methuen, London, 1966)
Isherwood, Christopher, *Lions and Shadows* (1938) (Methuen, London, 1953)
Isherwood, Christopher, *Mr Norris Changes Trains* (Hogarth Press, London, 1935)
Jacob, Naomi, *A Late Lark Singing* (The Book Club, United Kingdom, 1953)
Jameson, Storm, *Cloudless May* (Reprint Society, United Kingdom, 1943)
Jameson, Storm, *Journey from the North* (Volumes 1 and 2) (1969) (Collins and Harvill, United Kingdom, 1970 and reissued Pushkin Press, London, 2024)
Jameson, Storm, *The Hidden River* (Harper, London, 1955)
Jameson, Storm, *The Pot Boils: A Novel* (Constable and Co., London, *c.*1919)
Jerome, Jerome K., *Three Men in a Boat* (Arrowsmith, Bristol, 1889)

Johnson, Pamela Hansford, *This Bed Thy Centre* (Pan, United Kingdom, 1935)
Johnson, Pamela Hansford, *The Unspeakable Skipton* (Macmillan, United Kingdom, 1959)
Jordan, Elizabeth Garver, *The Wings of Youth* (Harper & Brothers, New York, United States, 1918)
Joyce, James, *Dubliners* (Grant Richards, London, 1914)
Joyce, James, *Ulysses* (Shakespeare and Company, Paris, France, 1920)
Lane, Margaret, *The Tale of Beatrix Potter* (1946) (Penguin, London, 1986)
Last, Nella, *Nella's Last War: The Second World War Diaries of Housewife 49* (Profile Books, London, 2006)
Lawrence, D.H., *Lady Chatterley's Lover* (Privately Published, Italy, 1928)
Le Gallienne, Richard, *Quest of the Golden Girl: A Romance* (The Bodley Head, London, 1896)
Lehmann, John, *New Writing* (paperback anthologies, London, John Lehmann Limited, 1936–1950)
Lehmann, Rosamond, *A Dream of Winter* (John Lehmann, London, 1946)
Lodge, David, *The Art of Fiction* (Penguin, London, 1992)
Lowndes, Susan (editor) *Diaries and Letters of Marie Belloc Lowndes* 1911–1947 (Chatto & Windus, London, 1971)
Mackworth, Cecily, *I Came out of France* (Routledge, London, 1941)
Magpie: The Complete Short Story Magazine (October 1951)
Mannin, Ethel, *Confessions and Impressions* (Hutchinson & Co. Limited, London, 1936)
Mansfield, Katherine, *Bliss and Other Stories* (1920) (Marshall Cavendish, United Kingdom, 1977)
Mansfield, Katherine, *In a German Pension* (*The New Age*, United Kingdom, 1911) (Reissued by Constable, London)
Mansfield, Katherine, *Je ne Parle Pas Francais* (Heron, United Kingdom, *c.*1920)
Mansfield, Katherine, *Psychology* (Publisher unknown, United Kingdom, 1920)
Mansfield, Katherine, *The Little Governess* (publisher unknown), United Kingdom, 1915)
Mantel, Hilary, *Giving up the Ghost: A Memoir* (2003) (4th Estate, London, 2013)
March, Joseph Moncur, *The Wild Party* (Covici Friede, New York, United States, 1928)
Marchant, Hilde, *Women and Children Last: A Woman Reporter's Account of Battle of the Britain* (Victor Gollancz, London, 1941)
Mason, A.E.W., *The Four Feathers* (Macmillan, London, 1902)

Massey, Philip, *Portrait of a Mining Town* (Fact, London, 1937)
Matthews, Dr Caroline, *The Experiences of a Woman Doctor in Siberia* (Mills & Boon, London, 1917)
Meredith, George, *Diana of the Crossways* (Constable and Co., London, 1885)
Meredith, George, *The Egoist* (Constable and Co., London, 1879)
Meredith, George, *The Tragic Comedians* (Constable and Co., London, 1880) (1940, London, Penguin)
Meyer, Martin, *Me of All People: Alfred Brendel in Conversation with Martin Meyer* (Cornell University Press, New York, United States, 2002)
Miller, Alice Duer, *Come out of the Kitchen! A Romance* (*Harper's Bazaar*, United States, 1916)
Milne, James, *The Memoirs of a Bookman* (John Murray, United Kingdom, 1934)
Mitchell, Gladys, *The Mystery of a Butcher's Shop* (1929) (Vintage, London, 2010)
Montgomery, L.M., *Anne of Avonlea* (L.C. Page & Co., United States, 1909)
Montgomery, L.M., *Anne of Green Gables* (L.C. Page & Co., United States, 1908)
Murger, Henri, *Scènes de la vie bohème* (*Le Corsaire*, Paris, France, 1851)
Nesbit, E., *The Railway Children* (Wells, Gardner, Darton and Company, London, 1906)
Nicholson, Helen, *Death in the Morning* (Lovat Dickson, United Kingdom, 1937)
Nicholson, Helen, *The Painted Bed* (Dodd, Mead & Co., United States, 1938)
Nicholson, Virginia, *Singled Out* (Penguin, London, 2007)
O'Brien, Kate, *Without My Cloak* (1931) (Penguin, London, 1949)
Olivier, Edith, *Without Knowing Mr Walkley* (Faber & Faber, London, 1938)
Orwell, George, *Down and Out in Paris and London* (Victor Gollancz, London, 1933)
Orwell, George, *Inside the Whale and Other Essays* (1957) (Penguin, London, 1974)
Orwell, George, *Keep the Aspidistra Flying* (Victor Gollancz, London, 1936)
Orwell, George, *The Collected Essays, Journalism and Letters of George Orwell: Volume 4 – In Front of Your Nose, 1945–1950* (Penguin, London, 1970)
Orwell, George, *The Road to Wigan Pier* (Victor Gollancz, London, 1937)
Owen, Wilfred, *The Collected Poems of Wilfred Owen* (Chatto & Windus, London, 1977)
Panter-Downes, Mollie, *The Shoreless Sea* (John Murray, United Kingdom, 1923)
Parker, Dorothy, *Big Blonde* (1929) (Penguin, London, 2022)
Parker, Dorothy, *The Lovely Leave* (1944) (Penguin, London, 1978)
Pitcher, Harvey, *When Miss Emmie was in Russia* (Eland, London, 1977)
Pitman, Sir Isaac, *Pitman's Shorthand and Typing Yearbook and Diary* (Sir Isaac Pitman & Sons, London, 1892)

Pontefract, Ella and Hartley, Marie, *Yorkshire Tour* (1939) (Smith Settle, Yorkshire, 2003)

Potter, Beatrix, *The Tale of Peter Rabbit* (Privately Published, London 1901)

Potter, Beatrix and Warne, Frederick, *The Tale of Peter Rabbit* (Privately Published, London 1902)

Powys, Phillipa, *The Blackthorn Winter* (1930) (reissued by The Sundial Press, United Kingdom, 2007)

Ratcliffe, Dorothy Una, *Dale Folk* (The Bodley Head, London, 1927)

Rhodes, Kathlyn, *Wild Heart of Youth* (Hutchinson, United Kingdom, 1925)

Rhys, Jean, *Quartet* (published in 1928 as *Postures*) (Andre Deutsch, United Kingdom,1969)

Rhys, Jean, *Wide Sargasso Sea* (1966) (Penguin, London, 1968)

Ruskin, John, *The Stones of Venice* (Smith, Elder & Co., London, 1851)

Sartre, Jean-Paul, The *Words* (*Les Mots,* 1963) (Penguin, London, 1974)

Sayers, Dorothy L., *Strong Poison* (1930) (New English Library, United Kingdom, 2003)

Scholes, Lucy (editor), *A Different Sound: Stories by Mid-Century Women Writers* (Pushkin Press, London, 2023)

Scott, Sir Walter, *Waverley* (Archibald Constable and Co., Edinburgh, 1814)

Simons, Judy, *Diaries and Journals of Literary Women from Fanny Burney to Virginia Woolf* (Macmillan, United Kingdom, 1990)

Sinclair, May, *The Combined Maze* (Harper & Brothers, New York, United States, 1913)

Sinclair, May, *Uncanny Stories* (Hutchinson, London, 1923)

Sitwell, Edith, *Facade and Other Poems* (1930) (Duckworth, United Kingdom, 1976)

Sitwell, Edith, *Gold Coast Customs* (Duckworth, United Kingdom, 1929)

Sitwell, Edith, *The Wheels* (Blackwell, London, 1916)

Smith, Nora K., *Strangers and a Sojourner* (Hodder & Stoughton, London, 1937)

Smith, Stevie, *Collected Poems and Drawings* (Penguin, London, 1971)

Smith, Stevie, *Novel on Yellow Paper* (Penguin, London, 1936)

Society of Authors, *Prospectus of the Society of Authors* (Bradbury Agnew, London, 1912)

St Clair Stobart, Mabel, *War and Women: From Experience in the Balkans and Elsewhere* (G. Bell & Sons, London, 1913)

Steen, Marguerite, *Phoenix Rising* (1952) (The Book Club, United Kingdom, 1953)

Stein, Gertrude, *The Autobiography of Alice B. Toklas* (1933) (Penguin, London, 2001)

Stein, Gertrude, *The Making of Americans: Being a History of A Family's Progress* (Contact Press, Paris, France, 1925)

Stein, Gertrude, *Three Lives* (Grafton Press, New York, United States, 1909)

Sterne, Laurence, *The Life and Times of Tristram Shandy, Gentleman* (Ann Ward, York, 1759)

Stopes, Marie, *Married Love* (Fifield & Co., United Kingdom, 1918)

Strachey, Lytton, *Eminent Victorians* (1918) (Dover Publications, United States, 2006)

Thirkell, Angela, *High Rising* (1933) (Virago, London, 2012)

Thompson, Flora, *Lark Rise to Candleford* (Oxford University Press, Oxford, 1945)

Tibble, J.W. and Tibble, Anne (editors), *John Clare: Selected Poems* (1951) (J.M. Dent & Sons, United Kingdom, 1965)

Trites, W.B., Love (Mills & Boon, London, 1917)

Tytler, Sarah, *The Countess of Huntingdon and her Circle* (Sir Isaac Pitman & Sons, London, 1907)

Uglow, Jenny, *In These Times: Living in Britain Through Napoléon's Wars, 1793–1815* (Faber & Faber, London, 2015)

Vaughan, Hilda, *The Soldier and the Gentlewoman* (1922) (Honno, United Kingdom, 2014)

Vaizey, Mrs George de Horne, *The Adventures of Billie Belshaw* (Mills & Boon, London, 1912)

Walbank, F. Alan, *Queens of the Circulating Library* (Evans Brothers, United Kingdom,1950)

Waugh, Alec, *Brief Encounter: A Novel* (W.H. Allen/Virgin Books, United Kingdom, 1975)

Wharton, Edith, *The Age of Innocence* (1920) (Wordsworth Classics, United Kingdom, 1994)

Williams-Ellis, Amabel, *The Big Firm* (Collins, London, 1938)

Woolf, Virginia, *A Room of One's Own* (Hogarth Press, London, 1929)

Woolf, Virginia, *Mrs Dalloway* (1925) (Penguin, London, 2019)

Woolf, Virginia, *The Common Reader* (1925) (Hogarth Press, London, 1968)

Woolf, Virginia, *The Waves* (Hogarth Press, London, 1931)

Wordsworth, William, *Preface to Lyrical Ballads* (1800 version) in Brett, R.L. and Jones, A.R., *Lyrical Ballads* (Routledge, London, 1971)

Wylie, I.A.R., *The Shining Heights* (Mills & Boon, London, 1917)

Poems Cited

Unless otherwise stated, individual poems are from Dowson, Jane (editor), *Women's Poetry of the 1930s: A Critical Anthology* (Routledge, London, 1996)

Ackland, Valentine, *Communist Poem* (1935)
Ackland, Valentine, *Journey from Winter: Selected Poems*
Ackland, Valentine, *Winter*
Ackland, Valentine, *Winter of Content* (1952)
Brooke, Rupert, *The Soldier* (1915)
Clare, John, *An Effusion to Poetry* (1820s)
Clarke, Gillian, *October* (from *Selected Poems* – see above)
Comstock, Gordon, *Mice*
Eliot, T.S., *The Waste Land* (1922)
Farjeon, Eleanor, *Easter Monday*
Farjeon, Eleanor, *First and Second Love* (1947)
Jameson, Storm, *El Heroe*
Jameson, Storm, *Port Bou*
Loy, Mina, *Lunar Baedecker* (1923)
Loy, Mina, *Last Lunar Baedecker* (1982)
Loy, Mina, *Three Moments in Paris* (1915)
Meredith, George, *Love in the Valley* (1851)
Meredith, George, *Modern Love* (1862)
Meredith, George, *The Lark Ascending* (1881)
Moore, Marianne, *Camellia Sabina* (1935)
Moore, Marianne, *England*
Moore, Marianne, *The Epicure's Guide to France* (1935)
Moore, Marianne, *Selected Poems* (1935)
Owen, Wilfred, *Anthem for Doomed Youth* (1920)
Owen, Wilfred, *Miners* (1918)
Owen, Wilfred, *Apologia Pro Poemate Meo* (1920)
Patmore, Coventry, *The Angel in the House* (1858)
Parker, Dorothy, *Anecdote*
Parker, Dorothy, *Death and Taxes*
Parker, Dorothy, *Enough Rope*
Parker, Dorothy, *Testament*
Parker, Dorothy, *Portrait of the Artist*
Sitwell, Edith, *Mariner Man*
Sitwell, Edith, *Minstrels*
Smith, Stevie, *Alfred the Great*
Smith, Stevie, *A Good Time was had by All* (1937)
Smith, Stevie, *Human Affection*

Smith, Stevie, *Not Waving but Drowning* (1957)
Smith, Stevie, *Testament*
Smith, Stevie, *Unser Vater* (*c.*1930s)
Wickham, Anna, *King Alfred and the Peasant Women*
Wickham, Anna, *The Silent Singer*
Beowulf
Lord's Prayer

Advertisements

Advertisement in *The Listener* in 1934 under the heading, 'How Many Stories There Are', announcement from the London School of Journalism

Reference Works

Baldwin, Dean R., *The Modern Short Story and Magazine Culture, 1880–1950*, (Edinburgh University Press, 2021)

Cooke, Rachel, *Her Brilliant Career: Ten Extraordinary Women of the Fifties* (Virago, London, 2013)

Davies, W.H., *The Autobiography of a Super-Tramp* (1908) (Parthian, Cardigan, 2013)

Döblin, Alfred, *Berlin Alexanderplatz* (1929) (Penguin, London, 2018)

Gibbs, Philip, *The Pageant of the Years: An Autobiography* (Heinemann, London, 1946)

Gostick, Chris, *Powys and Lord Jim* (The Powys Society, 2018)

Hall, Jean Graham and Smith, Gordon D., *R v Bywaters and Thompson (Then and Now)* (Barry Rose Law, United Kingdom, 1996)

Joannou, Maroula, *The History of British Women's Writing 1920–1945*
(Palgrave Macmillan, United Kingdom, 2018)

Kerbel, Sorrel (editor), *Jewish Writers of the Twentieth Century* (Fitzroy Dearborn, United States, 2001)

Moore, John, *Portrait of Elmbury* (1945) (Pan Books, London, 1953)

Moore, Marianne, *Complete Poems* (Faber & Faber, London, 1972)

Pearce, Robert, *Britain: Domestic Politics, 1918–1939* (Hodder & Stoughton, London, 1992)

Peterson, Linda H., *Victorian Women's Writing* (Cambridge University Press, Cambridge, 2015)

Pinkham, Lydia E., *Private Textbook on Ailments Peculiar to Women* (Lydia E. Pinkham Medicine Co., undated)

Preston, Paul, *A Concise History of the Spanish Civil War* (Fontana Press, London, 1996)

Priestley, J.B., *Delight* (Heinemann, London, 1949)

Priestley, J.B., *English Journey* (1934) (Mandarin, United Kingdom, 1994)

Reich, Nancy B., *Clara Schumann: The Artist and the Woman* (1985) (Cornell University Press, New York, United States, 2001)

Silkin, Jon (editor) *The Penguin Book of First World War Poetry* (Penguin, London, 1979)

Tannahill, Reay, *Sex in History* (1980) (Cardinal, United States, 1992)

Taylor, D.J., *Bright Young People: The Lost Generation of London's Jazz Age* (2007) (Vintage, London, 2008)

Taylor, D.J., *The Prose Factory: Literary Life in Britain Since 1918* (Chatto & Windus, London, 2017)

Taylor, Irene and Alan, (editors) *The Assassin's Cloak: An Anthology of the World's Greatest Diarists* (Canongate, United Kingdom, 2008)

Tolstoy, Leo, *Redemption* (Niva, Russia, 1899)

Tomalin, Claire, *Charles Dickens: A Life* (2011) (Penguin, London, 2012)

Watling, Sarah, *Tomorrow Perhaps the Future: Following Writers and Rebels in the Spanish Civil War* (Cape, London, 2023)

Winter, Genevieve, *110 Fiches sur les mouvements litteraires* (Bréal, France, 2011)

Articles and Essays

Aguirre, Mercedes, 'Sylvia Townsend Warner's Spanish Civil War Love Poems', (Introductory Essay)

Anonymous, 'Actress Claims Right to Box a Man's Ears', *Daily Express* (28 February 1938, p.11)

Anonymous, 'Clever Women and Immoral Women', *Hull Daily Mail* (31 July 1928, p.6)

Anonymous, 'Hint for Novelists', *Aberdeen Journal*, Issue 26,261 (2 March 1939)

Anonymous, 'How Many Stories are There?', *The Listener Supplement* (2 May 1934, p.xvii)

Anonymous, 'How to Write Crime Stories', *The Times* (6 November 1936, p.10)

Anonymous, 'Leader in the General Strike', *Daily Mail*, Special Issue, (May 1926, p.1)

Anonymous, 'One Slice or Two', *The British Worker*, Official Strike news bulletin, (6 May 1926, p.4)

Anonymous, 'Popular Novelists', *Derby Daily Telegraph* (24 March 1928 p.4)

Anonymous, 'Recent Verse', *The Times Literary Supplement* (17 January 1902 p.4)

Anonymous, 'When Women Write', *Aberdeen Journal* (13 June 1935, p.6)

Anonymous, 'Woman Novelists Honoured', *Bath Chronicle and Weekly Gazette* (29 March 1930, p.15)

Anonymous, 'Women Writers Uphold Prestige of Novel', *Derby Daily Telegraph* (11 October 1935, p.5)

Anto, Christina, 'The Probationer: Women and Romance in the Edwardian Era' (see https://cla.blogtorontomu.ca/the-probationer/.)

Baldwin, Dean R., 'Virginia Woolf and the Magazines', from his book, *The Modern Short Story and Magazine Culture, 1880–1950*, Chapter 10 (Edinburgh University Press, 2021)

Birch, Lionel, 'Anna Wickham: Poetess and Landlady' *Picture Post* (27 April 1946) (For the text, see 'The Neglected Books Page' at https://neglectedbooks.com.)

Bowker, Gordon, Obituary of Cecily Mackworth, 2006 (see https://www.stjohnstonandcarrigans.com/cecilymackworth.html.)

Bullough, Vera and Bullough, Bonnie, 'Reading *The Well of Loneliness* in America' *Signs*, Volume 2, Number 4, (summer 1977, pp.895–904)

Cavaliero, Glen, 'Powysiana: Collecting a Family', *Antiquarian Book Monthly Review*, Volume V, Number 1, Issue 55 (November 1978, pp.452–455)

Chesterton, G.K., 'Woman' (1905)

Day-Lewis, Cecil (editor), Wilfred Owen's poem, *Miners* (1918) (Lewis Chatto & Windus, London, 1977, p.92)

Duguid, Lindsay, 'No Love, Much Fidelity', *Times Literary Supplement* (5 May 2023, p.17)

Forbes, Rosita, 'A Woman Novelist's Desert Ordeal', *Nottingham Evening Post* (22 July 1930, p.8)

Fox, Lorna Scott, 'You Say You Want a Revolution', *Times Literary Supplement* (24 March 2023, pp.19–20)

Goldstone, Katrina, 'How to Disappear' Dublin Review of Books Essay on Stella Jackson. (see www.drb.ie/blog/writers-and-artists/2021/01/07/how-to-disappear.)

Groot, Gerald de, 'Gertrude Stein', (Kerbel, Sorrel – editor) – see *Jewish Writers of the Twentieth Century* (Fitzroy Dearborn, United States, 2001, pp.558–60)

Hamilton, Cicely, 'Woman's Place in France and Italy', *The Listener* Volume XI, Number 277 (pp.737–8)

Hentea, Marius, 'Late Modernist Debuts: Publishing and Professionalizing Young Novelists in 1920s Britain', *Book History*, Volume 14 (2011, pp.167–186)

Hilliard, Christopher, 'Producers by Hand and by Brain: Working Class Writers and Left Wing Publishers in the 1930s', *The Journal of Modern History*, Volume 78, Number 1 (March 2006, pp.37–64)

Jameson, Storm, 'Writing in Revolt', *Fact*, (July 1937 pp.9–18)

Joannou, Maroula, 'Literary Modernism and Women's Writing, 1920–1945', in her book *The History of British Women's Writing 1920–1945* (Palgrave Macmillan, United Kingdom, 2018)

Koelb, Tadzio, 'Show, Don't Tell', On the History of Writing Workshops, *Times Literary Supplement* (3 March 2023, p.12)

Lang, Andrew, 'Advice to Novelists', *Daily News* (2 October 1894)

Lehmann, John, 'Foreword', *Penguin New Writing*, Issue 1 (Penguin, London, 1940, pp.vii–viii)

Lehmann, Rosamond, *Penguin New Writing*, Issue 2 (Penguin, London, 1941)

Lehmann, John, 'Foreword', *Penguin New Writing* (Penguin, London, 1946, pp.7–8)

Lichtig, Toby, 'Edits and Ethics', *Times Literary Supplement* (10 March 2023, pp.14–15)

Lonsdale, Sarah, 'Harsh Testament', *Times Literary Supplement* (24 February 2023, p.8)

Lucarotti, Rolli, 'Introduction' to *Granite Island: A Portrait of Corsica* by Dorothy Carrington (Longman, London, 1971, pp.ix–xvi)

McCloskey, Donald N., 'The Unquashed Masses', *The Atlantic* (July 1994, pp.60–62)

Miles, Peter, Review of *The Will to Believe*, *Powys Review*, Number 13 (1983/1984, pp.84–5)

Mills & Boon, Advertisement, *The Times* (16 January 1917, p.4)

O'Faolain, Sean, 'Winifred Holtby's Last Novel', *The London Mercury*, (April, 1936, pp.643–644)

O'Farrell, Maggie, Introduction to *The Yellow Wallpaper and Selected Writings* by Charlotte Perkins Gilman (Virago, London, 2018, pp.vii–xii)

Orwell, George, 'Inside the Whale' (Penguin, 1974)

Orwell, George, 'Good Bad Books', *Tribune* (1945)

Orwell, George, 'Why I Write' *Decline of the English Murder* (Penguin, 1975) pp.180-188

Orwell, George, 'Writers and Leviathan', *The Collected Essays, Journalism and Letters of George Orwell: Volume 4 – In Front of Your Nose, 1945–1950* (Penguin, London, 1970, pp.463–470)

Pettitt, Clare, 'Bomb in the Biscuit Tin', *Times Literary Supplement* (10 March 2023, p.18)

Pontefract, Ella, 'Dales Folk', *The Yorkshire Dalesman*, Issue 1 (April, 1939, pp.4–5)

Rankin, John, 'Hardship and Courage on the Clydeside – What the Pinch Really Feels Like', *The Listener* (2 May 1934, p.743)

Robertson Scott, J.W., 'Three Quarters of a Century', *The Countryman*, Volume XXIII (April–May 1941, pp.28–33)

Sherard, Robert H., 'The Child Slaves of Britain', *The London Magazine* (February 1904, pp.3–9)

Shoard, Marion, 'Why Eleanor Farjeon Should be Considered One of the Dymock Poets', *The Newsletter of the Friends of the Dymock Poets*, Number 60 (January 2014)

Taylor, D.J., 'Such, Such Were the Joys', *Times Literary Supplement* (17 March 2023 p.13)

'The Idlers' Club', *The Idler* (Chatto & Windus, London, 1893, p.108)

'The Spell of the Black Woman: A Remarkable Novel', *Hull Daily Mail* (17 March 1916, p.5)

Walpole, Hugh, 'Why Write a Novel?', *The Times* (14 October 1933, p.9)

Willson, Dr Flora, 'The Muses at a Football Match', *The Times Literary Supplement* (10 March 2023, p.9)

Wyndham, Francis, Introduction to *Wide Sargasso Sea* by Jean Rhys (Penguin, London, 1968, pp.5–11)

Archive Material

Brown, Marie (1877–1955), a sub-collection at the Leeds Russian Archive, covering the years 1920–1984. The material includes letters and cuttings.

Gregory, Alyse, 'Madeleine Walker-Curry' Beinecke Library YCAL Mss 163, Box 13, Folder 224: letters from Madeleine Walker-Curry to Alyse Gregory.

Marx Memorial Library: *Spanish Collection* SC 59879

The Writers' Club, London University, School of Economics, Reference: 6WCW, 1891–1900. The archive has forty-eight letters addressed to Florence Routledge, the daughter of the publisher George [Routledge (1812–1888)]. The archive note has this:

'Founded in 1892 by Frances Low at 10, Norfolk Street.

many well-known writers were members and a quiet room was reserved for writing. The suite included a writing room, dining room, kitchen, cloakroom and two reception rooms. At Homes were held every Friday afternoon when guests (including men) could be invited to tea ... The Writers' Club was still in existence in the 1920s.'

Journals, Magazines, Newspapers and Periodicals

Aberdeen Journal

Antiquarian Book Monthly Review

Bath Chronicle and Weekly Gazette
Book History
Blackwood's Magazine
Cornhill Magazine
Daily Chronicle
Daily Express
Daily Mail
Daily Mirror
Daily News
Derby Daily Telegraph
Editions de Montagne
English Review
Fact
Harper's
Harper's Bazaar
Horizon
Hull Daily Mail
Jack's Reference Book for Home and Office (1930)
Le Corsaire
Left Review
Left Review Authors Take Sides on the Spanish War
London Evening News
McClure's Magazine
New Commonwealth
New Writing (John Lehmann Limited, 1936 –1950)
Nottingham Evening Post
Pearson's Weekly
Penguin New Writing, Issues 1 and 2
Picture Post
Powys Review
Punch
Review of Reviews (W.T. Stead)
Rhythm (John Middleton Murry)
Scrutiny
The Atlantic
The British Worker
The Bystander

The Countryman
The Dial
The English Woman's Journal
The Englishwoman's Review
The Evening Standard
The Express
The Harmsworth's Magazine
The Idler
The Journal of Modern History
The Listener
The Listener Supplement
The London Magazine
The London Mercury
The Monthly Packet
The New Age (A.R. Orage)
The New Statesman
The New Yorker
The Newsletter of the Friends of the Dymock Poets
The Observer
The Paris Review
The Pelican
The Sphere
The Strand
The Suffragette
The Times
The Times Literary Supplement
The Yorkshire Dalesman
Time and Tide
Tribune
Vanity Fair (Articles by Dorothy Parker, 1918–1920)
Vogue
Windsor Magazine
Women's Own
Women Today
Yorkshire Post
Yorkshire Evening Post

Plays

Christie, Agatha, *The Mousetrap* (1952)
Cartland, Barbara, *Blood Money* (1926)
Henrik, Ibsen, *Hedda Gabler* (1891)
Pinter, Harold, *The Caretaker* (1960)
No More Fun

Films

Colliery Disaster (J.E. Samuel)
Drifters (John Grierson, 1929)
Educating Rita (1983)
Four Sons (1928)
Keeper of the Flame (1942)
Night Mail (1936)
Sweat (Fred Urquhart)
The Deserter (Stephen Spender)
The Cobbler and the Machine (Mulk Raj Anand)
The Lodger: The Story of the London Fog (1927)

Television Programmes

Dickson of Dock Green, BBC
Downton Abbey
Pub and the People: Worktown (1943)

Radio Broadcasts

Light Programme (BBC, 1930s)

Songs

Lily the Pink, The Scaffold

Special Publications

de Maupassant, Guy, *Yvette* (1884) (Flammarion: Selection Collection, France, 1938)

Unpublished Material

Gibbs, Sir Philip, Five letters to an aspiring author, 1951–1953 (Author's archive)

Hartmann, Laura A., *Say that we Saw Spain Die: British and American Women Writers and the Spanish Civil War*, Master of Arts Thesis, Virginia Polytechnic Institute, 2008

Letter from Ewart Milne (Author's archive)

Online Sources

http://furrowedmiddlebrow.blogspot

https://archives.bristol.gov.uk/records/40145

https://archiveshub.jisc.ac.uk/search/archives (For the Society for Promoting the Employment of Women.)

https://spartacus-educational.com/frank_crowninshield.htm (On Crowninshield and the first stage of Dorothy Parker's career.)

https://uclpress.scienceopen.com/hosted-document (This is on Sylvia Townsend Warner and Spain.)

https://www.cambridge.org/core/books/cambridge-companion-to-victorian-womens-writing (Easley, Alexis, 'Making a Debut', Cambridge University Press)

https://www.lesleyahall.net ('The middle brows'.)

https://www.poetryfoundation.org

https://www.poetryfoundation.org/poets/mina-loy

https://www.shakespeare.org.uk (For Marie Corelli at Stratford.)

https://www.wikipedia.org

Ephemera

List of Artistes, The Premier Provincial Entertainment and Concert Bureau brochure (*c.*1910)

Publishing lists of Pitman, in Maskell, Henry P. and Gregory, Edward W., *Old Country Inns* (Sir Isaac Pitman & Sons, London, 1910)

Images and Photographs

All images and photographs in the plate section include an appropriate credit to the copyright holders.

Index